THE BUSINESS OF REASON

International Library of Philosophy and Scientific Method

EDITOR: TED HONDERICH

A Catalogue of books already published in the
International Library of Philosophy and Scientific Method
will be found at the end of this volume

THE BUSINESS OF REASON

edited by

J. J. MACINTOSH

and

S. COVAL

. . . a great, perhaps the greatest, part of the business of our reason consists in analyses of the concepts which we already have . . .

IMMANUEL KANT

NEW YORK

HUMANITIES PRESS

First published
in the United States of America 1969
by Humanities Press Inc.
303 Park Avenue South
New York, N.Y. 10010

Library of Congress Catalog Card No. 68–27430

Printed in Great Britain

CONTENTS

PREFACE

PEOPLE SOMETIMES TALK about 'linguistic philosophy' or 'Oxford philosophy' or 'analytic philosophy' as if there were to be found in Oxford or elsewhere recognizable groups of philosophers who either fitted themselves into, or who could be forced into, these uncomfortable pigeon-holes. It seems doubtful whether many philosophers themselves believe in the existence of such groups, since they know that they themselves are only trying to solve philosophical problems as best they can, much as philosophers always have, and it seems fairly obvious that their colleagues are doing the same. Some philosophers are more conscious of, and sometimes more explicit about, the method they are employing. But this is not enough to make it a different method.

Philosophers in Oxford and elsewhere are not *only* interested in words, but they do recognize that often the most straightforward or the most productive way of approaching a philosophical problem is through a discussion of the way we talk, and that often a linguistic investigation is a necessary or a useful preliminary to philosophical discussion. To say that these philosophers are *only* interested in words is like saying that chess-players are *only* interested in openings. They are, of course, interested in the analysis of concepts: if clarity is not enough, what needs to be added to it is ingenuity and if possible profundity, not subsequent obscurity. But such analysis, as our title indicates, has been recognized as the task of philosophers for some time.

The suggestion being made is not that it is impossible to have recognizable schools of philosophy, of course. It is possible to have such schools; it is even possible to have them on purpose. Only, it seems doubtful whether the 'linguistic school' is such a school. At any rate, whether or not one believes in the existence of such a group among older philosophers, it is interesting to see what younger philosophers are doing: if one does have such a belief, to see how far they have been corrupted by their mentors; and if one does not, to see to what extent this lack of a unified policy leaves a gap which they will be inclined to fill.

Partly with this in mind, we invited papers[1] from various young and comparatively unpublished philosophers. This volume is the result. Our contributors are all English-speaking philosophers. They come from Great Britain, the United States, New Zealand, Australia, and Canada. All but two spent some time in Oxford in the early 1960s, though their present whereabouts are as geographically diverse as their origins.

We placed certain minimal restrictions, couched rather vaguely, on our contributors, by suggesting that their papers should not be exclusively historical nor tied too closely to comment on contemporary philosophers. Nor, we suggested, should they deal with topics in the field of formal logic. We did not choose a central theme, nor did we ask our contributors to restrict themselves with regard to theme or treatment in ways other than those mentioned.

This course of action would, we hoped, yield a selection of the sort of philosophical topics that young philosophers find interesting, discussed in the way or ways that they find most profitable. In the event the topics they chose were as heterogeneous as their backgrounds: ethics and materialism, aesthetics and the philosophy of science, meaning and existence, persons, machines and the philosophy of language. As might have been expected, the treatments given these diverse topics are as diverse as the topics themselves. If there ever was a school of philosophy which concerned itself exclusively with language, it seems to have disappeared. This, however, is something which it is not necessary to argue: the evidence lies at hand, and the conclusions to which it points can be drawn by readers at least as well as by editors.

J. J. MACINTOSH

[1] In 1962. The delay in publication is due in part to the editors (though not the editor of the series), in a much smaller part to some of the contributors, and in a somewhat larger part to circumstances which would have required a massive expenditure of energy to be brought within our control.

LIST OF CONTRIBUTORS

Peter Achinstein
Johns Hopkins University, Baltimore

Keith Campbell
University of Sydney

S. Coval
University of British Columbia

Cora A. Diamond
University of Aberdeen

Jerry A. Fodor
Massachusetts Institute of Technology

J. C. Gosling
St. Edmund Hall, Oxford

Andrew Harrison
University of Bristol

Don Locke
University of Warwick

J. J. MacIntosh
University of Calgary

Brian Medlin
Flinders University of South Australia

Kai Nielsen
New York University

Bede Rundle
Trinity College, Oxford

M. J. Scott-Taggart
University of East Anglia

C. C. W. Taylor
Corpus Christi College, Oxford

ON THE CHOICE OF FUNCTIONAL HYPOTHESES[1]

PETER ACHINSTEIN

I

SUPPOSE THAT A scientist tries to discover how a certain physical quantity y changes in magnitude with another quantity x (e.g. how the length of a bar of copper changes with temperature, how the volume of hydrogen changes with pressure, how the distance covered by a freely falling object changes with time). For this purpose a number of tests are made at each of several different values of x and the corresponding values for y noted. Let us imagine a very simple case in which the results are given in the table at the left.

x	y
1	7
2	11
3	15
4	19
5	23
6	27
7	31

Such information could be depicted by employing a Cartesian coordinate system and plotting the observed values of x and y as points on a graph. On the basis of the recorded evidence, the natural hypothesis to adopt is that the relationship between the above quantities x and y can be expressed by the equation $y = 4x + 3$, and illustrated by drawing the smoothest curve (a straight line) through the points on the graph. Analogous examples are readily constructed for sets of magnitudes with different values. In each case the most acceptable procedure seems to involve drawing the smoothest curve which fits the data and adopting the corresponding hypothesis. The question I want to consider is what type of justification is to be given for selecting hypotheses on this basis. (In what follows, the expression *functional hypothesis* will be used to refer to those propositions which describe a functional relationship between various physical quantities.) I want to examine a number of important attempts to provide general criteria for determining the acceptability of hypotheses, suggest why each of these fails to give a completely satisfactory answer to our question concerning functional hypotheses, and finally offer what may be a more adequate solution. I shall not complicate the issue by considering cases in which the most acceptable curve in a given situation does not fit all the observed points precisely (but only within the limits of experimental error). My concern will be with the least complex type of case, viz. that in which all the points lie on the chosen curve. Moreover, although the example employed refers to the case of a linear hypothesis, what is said should be applicable to any functional hypothesis which in a given situation is deemed most acceptable on the basis of the data.

II

Let us begin, then, by considering the following position which might be called simple inductivism: the acceptability of a hypothesis depends upon the number of its positive and negative instances in such a way that the greater the number of positive instances, where no negative instances have been observed, the better confirmed, and hence the more acceptable, the hypothesis. For purposes of discussion, we may consider a positive instance of a hypothesis of the form 'All *A* is *B*' to be something which is both *A* and *B*, and a negative instance to be an *A* which is not *B*.[2] Now, with respect to our initial example, since all pairs of recorded values of x and y have the property of satisfying the formula $y = 4x + 3$, these constitute positive instances of the hypothesis that all such pairs (including the unrecorded ones) satisfy this formula. Hence, because there are no negative instances, the hypothesis in question is highly confirmed by the evidence, and for this reason it is acceptable.

The difficulty with such reasoning is that it can be used to show that innumerable alternative hypotheses are equally acceptable. For the observed points lie on an infinite number of different curves and thus constitute positive instances for an infinite number of mutually incompatible hypotheses, each of which represents values of y as a function of x. Hence, from the simple inductive standpoint, each of these functional hypotheses is equally confirmed by the evidence, since each has the same number of positive instances, and no negative ones. Consequently, no reason has been given for thinking that the linear hypothesis is more acceptable than any of the others that are compatible with the data.

The failure of the simple inductivist position to account for the choice of the linear hypothesis in our example may lead one to pursue an entirely different approach. The reason for adopting the linear hypothesis in such a case, it might be suggested, is not that it has many positive instances and no negative ones but rather that it is the *simplest* hypothesis compatible with the evidence.[3] Surely, it will be argued, considered by itself, a linear functional relationship is simpler than any other one which would be satisfied by the pairs of values recorded, and for this reason the corresponding hypothesis is to be preferred. To render such a viewpoint precise it would be necessary to specify criteria to be used in determining the relative simplicity of individual hypotheses expressing functional relationships. Nevertheless, it might be argued, the concept of simplicity is applicable to such hypotheses and must be recognized as central in enabling us to understand why one functional hypothesis is to be preferred over another.

The view that the scientist chooses a particular functional hypothesis because it is the simplest one compatible with the evidence—stated in this unqualified fashion—is open to serious challenge. For it fails to distinguish two types of cases: those in which there is a large quantity of evidence (a large number of recorded associated values of x and y) that strongly supports a particular hypothesis, and cases in which the evidence is meagre and therefore does not lend strong support. Let us suppose, e.g., that in both types of situation a certain linear hypothesis is the simplest one compatible with the evidence. We might even agree that it is the most acceptable hypothesis in each case. But the point is that the reasons for its acceptability are different in each case. In the first, the scientist has amassed a substantial amount of evidence which, he would claim, supports the linear hypothesis. In the second case, whatever his reasons for accepting this hypothesis, they do not include reference to a large amount of evidence in its favor. Obviously, a major problem lies in understanding the nature of the support provided by the data, if, as indicated above, it cannot be analysed by simple inductive means. But whatever the analysis, it would seem incorrect to maintain that the quantity of the data is not at all a relevant consideration in determining the acceptability of a hypothesis, and therefore to claim that the reasons for selecting the linear hypothesis in the cases cited above are identical. The unqualified simplicity view, according to which the acceptability of a hypothesis compatible with the evidence depends solely on its simplicity, ignores the factor of quantity in the data, and hence fails to distinguish these cases.

III

In seeking to establish a basis for choosing among competing functional hypotheses, we have considered two positions, neither of which provides a satisfactory answer. These positions were rather crudely formulated, and it is natural to expect that views more completely and precisely developed will serve better to clarify the situation. In this section and the next a number of such positions will briefly be examined.

One of the most elaborate and precisely formulated systems of induction is that of Carnap.[4] This scheme specifies a set of conditions on the basis of which a confirmation function is to be constructed. Such a function, defined for sentences of a formal language, determines the numerical degree to which any sentence in that language confirms any other. The conditions stipulated by Carnap yield the following theorem:

> As the amount of evidence increases for or against a hypothesis attributing a property to an unexamined individual, the degree of confirmation of this hypothesis depends more and more upon the relative frequency of the individuals observed to have that property, and less and less upon other factors; in the limit the degree of confirmation is equal to this relative frequency.[5]

Accordingly, if *a*) functional properties of the form 'satisfies the relationship $y = f(x)$' could be expressed in the type of language Carnap considers, and if *b*) such properties were subject to the theorem cited above, then the degree of confirmation of the hypothesis that the next pair of associated values of x and y observed will also manifest this property would depend almost entirely upon, and be approximately equal to, the relative frequency of such pairs which have been observed to have this property, provided that the number of pairs recorded was considerable. Under these assumptions, since in any particular example the entire set of point-pairs recorded will satisfy innumerably many functional properties, the degree of confirmation of all hypotheses of the type in question will be approximately equal. In such a case, a linear hypothesis could be expected to receive no more confirmation than other functional hypotheses equally satisfied by the evidence; thus Carnap's scheme would provide no reason for choosing the hypothesis that the next pair of observed points will satisfy a linear relationship over any other hypothesis compatible with the data.

In point of fact, however, neither assumption *a*) nor assumption *b*) above can be made with respect to Carnap's system as presently expounded. As for assumption *a*), Carnap's theory has not been developed to the extent that it can be applied to sentences expressing functional hypotheses. Nor do the extensions of this scheme provided by Kemeny[6] and Putnam[7] remedy the situation, since the languages for which these authors are able to define confirmation functions, although richer than Carnap's, do not employ primitive expressions for functors (e.g. 'length', 'mass', 'temperature') with real numbers as values. As for assumption *b*), it should be noted that in the present system the theorem cited above holds only for molecular properties (properties which can be defined by the use of primitive predicates and truth-functional connectives). And since functional properties require the use of identity in their definitions, they would not be classified as molecular, and hence would not be subject to this theorem. Nevertheless, because hypotheses involving quantitative (non-molecular) properties are capable of expressing scientific laws, it would seem necessary, and consonant with the basically inductive character of Carnap's scheme, to require that in a more fully developed system such hypotheses be capable of receiving confirmation from their instances.[8] But, following Carnap's present inductive procedure, if the confirmability of functional hypotheses is achieved by allowing predicates used to express such hypotheses to satisfy the theorem cited above (i.e. by allowing the degree of confirmation of a hypothesis attributing a predicate of this sort to an unexamined individual to depend largely upon the number of individuals observed to have or lack the property designated by that predicate), then, as we have seen, the resulting system will accord approximately equal degrees of confirmation to competing functional hypotheses on the basis of evidence reporting a large number of different observations.

For these reasons, then, Carnap's system is not at present capable of showing why a linear hypothesis is to be preferred in a case of the sort originally cited.

Perhaps, however, other inductive theories are more successful. Another author working within this general type of framework is Reichenbach.[9] He propounds what has been referred to as the 'straight rule' of induction. According to this rule, if the observed relative frequency of a certain property in a given series is a specific fraction (and if nothing is known about second-level probabilities), we are to predict that the limit of the relative frequency of the property in the series will be equal to that fraction.

An unqualified use of this rule, however, yields unacceptable consequences in the case of functional hypotheses. Thus, in our earlier example, the observed relative frequency of the property 'satisfies a linear relationship' is 1, but so is the observed relative frequency of many other properties as well. Hence, unrestricted use of Reichenbach's rule, in a case in which nothing is known about what he terms 'second-level probabilities', will result in incompatible assertions.

Unlike Carnap and most inductive theorists, Reichenbach does, however, go on to discuss the problem of choosing among functional hypotheses. He offers a solution by providing what he calls an inductive justification for choosing the simplest curve (an argument, he claims, that is not based on appeal to mere convenience).[10] The justification involves three steps. First, given any set of points plotted on a graph, we are warranted, as an initial approximation, in joining such points by a chain of straight lines. The procedure of drawing and later correction is justified, according to Reichenbach, on the grounds that it must eventually lead to the true curve representing the quantities tested, if there is such a curve. However, since constructing a chain of straight lines will not by itself generally yield the simplest curve, a second step is required. This involves choosing a curve which is sufficiently like that constructed by the first procedure, except that it is to have a continuous derivative, and hence must itself be a continuous curve. The justification for this is that scientists seek not only laws governing the quantities tested but also laws governing the derivatives of these quantities, where such laws are to be represented by continuous functions. Recognizing, however, that even the second step will not determine a unique curve (since innumerable curves with continuous derivatives will approximate the chain of straight lines constructed), Reichenbach introduces a third step, which involves choosing any one of the resulting curves merely 'from the viewpoint of convenience'.[11] This procedure is deemed legitimate because all of these resulting curves, being quite similar, will not yield predictions that are vastly different.

Whatever its merits, it should be noted that this method of justifying the choice of the simplest curve can hardly be classified as inductive, i.e. as proceeding by appeal to a principle of induction (such as the 'straight rule' formulated above). The most that can be said is that the justification that Reichenbach offers for constructing a chain of straight lines (in the first step) is the same type of ('pragmatic') justification which he presents for utilizing his rule of induction, viz. that by doing so we are bound to be successful in the long run, if success is possible.[12] However, although the proposed justifications for the first step above and for the rule of induction are similar in kind, this does not warrant the inference that the former procedure has been justified by appeal to a principle of induction.

Even more important, however, is the fact that the argument in favor of connecting the recorded points by a chain of straight lines does not establish the desired conclusion. For precisely the same reasoning can be used with respect to innumerably many procedures which, given a set of observed points, bid us construct curves of many different sorts, where these curves pass through all the points plotted.[13] These methods will be 'self-correcting', and, since they prescribe curves satisfying all the recorded points, must eventually (i.e. in the limit) lead to the true curve, if there is one; and each will yield quite different predictions concerning unobserved cases.

Finally, the appeal to convenience in the third step runs counter to the avowed aim of providing an entirely inductive justification for choosing the simplest hypothesis.

Reichenbach's proposals, then, are not sufficient to justify the choice of a functional hypothesis. Neither his principle of induction nor the allegedly inductive justification for adopting the simplest curve provide the basis for a solution to our problem.

Moreover, it is doubtful that a purely inductive justification could be given. For, suppose it were argued that we are warranted in selecting the simplest functional hypothesis consistent with the recorded data on the grounds that the frequency of success in the case of such hypotheses has been high. We might imagine that we have acquired detailed information about functional hypotheses proposed within the various sciences, and about the degree of success of these hypotheses. Suppose we construct a graph whose x-coordinate is divided into finite segments, one for each science considered. This coordinate will represent the set of *simplest* functional hypotheses proposed in different areas of the various sciences on the basis of sets of data which in each case, let us say, are of comparable quantity. The y-coordinate will represent the degree of success of these hypotheses. If, indeed, the simplest functional hypotheses so far proposed have been the most successful, we can indicate this fact by plotting the appropriate points on the graph. The result will be a set of points lying on some curve C whose distance from the x-coordinate is considerable and (if we assume approximately equal success) fairly constant, where C is the smoothest curve connecting the recorded points. Now, to justify the choice of the simplest functional hypotheses on purely inductive grounds is to argue that since the recorded points satisfy the hypothesis corresponding to this curve C, the unrecorded ones do also. This means connecting the recorded points by the curve in question, and hence accepting a certain hypothesis about the success of functional hypotheses not yet proposed. But, of course, the points plotted on this 'success' graph lie on an infinite number of different curves, many of which indicate a low success rate for simple functional hypotheses not yet proposed. And a purely inductive argument—one based on Reichenbach's rule of induction or on Carnap's principles of confirmation—is unable to provide a reason for choosing one of these curves over the others. Such an argument, therefore, would not succeed in demonstrating the preferred status of the simplest functional hypotheses.

IV

In order to determine whether a more adequate method for dealing with functional hypotheses can be found, I turn now from inductive systems to theories of confirmation founded on considerations of simplicity. One of the best-known theories of this sort is that of Popper.[14] Popper identifies the simplicity of a hypothesis with its empirical content which he equates with its degree of falsifiability: the more falsifiable a hypothesis, the more it says about the world of experience by restricting the physical possibilities to a minimum. The extent of systematization which a hypothesis achieves by means of its restrictive character constitutes the measure of its simplicity.

In the case of functional hypotheses, Popper suggests that degree of falsifiability is to be determined by reference to the 'dimension' of the type of curve in question: if d points are necessary and sufficient to determine a particular curve of a certain type, then the set of curves of that type is d-dimensional. Thus, e.g., the expressions 'straight line', 'circle through one given point', and 'parabola through two given points' designate sets of curves each of which is two-dimensional. To falsify a functional hypothesis describing one of these curves, three observations would be necessary. Accordingly, Popper suggests, one functional hypothesis is simpler than another if the type of curve it describes is of lower dimension, and hence is more readily falsified, than the other. On the basis of this theory, he shows how a system of confirmation can be constructed, according to which the more falsifiable, and hence the simpler, hypothesis which is subjected to tests aimed at falsifying it, and which remains unrefuted by these tests, is the better-confirmed hypothesis.[15]

Popper's scheme may indeed be capable of handling certain types of functional hypotheses. Nevertheless it does not seem to provide a completely satisfactory answer to our problem. For it is not able to deal with cases, such as the one cited in our original example, in which we are asking why, given the specific evidence we have, ought we to accept one particular curve (e.g. the one whose formula is $y = 4x + 3$) rather than other particular curves. Hypotheses in such cases concern specific curves whose parameters have been assigned definite values, rather than general sets of curves with unspecified parameters. Such hypotheses, which will be called *particular* functional hypotheses in what follows, are zero-dimensional according to Popper's classification. All of them are refuted by a single observation, and hence all are equally falsifiable.[16] In Popper's scheme, then, competing particular functional hypotheses will receive equal confirmation from observations designed to refute them.[17] Thus, in a case of the type originally cited, this system would provide no more reason for accepting the hypothesis that the physical quantities x and y are related according to the formula $y = 4x + 3$ than for accepting any other particular functional hypothesis equally satisfied by the data.

Nor will it be of any help to point out that according to Popper's theory the hypothesis that the general form of the curve is linear is simpler than alternative hypotheses about its general form. For such information is relevant for choosing among particular functional hypotheses only if it warrants the inference that the particular linear hypothesis we are considering is simpler than other particular non-linear hypotheses. But this inference cannot be made, since in Popper's scheme all particular functional hypotheses are equally simple.

It might be objected, of course, that the present lacuna is not serious, since the functional hypotheses of major concern to scientists are those dealing with the general form of curves rather than with specific curves: the important question is the general manner in which one quantity varies with another, and not the specific values of the parameters involved.

It must certainly be admitted that in many scientific contexts interest is focused upon the general form of the functional relationship between two quantities. Nevertheless, in numerous instances the specific function is sought as well. For it is only when the parameters in the equation have been assigned definite values that a functional hypothesis can be used to achieve one of the important aims of science, viz. that of affording a basis for specific predictions. The physicist, e.g., wishes to learn not only that the relationship between temperature and length of a solid substance is (approximately) a linear one but also the specific linear relationship for particular substances. Accordingly, he attempts to determine the value of the parameter (the coefficient of linear expansion) for various elements; and by this means he seeks to construct particular functional hypotheses which can be used to predict, e.g., how a copper bar of a certain standard length will increase in size at various temperatures. Moreover, in many scientific contexts, a hypothesis which expresses the general form of the curve for substances of different sorts is proposed only after particular functional hypotheses have been formulated and tested. In such instances sets of specific points may be plotted on graphs and particular curves drawn through these points. This procedure of fitting a specific curve through a set of points, and thereby adopting a particular functional hypothesis, is just as much in need of justification as are cases involving more general hypotheses.

For these reasons, then, it seems important that a theory of confirmation based on simplicity be able to justify the choice of particular as well as general functional hypotheses. Popper's theory, since it is unable to do the former, does not afford an entirely adequate basis for the solution of our problem.

Another important attempt to provide a theory of confirmation founded on principles of simplicity is that of Barker.[18] Utilizing Kemeny's concept of logical measure,[19] Barker proposes that the extent to which evidence confirms a hypothesis is to be determined by considering the logical measure of the entire system of propositions to which the hypothesis and evidence belong. With reference to a language containing a finite number of extralogical predicates, the logical measure of one system (i.e. one set of postulates) is greater than that of another system if, for every sufficiently large universe, the one allows more models than the other (i.e. if the conjunction of sentences expressing one set of postulates can, under various interpretations of all the extralogical terms in the language, come out true in more ways than the conjunction of sentences expressing the other set of postulates). The lower the logical measure of the system, and hence the more uniformity it imposes on the world, the greater its simplicity. And if there is a system containing a hypothesis plus all the available evidence that is simpler than any system containing the negation of that hypothesis plus the evidence, we may say that the hypothesis in question is better confirmed than its negation.[20]

These ideas can be illustrated as follows. Suppose that our language contains two extralogical predicates, P_1 and P_2, and that the universe consists of just three individuals. Then there are 64 ($=4^3$) possible assignments of these predicates and their negations to the three individuals, i.e. there are 64 models. Consider two general statements that might be formulated in this language: 'Any P_1 is also P_2', to be called S_1, and 'At least one P_1 is not P_2', to be called

S_2. For our three-membered universe, S_1 comes out true in 27 ($=3^3$) models, because in each of these there is no P_1 that is not P_2; S_2 comes out true in 37 ($=4^3 - 3^3$) models, since in every other model any individual that is P_1 is also P_2. But now whatever the size of the universe, provided that it is finite and greater than two members, S_2 will come out true in more models than S_1. (S_2 will come out true in $4^N - 3^N$ models, S_1 in 3^N models, where N is the number of individuals in the universe.) Accordingly, the logical measure of S_2 is greater than S_1. Suppose, then, that we have obtained evidence which says that some individuals that are P_1 are also P_2, there being no evidence reporting individuals that are P_1 but not P_2. Consider the system consisting of S_1 plus the evidence and also the system consisting of S_2 plus the evidence. Which system is preferable? The answer is the former, since for any sufficiently large universe (in this case, any universe with more than two members), the logical measure of this system will be lower than that of the latter system. The former system will preclude more models and hence will be the simpler system. Moreover, S_1 will be better confirmed than S_2 on the basis of the sort of evidence envisaged, since S_1 plus this evidence will belong to some system which is simpler than any system to which S_2 and the evidence belong; and the greater the number of P_1's reported not to be lacking in P_2, the greater the confirmation of S_1 by contrast with S_2.

This theory as outlined is not yet applicable to languages containing functors and mathematical expressions; hence, as it stands, it cannot be used to compare the confirmation of various hypotheses about the curve that should be fitted through a set of points. Nevertheless, Barker offers considerations designed to show that his theory, when further elaborated, might well prove capable of providing a basis for choosing among functional hypotheses. Thus suppose our evidence consists of points plotted on a graph, all of which lie on a straight line. Then, says Barker:

> We might conjecture that the relation is a linear one; or we might suppose it to be some more complicated relationship which mathematical ingenuity may invent. How do these competing hypotheses compare with respect to their simplicity? This much at least we can say: the hypothesis that this relationship is linear is a hypothesis which, when conjoined with the evidence, is consonant with only one type of structure of the universe, with respect to these two quantitative properties;

whereas the hypothesis that the relationship should be represented by an equation of some more elaborate form is a hypothesis which, even when conjoined with the evidence, still is consonant with many different types of structure of the universe. The former hypothesis may be expected to exclude more models than would the latter, and in this sense the former should be accounted the simpler and more acceptable hypothesis. This informal consideration at least does suggest that the proposed criterion of confirmation may give us a reason for preferring the hypothesis here which intuitively and mathematically does seem the simpler (*ibid.*, p 186).

Barker's scheme appears to have advantages over the unqualified theory of simplicity considered earlier. Still there is reason to believe that it cannot be applied to the problem of choosing among competing functional hypotheses. For the simplest system (or systems) containing a certain (general) functional hypothesis *h*, together with the evidence, will presumably also contain some *particular* functional hypothesis which is compatible with the data and which logically implies *h*. This is so because a system containing such a particular functional hypothesis will exclude many more models, and hence be much simpler, than a system containing only the general functional hypothesis. For the same reason, the simplest system(s) containing the negation of *h* will also contain some particular functional hypothesis which is compatible with the data and which implies the negation of *h*. But a *particular* functional hypothesis plus the evidence is compatible with only one type of curve. Following Barker's argument in the passage quoted, a system containing such a hypothesis would allow only a single type of structure of the universe, with respect to the functional properties possible. There would be no system containing *h* plus the evidence that would be simpler than *every* system containing the negation of *h* plus the evidence, since in both cases the simplest systems (containing *h* or containing the negation of *h*) would allow only a single structure to the universe with respect to the functional properties in question. Therefore, according to Barker's scheme, hypothesis *h* and its negation would be equally confirmed, and we would be provided with no more reason for choosing *h* than for choosing its negation (or any hypothesis implying its negation), no matter how much more preferable *h* might appear to us to be.

For this reason I conclude that although Barker's theory represents an important contribution to the task of utilizing the notion of simplicity in comparing the confirmation of certain types of hypotheses, it cannot be employed in the context of the present problem.

V

It may be suggested at this point that a basis for choosing among functional hypotheses is to be found not by instituting revisions within a theory of confirmation; it is to be found, rather, by utilizing a particular confirmation system as presently conceived (although extended to richer languages) together with a theory of *rational decision.* A theory of rational decision consists of a rule, or set of rules, for determining which hypothesis ought to be accepted on the given evidence. These rules, according to Carnap, are not part of a theory of confirmation itself; they are to be thought of only in connection with the practical application of that theory to the task of determining which hypothesis to add to our corpus of beliefs. The suggestion that considerations of simplicity are to be included within rules of rational decision rather than within a theory of confirmation has been made by a number of authors. Thus, e.g., in the course of a discussion of the relevance of simplicity to induction, Kemeny[21] formulates the following decision rule:

> From a set of hypotheses select the simplest one having a high degree of credibility,

where the degree of credibility is to be determined by employing an inductive system of confirmation, such as Carnap's. Hempel[22] is another author who makes reference to decision rules, and also suggests the possibility of using these in conjunction with Carnap's theory of confirmation in order to provide a basis for choosing among competing functional hypotheses.

The essential idea behind the approach is this. Suppose that we are to choose one from a set of mutually exclusive and exhaustive courses of action, which may have many different outcomes. By means of a theory of inductive confirmation ('logical probability'), such as Carnap's, we can determine the probability that a particular action will have a certain outcome, for each action and outcome. The particular action which constitutes the most rational choice for us depends upon the value or utility we attribute to the various outcomes. If it is possible to assign numerical measures to these utilities, then by employing a quantitative theory of confirmation we can determine the probability of achieving a certain utility value by pursuing a particular course of action; and on this basis a rule of rational decision can be formulated. Carnap, e.g., proposes the following rule:

> Among the possible actions choose that one for which the probability-estimate of the resulting utility is a maximum.[23]

This general procedure can be applied to the case of hypothesis selection as follows. Suppose that we are considering a set of hypotheses h_1, h_2, . . ., which, on the evidence, are mutually exclusive and exhaustive. With respect to these hypotheses the following courses of action are possible: accept h_1 and add it to our body of beliefs; accept h_2 and add it to our body of beliefs; etc.; accept none of the hypotheses. The possible outcomes are these: adding h_1 to our body of beliefs, where h_1 is true; adding h_1 where h_1 is false; adding h_2 where h_2 is true; adding h_2 where h_2 is false; etc.; leaving our body of beliefs unchanged. To utilize a rule of rational decision in determining which course of action to adopt, we must assign utilities to the various possible outcomes. According to Hempel, such utilities 'should reflect the value or disvalue which the different outcomes have from the point of view of pure scientific research rather than the practical advantages or disadvantages that might result from the application of an accepted hypothesis, according as the latter is true or false'.[24] These utilities Hempel classifies as purely scientific or epistemic. It is at this point, it might be suggested, that considerations of simplicity will prove relevant. For the epistemic utility of adding one hypothesis may be greater than that of adding another hypothesis, if, other things being equal, the former hypothesis is simpler than the latter. This will reflect one of the important aims of scientific pursuit, viz. that of providing maximally simple theories. Obviously the problem remains of how to construct a utility function which will take into account the relative simplicity of hypotheses. Nevertheless, it might be urged, the present line of approach is one which appears promising, and may well be expected to provide a rational basis for choosing among competing functional hypotheses.

Plausible though such an approach might seem, the proposal to solve the problem we are considering by formulating decision rules to be used in conjunction with an inductive theory of confirmation, rather than by introducing basic modifications within such a theory, leads to serious difficulty. For, the result of this procedure will be that the most rational course of action in the case of choosing among functional hypotheses is to refrain from adopting any hypothesis at all. Let us see why this is so.

Suppose that a particular inductive system of confirmation is enriched to the extent that functional hypotheses can be expressed in the language for which confirmation functions are defined. Suppose, furthermore, that a principle basic to most present schemes is retained, according to which the degree of confirmation of a hypothesis attributing a property to an unexamined individual depends in large measure upon the number of individuals observed to have or lack that property (the dependence being greater the larger the sample). Then, since all competing functional hypotheses describing the coordinates of an unexamined point will have the same number of positive instances (i.e. the same number of points satisfying the various curves), and no negative instances, the degree of confirmation of each of these hypotheses will be approximately the same, if the quantity of data is considerable. And since, no matter what the evidence, there will be an infinite number of such hypotheses, or at least a very large finite number (if we manage to restrict the number of competing hypotheses in some way), and these hypotheses will be mutually exclusive, the degree of confirmation of any particular hypothesis, on the basis of the evidence, will be either zero or close to it.[25] Suppose, now, that a utility function is defined, based on considerations of simplicity. This utility function will assign a numerical value to each outcome. Thus, we may suppose that the highest value u_1 will be assigned to the outcome of adding the simplest hypothesis h_1 to our body of beliefs, where h_1 is true; and, following the usual procedure, a value (or disvalue) of $-u_1$ (minus u_1) will be assigned to the outcome of adopting h_1, where h_1 is false. The assignment of utility values will proceed accordingly for each hypothesis, where utility values will be less in the case of more complex hypotheses. Finally, a value of 0 (no gain, no loss) will be assigned to the outcome of leaving our body of beliefs unchanged by adopting no hypothesis at all. Since, as we have seen, the degree of confirmation of each competing functional hypothesis will be very small, and in any case less than one-half, the rule of decision to adopt that course of action for which the probability-estimate of the resulting utility is a maximum will necessitate our choosing the very unheroic course of adopting no functional hypothesis at all; for it will turn out that the latter choice has the highest estimate of resulting utility.

This is demonstrated as follows: Let A_i be the choice of adopting hypothesis h_i, and let a_i be a sentence describing A_i. Let O_i be the outcome of adopting hypothesis h_i, where h_i is true, and let o_i be a sentence describing O_i. The outcome of adopting hypothesis h_i, where h_i is false is $\sim O_i$, which is described by the sentence $\sim o_i$. Let u_i be the utility associated with outcome O_i, and $-u_i$ the utility associated with $\sim O_i$. The probability-estimate of the utility (*est. util.*) associated with choice A_i is given as follows (where e represents the total evidence, and c is an inductive confirmation function):

$$(1)\quad \textit{est. util.}\ (A_i, e) = c(o_i, e \,.\, a_i)u_i + c(\sim o_i, e \,.\, a_i)\,(-u_i)$$

According to a theorem of probability, $c(\sim h, e) = 1 - c(h, e)$. Hence, from (1) we have

$$\textit{est. util.}\ (A_i, e) = c(o_i, e \,.\, a_i)u_i + [1 - c(o_i, e \,.\, a_i)]\,(-u_i)$$

Let $x = c(o_i, e \,.\, a_i)$. Then we have

$$\begin{aligned} \textit{est. util.}\ (A_i, e) &= xu_i + (1 - x)\,(-u_i) \\ &= (2x - 1)u_i \end{aligned}$$

Hence, *est. util.* $(A_i, e) \geqslant 0$ if and only if $(2x - 1)u_i \geqslant 0$. But since $u_i > 0$, it follows that

$$\textit{est. util.}\ (A_i, e) \geqslant 0 \text{ if and only if } x \geqslant 1/2$$

Since for any competing functional hypothesis h_i, $c(o_i, e \,.\, a_i)$ can be expected to be very low, and in any case less than $1/2$ (see above), it follows that for any such hypothesis h_i, $x < 1/2$. Consequently, *est. util.* $(A_i, e) < 0$. But, since the estimated utility of adopting no hypothesis at all must be 0 (because the utility value assigned to the corresponding outcome is 0), it follows that the latter course of action has a higher estimate of resulting utility than does the adoption of any hypothesis.

It is for this reason that the proposal to conjoin an inductive system of confirmation, as presently conceived, with a decision theory of the sort outlined by Carnap, seems to me insufficient for enabling us to justify the choice of a functional hypothesis. This fact, of course, does not impugn the value of decision theory. But it does seem to suggest that a solution to our problem will not be found merely by employing rules of acceptance which are based upon an inductive theory of confirmation, unless that theory undergoes some basic modifications.

VI

So far we have considered whether theories of confirmation based on induction, those founded on principles of simplicity, and decision theory conjoined with an inductive system of confirmation can be used to justify the choice of a functional hypothesis. Reasons have been suggested for doubting that such theories, as presently conceived, provide a satisfactory solution. Systems of induction, such as Carnap's and Reichenbach's, as well as theories of confirmation based on simplicity, such as those of Popper and Barker, seem unable in all cases to assign different amounts of support to competing functional hypotheses. And the attempt to combine an inductive system of confirmation with principles of decision theory leads to a negative result.

It is time to take positive steps. Instead of attempting at the outset to utilize confirmation theory in conjunction with rules of rational decision, it will now be proposed that modifications first be made within some of the basic assumptions underlying confirmation theory itself. Such modifications, I suggest, should incorporate principles of simplicity within the basic rules of confirmation, and should also reflect the fact that the quantity of data is relevant in determining the acceptability of a functional hypothesis. With this in mind, I propose that the basic rules of confirmation satisfy the following principle:

> With respect to a curve-fitting situation in which the data (a class of points) satisfy a set of mutually exclusive functional hypotheses, it is the simplest hypothesis, and only the simplest hypothesis, which receives positive support from these data. The nature of this support is inductive, in the sense that, other things being equal, the greater the

number of observed instances of this (simplest) functional hypothesis, the higher its degree of confirmation. (If several hypotheses are equally simple, and simpler than all the rest, and if each has the same number of positive instances and no negative ones, then each receives support from the data, though none receives more support than any other.)

I have added 'other things being equal' to the above principle, since obviously there are factors other than simplicity and the number of instances which can affect the confirmation of a hypothesis. One needs to consider, as well, how *varied* the instances are (e.g. whether observations were made at quite different values of the quantities, under different conditions, etc.); whether there are known *analogies* between these instances and others for which information is possessed; and also the effect of accepted *theories* on the hypothesis being considered.[26]

Suppose, then, that we have obtained data of the sort given at the beginning of the paper: The recorded points all lie on a straight line. And suppose either that nothing is known about the additional factors I have just mentioned or that what is known about these does not provide more support for the linear hypothesis than for others. The question, then, is this: why do we choose to accept the linear hypothesis when we have obtained a large number of points all of which lie on a straight line? The above principle provides an answer, as follows: because that hypothesis is the simplest one compatible with the evidence, and hence its instances, of which there are many, provide support for it; the instances of alternative hypotheses compatible with the data do not provide support for these hypotheses since these hypotheses are less simple than the linear one. In formulating rules of confirmation, the principle expressed above is to be adopted, I suggest, because it reflects the actual scientific practice of accepting the simplest functional hypothesis and maintaining furthermore that this hypothesis is indeed supported by the evidence, whereas other hypotheses, though compatible with the evidence, are not.

Accordingly, those who emphasize the role of induction are certainly correct when they claim that it is the observed instances of a functional hypothesis which are necessary to provide support for it, the extent of this support depending, among other things, on the number of such instances. And those who stress the importance of simplicity in curve-fitting problems are quite right in maintaining that the simplest hypothesis compatible with the data is, other things being equal, the most acceptable. The answer to the question of how to justify the choice of a functional hypothesis lies in combining the truths implicit in each position in the manner suggested. In accordance with this proposal, it should be noted that instances of a hypothesis do not always provide support for it; in other words, not all observed regularities—but only those meeting certain conditions which need to be specified—can be projected.[27] In the case of functional hypotheses, the condition we have imposed reflects the claim that only the simplest observed regularity can legitimately be projected.

If this proposal were to be adopted by an inductive theory of confirmation, some basic changes within that theory would be required. Thus, suppose we wish to define a confirmation function for a language rich enough to express functional hypotheses of some science, say physics. The language will contain the requisite mathematical expressions as well as symbols for functors (such as 'length', 'temperature', 'mass'). On this basis *functional predicates* could be defined. Thus, where P_i is such a predicate, a statement of the form $P_i x,t$ would mean 'x satisfies curve P_i at point t'. For example, let $T(b)$ mean 'the absolute temperature of b', and let $L(b, t)$ mean 'the length of b at (temperature) t'. Let us now define the functional predicate P_1 as follows:

$$P_1 b,t \equiv [t = T(b) \equiv L(b,t) = L(b, 0)\,(1 + 16{\cdot}7 \times 10^{-6}\, t)]$$

The functional hypothesis expressing the law of linear expansion for copper can be formulated in this way: $(x)\,(Cx \supset (t)P_1 x,t)$. And the fact that a given bar of copper b has been tested at various temperatures $t_1, t_2, \ldots t_n$, and has been found to satisfy this law at these temperatures is expressed as follows:

$$P_1 b,t_1,\ P_1 b,t_2,\ \ldots\ P_1 b,t_n.$$

Now, the problem of choosing among competing functional hypotheses stems from the fact that a given individual b may satisfy innumerably many functional predicates at the same points. Thus, in our copper example, since the observations made on the sample b of copper satisfy many different equations, each of the following conjunctions correctly describes the data: $P_1 b,t_1, \ldots P_1 b,t_n, P_2 b,t_1, \ldots P_2 b,t_n, P_3 b,t_1, \ldots P_3 b,t_n$, etc., where P_1, P_2, P_3, etc., are the different functional predicates satisfied by *b* at all the observed points.

Suppose, however, that we could order the various functional predicates according to the simplicity of the curves they are used to define. That is, P_i would be earlier in the ordering, and hence simpler, than P_j if the curve represented by the hypothesis that an individual (or each individual) of a certain sort satisfies, at all points, the predicate P_i is simpler than the curve represented by the hypothesis that an individual (or each individual) of that sort satisfies, at all points, the predicate P_j. In accordance with the proposal of the present section, we could say that although individual *b* satisfies many different functional predicates at the same points, it is only the simplest of these predicates which can be projected. That is, if P_s is the simplest of the functional predicates which *b* satisfies at the observed points, then the functional hypothesis that *b* satisfies P_s at all points—and only this hypothesis—receives increasing positive support from the evidence (i.e. as more and more points are recorded which satisfy P_s). And if *b* satisfies a number of different predicates that are equally simple, and simpler than the rest, then the corresponding hypotheses, and only these, receive increasing positive support. Thus, a confirmation function defined for the type of language in question would be required to satisfy the following condition:

> If *h* is a functional hypothesis ascribing a functional predicate *P* to a given individual *b* at all points (or at an unexamined point), and *e* is evidence ascribing the same functional predicate *P* to *b* at various points, then as the evidence *e* reports that *b* is observed to have *P* at more and more points (where *e* is the total evidence), the degree of confirmation of *h* on *e* increases *if and only if there is no functional predicate simpler than* P *which* b *manifests at all the points reported in the evidence.*

A confirmation function defined so as to satisfy this condition, and others of a similar nature, would thus be expected to accord a considerable measure of confirmation to a functional hypothesis on the basis of a set of data if and only if that hypothesis is the simplest one compatible with the data and the data are numerous.

Obviously, to construct such a function a number of major problems must first be solved. It must be determined how in principle to define a confirmation function for a language which contains expressions for functors with real numbers as values. The task of extending the definition of confirmation functions to richer languages is one of the main problems currently besetting confirmation theorists. Although progress has been made in recent years, in no cases are the languages strong enough to express many important quantitative statements of science, including functional hypotheses. Another problem is that of formulating criteria of simplicity which allow an ordering of algebraic as well as transcendental curves. Proposals have been offered in this area, but these have generally been limited in scope to polynomials, and in some cases do not prove adequate even for curves of this type.[28]

If a solution to these problems is forthcoming, and a confirmation function defined so as to incorporate the proposals of the present section, the resulting system could be combined with a decision theory; and the consequences would be of a sort more acceptable than previously. For, given a confirmation function of the type envisaged, if in a certain case the data were numerous, then the simplest functional hypothesis compatible with these data would be expected to receive a high degree of confirmation (certainly greater than one-half). And if the highest measure of utility is assigned to the outcome of accepting the simplest hypothesis h_s, where h_s is true, then this outcome will have the highest estimate of resulting utility. Consequently, the adoption of the simplest hypothesis in such a case would be prescribed by Carnap's decision rule.

The task of constructing a confirmation function capable of accommodating functional hypotheses still lies ahead. The present proposals indicate what sort of assumptions may be needed for this task. However, the aim of this section has been neither to advocate nor to criticize the idea of a confirmation theory of the sort envisaged by Carnap. It has been, rather, to argue that, in the case of functional hypotheses at least, any adequate expression of the principles of confirmation, whether these are stated in the formal way required by confirmation theory or in a more informal, intuitive way, will need to include considerations of simplicity as well as of quantity in the data. What I have tried to do is to suggest how the relationship between these factors should be expressed by such principles.

NOTES

[1] I am indebted to S. F. Barker for his valuable comments.

[2] For a detailed account of the notion of positive instance see Carl G. Hempel, 'Studies in the Logic of Confirmation', *Mind*, vol. 54 (1945), pp 1–26, 97–121. In accordance with Hempel's proposal, the stipulation above would provide a sufficient though not a necessary condition for being a positive instance of a generalization.

[3] Usually 'compatibility' in such contexts is taken to mean 'within the limits of experimental error' rather than 'exactly in accord with the data'. However, since we are not considering cases involving experimental error, compatibility in what follows can be construed in the stronger sense.

[4] Rudolf Carnap, *The Continuum of Inductive Methods* (University of Chicago, 1952); *Logical Foundations of Probability* (University of Chicago, 1950; 2nd edn., 1962).

[5] More precisely, the theorem can be expressed as follows. Where h_M is a hypothesis attributing the predicate M to an unexamined individual, and e_M is evidence which attributes either M or its denial to each of the individuals observed, then, if c is a confirmation function which is defined for a specified language and which satisfies Carnap's requirements,

$$\lim_{s\to\infty} c\,(h_M, e_M) = s_M/s,$$

where s is the number of individuals in the observed sample, and s_M is the number of these which have M.

This theorem follows from theorem 9–8 in Carnap's *Continuum of Inductive Methods* (p 30); it holds for all confirmation functions in this system with one exception (the so-called Wittgenstein function, which, however, Carnap finds unacceptable—see *ibid*, p 38). Carnap constructs his system in such a way that the choice of a particular confirmation function is made to depend upon the choice of one parameter in a certain equation; the smaller the parameter selected, the faster is the convergence in the above theorem. A similar theorem, but applying only to primitive predicates in what Carnap calls a 'family of predicates', is derivable in a later system which he develops in *The Philosophy of Rudolf Carnap*, ed. Paul Arthur Schilpp (Illinois, LaSalle, 1963). See prop. (7), p 976.

[6] John G. Kemeny, 'A Logical Measure Function', *Journal of Symbolic Logic*, vol. 18 (1953), pp 289–308.

[7] Hilary Putnam, 'A Definition of Degree of Confirmation for Very Rich Languages', *Philosophy of Science*, vol. 23 (1956), pp 58–62.

[8] Carnap classifies predicates into three types: purely qualitative, purely positional, and mixed. And he maintains that all purely qualitative predicates are inductively projectible, and therefore subject to a theorem of the sort indicated above. But predicates of the form 'satisfies functional relationship $y = f(x)$' would appear to be purely qualitative in Carnap's sense, since their definitions make no reference to particular individuals or specific positions. If so, then in a more fully developed system they would be subject to the theorem specified.

[9] Hans Reichenbach, *Experience and Prediction* (Chicago, 1938).

[10] *Ibid,* pp 375 ff.

[11] *Ibid,* p 380.

[12] *Ibid,* pp 348–57.

[13] Given a set of observed points, Reichenbach's argument for the initial step can be used to choose any curve whatever whose defining function f satisfies the following condition: where (x_0, y_0) represents the values of the quantities x and y at any observed point, $\lim_{x \to x_0} f(x) = y_0$, for each such (x_0, y_0).

[14] Karl Popper, *The Logic of Scientific Discovery* (London: Hutchinson, 1959).

[15] *Ibid,* pp 399–401.

[16] Popper does maintain (*op. cit.,* p 134) that in certain cases the degree of falsifiability of two functional hypotheses should be compared by considering not only the dimensionality of the curves in question but also what he calls the 'generality' in the definitions of these curves, i.e. 'their invariance with respect to coordinate transformations'. But he never indicates exactly how we are to combine this criterion with the dimension criterion of falsifiability. Moreover, since any two polynomials, e.g., all of whose parameters have been specified have zero-generality, according to Popper's definition, the additional criterion which he suggests does not appear to alter the initial results with respect to particular functional hypotheses.

[17] Thus, consider one of Popper's definitions of a confirmation function c (*op. cit.,* p 400):

$$c(x, y) = \frac{p(y, x) - p(y)}{p(y, x) + p(y)} (1 + p(x)p(x, y)),$$

where p is a probability function. If x is a functional hypothesis which logically entails the data y, then, since $p(x, y) = p(x, y)/p(y)$, we can introduce the following simplification:

$$(1) \qquad c(x, y) = \frac{1 - p(y)}{1 + p(y)} \left(1 + \frac{p(x)p(x)}{p(y)}\right)$$

Now, according to Popper, the simplicity of a hypothesis is measured in terms of its absolute probability (where lower probability values indicate greater simplicity). Hence, since competing *particular* functional hypotheses are equally simple on Popper's criterion, where x_1 and x_2 are any two such hypotheses, and y describes a set of points satisfying both hypotheses, it follows from (1) above that $c(x_1, y) = c(x_2, y)$.

[18] S. F. Barker, *Induction and Hypothesis* (Ithaca, 1957).

[19] John G. Kemeny, 'Two Measures of Complexity', *Journal of Philosophy,* vol. LII (1955), pp 721–34.

[20] Barker, *op. cit.,* p 181.

[21] John G. Kemeny, 'The Use of Simplicity in Induction', *Philosophical Review,* LXII (1953), pp 391–408.

[22] Carl G. Hempel, 'Inductive Inconsistencies', *Synthese,* vol. XII (1960), pp 439–69.

[23] Rudolf Carnap, *Logical Foundations of Probability,* p 269.

[24] 'Inductive Inconsistencies.'

[25] Hence, Kemeny's decision rule (which makes no reference to utility)

would not allow the adoption of any of these hypotheses, since none has a high degree of confirmation.

[26] See my 'Variety and Analogy in Confirmation Theory', *Philosophy of Science,* vol. 30 (1963), pp 207–21; also my 'Rudolf Carnap', *Review of Metaphysics,* vol. XIX (1966), pp 517–49, 758–79, and esp. 769 ff.

[27] A point emphasized by Nelson Goodman; see his *Fact, Fiction, and Forecast* (Cambridge, 1955), chapter 3.

[28] For a discussion of some of the problems involved see Robert Ackermann, 'Inductive Simplicity', *Philosophy of Science*, vol. 28 (1961), pp 152–61.

DIRECT REALISM AND PERCEPTUAL ERROR

KEITH CAMPBELL

UNDER CERTAIN CIRCUMSTANCES normal human observers misperceive their environment. Fatigue, hunger, emotional agitation, expectation, desire, and reward, all have some effect on our perception of the world. As concrete examples of such phenomena, let us take the expectation effects of colour and shape constancy. In experiments, one group of subjects was presented with what they knew to be familiar objects under unusual conditions of illumination or perspective. Another group was presented with the same objects under the same conditions, but were not told what they were. The subjects were asked to match the appearances of the objects with sample colours and shapes. The first group consistently matched the appearances with shapes and colours closer to the appearances the objects have under normal conditions than did the second group; but the matchings made by the latter accorded better with the findings of instruments and of optical theory.[1] The first group of subjects were judged to be committing systematic perceptual errors.

By means of investigations like the ones just mentioned, human beings can discover systematic errors in their own perception. They can even learn to correct in appropriate circumstances and so err no longer. Any satisfactory account of perception must be able to accommodate the two facts: that we make the errors of the colour and shape constancy effects, and that we can discover this. To effect this accommodation, more general requirements must be satisfied. Any satisfactory theory must be compatible with, and preferably furnish an explanation for, the truths:

A. It is possible for a human observer both to perceive an object correctly and to misperceive it.

B. It is possible, at least in some cases, to distinguish between veridical and erroneous perception of an object.

In what follows, *a theory of perception* means a philosophical theory specifying:

1) what are the immediate data of sense, i.e. what knowledge (if any) is obtained by means of the senses alone, i.e. what knowledge (if any) is prior to all inference or hypothesis;[2] and

2) the manner in which the immediate data of sense relate to our natural pre-scientific knowledge of the world.

The theories which have recurrently found favour among philosophers may be grouped under three heads according to their ontological commitments, as

PHENOMENALIST: theories committed only to impressions of sense (fleeting, private entities, dependent on being perceived for their existence), and logical or psychological constructions out of them.

REPRESENTATIVE REALIST: theories committed to both impressions of sense and independent bodies (public, enduring substances having variable states).

DIRECT REALIST: theories committed only to bodies and their states.

Apart from theories of these three types, there are further accounts of perception which might be called the

THESES OF POLYMORPHISM: one (or both) of the questions 'What are the immediate data of sense?' and 'How do such data yield knowledge of the world?' has no single answer both correct and non-trivial.

The Theses of Polymorphism are serious suggestions and one of them may even be true, but they do not form a fourth group straightforwardly rival to the traditional three. Where such a thesis is more than a mere denial that any epistemology for our common knowledge is possible, it must offer general accounts of the several and various grounds of knowledge which any unified doctrine of perception culpably fails to distinguish. Any epistemology to which a Thesis of Polymorphism could give rise will inevitably be more complex, and any part of it less general, than a theory which treats perception in a single fashion. But simplicity and generality are virtues in theories of any kind. So the proper strategy is to regard the Theses of Polymorphism as last resorts, and to embrace one only when the inadequacy of every plausible unitary theory of perception has been established.

Now, any adequate theory of perception must be able to accommodate in a convincing fashion truths *A* and *B* above, namely that humans can both perceive veridically and misperceive an object, and that they can sometimes distinguish veridical from erroneous perception. This provides two touchstones which may be applied to a theory, in a preliminary way, by attending solely to its ontological commitments. These conditions on any adequate theory—being compatible with *A*, and being compatible with *B*—are henceforth labelled *CA* and *CB* respectively.

CA is satisfied by any theory which holds that perceived objects and perceivers are relatively stable and independent of any perceiving of them, and which embraces the general causal doctrine:

> Whenever an observer *S* perceives an object *O*, *O* is a causal condition for *S*'s perception of *O*.

Where *O* is an independent body or a state of such a body, the general causal doctrine suffices for the satisfaction of *CA*. For no details are specified in the causal connection between *O* and *S*'s perception of *O*. *O* can still be a causal condition for *S*'s perception of *O* although change in the relevant conditions other than the presence and nature of *O* results in the production of a different effect. That is, *O* can be perceived differently, or not at all, as these conditions vary. Whence, if in perception of *O*, *O* acts on *S*, two possibilities are open: that *O* should act on *S* so that *S* entertains true beliefs about *O* gained in that perception, or, that *O* should act on *S* so that *S*'s beliefs about *O*, so gained, are false. But this, precisely, is the satisfaction of *CA*; for the truth and falsity of such beliefs is a sufficient condition for *S*'s perceiving *O* correctly or incorrectly.[3]

The general causal doctrine is to be contrasted with the more common, more restricted doctrine that in all and only cases of *veridical* perception the object *O* is causally responsible for *S*'s perception of it.[4] Conflict between the general and the more restricted doctrine stems from different decisions on the use of the technical term 'perceive'. To decide in favour of the general doctrine and build causal history into the unqualified notion of perception has its advantages.

If the essential causal rôle of *O* is made a peculiarity of veridical perception, it becomes possible for *S* to misperceive *O* in the case where *O* plays no such part. But then we must resort to some *ad hoc* expedient to avoid having to admit the strict propriety of such locutions as 'I made a mistake in seeing the Lord Chief Justice last night' in the situation where I caught a glimpse of a film of Mme Tussaud's, thought I saw the man himself, and was mistaken about the length of the wig on the waxwork.

The restricted doctrine is further open to criticism in inviting, although not requiring, the introduction of ethereal, private entities into accounts of perception. For 'misperceive' is a transitive verb. If cases where what is thought to be perceived does not exist at all (hallucinations of Oliver Cromwell) may nevertheless be cases of misperception, there is a temptation to furnish a seeming-Oliver-Cromwell as the grammatical object of the verb, and as the immediate object of the misperception. If the object misperceived must play a causal part in the misperception of it, this move is blocked—having hallucinations is not a case of perceiving at all, not even of misperceiving. Both these difficulties are avoided if neither '*S* perceived *O*' nor '*S* misperceived *O*' is allowed in describing a perceptual situation in which *O* plays no essential causal rôle, no matter what *S* takes himself to be perceiving. We may in such cases say '*S* perceived (misperceived) *P* as an *O*' or intransitive verbs may take the place of 'perceive' and 'misperceive' in our description of them.

A more serious objection to restricting the essential causal rôle of *O* to those cases in which perception of *O* is veridical is that under the restriction any satisfaction of *CA* will be very awkward. It will be awkward even where *O* is an independent body or state of such a body, the case in which the general causal doctrine satisfies *CA* so readily.

Note first that the restricted doctrine (that in veridical perception *O* plays an essential causal rôle in perception of *O*) specifies a necessary, but not a sufficient, condition for veridical perception. For in the shape- and colour-constancy experiments which form our point of departure, the objects *mis*perceived played such a causal rôle in perception of them. So to show that an error occurred in perception of *O* does not show that *O* was not an essential causal agent in the perception of *O*, hence does not show that it was not *O* that was perceived.

Suppose now that while in Trafalgar Square I believe myself to be on Fish Hill. Having read of the ball in flames to be found on the Monument, and believing Nelson's Column to be the Monument, I look up and 'see' the flaming ball. It is established that it was Nelson on his column which I mistook for the ball in flames. For a theory containing the general causal doctrine this case can be straightforwardly accommodated:

I made an error in perceiving the statue of Nelson as a ball in flames.

But a theory containing the restricted doctrine allows that misperceived objects need play no causal rôle in their misperception. It thus fails to exclude:

i) I made an error in perceiving a ball of flames.

It was the statue of Nelson I mistook for the ball, and as argued above, the restricted causal doctrine does not show that an object misperceived is not, properly speaking, perceived at all. So the theory also fails to exclude:

ii) I made an error in perceiving the statue of Nelson.

But both phenomenologically and on optical grounds:

iii) There was only one object of my misperception.

An account of the incident embracing these three propositions and satisfying *CA* is possible. But it will be a very awkward one, to say the least.

To repeat how *CA* can be satisfied by theories according to which the world is composed of independent substances, and which adopt the general causal doctrine:

When *S* perceives *O* as an *O′*, '*O*' and '*O′*' both refer to independent bodies (or their states). It is true that *S* perceives *O* as an *O′* if as the result of an action on *S*'s senses in which *O* plays an essential causal rôle, *S* comes to believe that *O* is an *O′*, whether *O* is an *O′* (veridical perception) or is not (misperception).

Two consequences of this doctrine are:

When *S* believes he is perceiving *O*, he may not be perceiving *O*.

and

When *S* believes he is perceiving *O*, he may be perceiving nothing at all.

This way of satisfying *CA* is clearly open to theories of perception of either Direct Realist or Representative Realist type. But no theory according to which the world is constructed from sense impressions can avail itself of the general causal doctrine. For then in our formula:

S perceives *O* as an *O′*, '*O*' refers to a set of actual and possible sense impressions, and '*O′*' refers to such a set, or to a member of such a set. In this case '*S* perceives *O*' is glossed as 'one member *b* of the set of impressions {*a, b, c, d, . . .*} now here occurs'. But as {*a, b, c, d, . . .*} can never sensibly be said to be the cause of the occurrence of *b,* the general causal doctrine can never figure in any Phenomenalist theory.

Phenomenalist theories may nevertheless satisfy *CA*. The perceptual errors of the shape-constancy effect admit of description in a familiar style thus:

A subject *S* who knew that *O* was a familiar object had sense impression sdS_1, the apparent shape of (and member of the construct which is) the familiar object *O*, and at t_2 sense impression sdS_2, the apparent shape of (and member of the construct which is) the shape sample *Q*, such that sdS_1 and sdS_2 were identical in shape. Other matchings at other times and by other subjects of sense impressions, properly considered to be normal impressions for the construct which is *O*, matched the apparent shape of *O* with that of a different shape sample *Q′*. This gave *S* (and others) reason to think that sdS_1 must be judged an abnormal impression in the set which is *O*. Strictly, of course, both 'matching' and 'other subjects' must also be rewritten in phenomenalese, making the description even more cumbersome. Let us assume this is possible.

To cope with misperception, appeal is made to difference of status among members of the set of impressions which is *O*, some being accorded central, normal status, and some being considered peripheral and abnormal. The members are classed according to the accuracy of predictions based on them concerning the occurrence and content of further impressions under specified conditions. The claim:

Objects are sets of impressions of varying status,

makes possible both perceptual error and perceptual success. Misperception is not misperception of the immediate object of perception, for the immediate object is precisely one about which such error is impossible. Misperceptions are rather misjudgments of the set to which a sense impression belongs, or of its status within that set. In veridical perception these ordering judgments are correctly made. To the Realist contention that *O* may appear to *S* to be what it is not, and in any particular case *S* may not realize this, corresponds in Phenomenalist theories the claim that the members of *O* given to *S* may be normal or abnormal, and *S* may not know what a particular member's status is.

Theories of perception of all three classical types may therefore admit the truth that human beings can both perceive veridically and misperceive an object. But we require more of a theory of perception than mere compatibility with this truth. We require further at least that the theory should allow for the provision of an explanation of those particular vagaries in the accuracy of perception (e.g. the occurrence of colour and shape-constancy effects) which experiment discovers.

Realist theories, whether Direct or Representative, are in a strong position here. Since human beings perceive by means of sense organs, Realists can claim that variations are to be found in the fine structure and functioning of the sense organs and central nervous system of observer *S* which can be correlated with, and used to explain, the variations in the accuracy with which *S* perceives *O* under various conditions. These neural variations may themselves admit of explanation. We may of course never find satisfactory explanations of, e.g., the shape-constancy effect along these or any other lines. But where our theory of perception is a Realist one, such explanations are at least possible. And that is all that is here being demanded.

But Phenomenalist theories cannot take the same line. For the sense organs of *S* are on such accounts themselves constructions out of impressions of sense. Terms for the sense organs, like all terms for independent bodies, are theoretical terms referring to constructions. Furthermore, they are theoretical terms after the model of 'gravitation' rather than 'virus'. There is no question of any entity, in principle directly observable, over and above the phenomena the terms serve to connect.

Talk of the fine structure of sense organs, if admitted at all, could therefore be interpreted only as a refinement of an admittedly ideal model. Such talk would explain in the sense in which the law of inverse square decay, a refinement of the gravitation model, explains the planetary orbits. Such explanation exhibits the phenomena as in orderly connection.

The effect of any reply to the question 'Why, in the shape-constancy effect, for example, do impressions obtained in conditions C_1 differ from impressions obtained in C_2, if impressions gained under both sets of conditions all belong to the same construct?' is to show that such differences are to be expected as part of the ordinary run of things. Impressions, it must be held, just happen to form the orderly sequences on which our expectations are based.

This is unsatisfactory. For the explanations whose possibility is demanded are stronger ones which make the orderliness itself intelligible, and not a mere brute fact. On a Phenomenalist metaphysic, neither the fine structure of the sense organs and of the central nervous system nor anything else can furnish material for a real mechanism connecting the phenomena discovered in the shape-constancy effect. The stronger sort of explanation is impossible in any Phenomenalist theory. So although Phenomenalist theories meet the minimum requirement (*CA*) that they be compatible with the truth that we perceive both aright and awry, they fail the further requirement of admitting suitable explanations of this. They are therefore inadequate.[5]

This first touchstone, the ability properly to accommodate *A*, does not make any distinction between Direct and Representative Realist theories. So let us now turn to the second test, the condition *CB*:

> It must be possible to distinguish between veridical and erroneous perception.

Truistically, the true and false beliefs, gained by observation, through which veridical and erroneous perceptions are specified, are alike gained in observation. So to distinguish veridical from erroneous perception, we must be able to distinguish between those conditions of observation which give rise to error, and those which do not. Our second touchstone for theories of perception thus becomes:

> It is possible to distinguish between standard and non-standard conditions of observation.

The distinction made must be such that any systematic errors we discover (for example, the shape- and colour-constancy errors) occur under non-standard conditions.

Notoriously, whatever distinction is drawn among conditions of observation cannot be arbitrary or *ad hoc* but must be buttressed by reasons. For otherwise no defence can be made to that sceptical species of the Argument from Illusion according to which, because not all our perceptions are veridical, it is unphilosophical to trust any particular one of them. This argument depends precisely upon our inability to make any reasoned distinction among various conditions of observation.

Attempts to base the distinction between standard and non-standard conditions on the relative predictive success of perceptual beliefs about *O* obtained under various conditions are incurably circular. For predictive success or failure can only be determined by later observations of *O* which are themselves made under standard conditions.[6]

Attempts to specify standard conditions by listing and excluding the conditions under which perceptual errors may arise are no more successful. They fail either through circularity or through our inability to know that the list is complete.

But a distinction between the qualities of *O* as it is in itself, and the qualities *O* has relative to some observer or observers (one of the distinctions the primary/secondary dichotomy has been used to mark), can be used as a basis for the distinction between standard and non-standard conditions.[7]

For standard conditions of observation of *O* can then be defined as those under which the immediate data of the observation are compatible with what is known of *O*'s primary qualities (and also with more general knowledge of, e.g., the behaviour of propagated light).[8]

The definition of 'standard conditions of observation' which rests upon the primary/secondary dichotomy of qualities will enable us to distinguish standard from non-standard conditions and so satisfy our second touchstone only if further:

We can distinguish primary from secondary qualities

and

The real primary qualities of an object can be discovered.

To make good a claim to distinguish primary from secondary qualities we must produce a criterion. It has always been a mark of primary qualities that they are detectable by more than one sense. This is a special case of the more general mark that there is more than one item in the list of possible modes of sensation a perceiver must lack if a quality is to be imperceivable for him.

Adopting this more general mark as our criterion:

Primary qualities are those which are not dependent on the particular sensible constitution of man or any other perceiver for their detectability. Such qualities can be discovered by any creature able to make sufficiently fine discriminations, no matter what particular qualities its senses are able to detect immediately; they may be tagged as *neutral with respect to perceptual mode*. On this criterion, extension, figure, and motion are primary qualities, colour and felt temperature secondary; that is, this criterion effects something very like the traditional division.

Now on a Representative Realist theory of perception it is not reasonable to accept this or any other criterion whereby to distinguish primary from secondary qualities. For on such a view, according to which *S* perceives *O* by having sense impressions 'of' *O*, all perceived qualities must be in our sense secondary. All perceived qualities must be considered qualities of *O* in relation to *S*, in so far as they are qualities of *S*'s impressions of *O*. No matter what our theory, neutrality with respect to perceptual mode will be a feature of some of *O*'s perceived qualities and not of others. But possession of this feature can be no ground for holding that a quality belongs to *O* as it is in itself. Neutrality with respect to perceptual mode distinguishes rather a sub-species of secondary quality. So for any other proposed criterion whereby primary qualities are to be determined; all distinctions among qualities become distinctions between varieties of secondary quality.

We may describe the failure of Representative Realist theories at this point in either of two ways. They may be said to admit no distinguishing of primary from secondary qualities, and hence no distinguishing among conditions of observation. Or a criterion such as that of neutrality with respect to perceptual mode may be deemed to distinguish 'apparent primary' from 'properly secondary' qualities. But then the real primary qualities of an object can never be discovered. Where not *O* but impressions of *O* are the objects of perception, it cannot even be known whether *O* really has in itself any quality whatever under the same determinable with an apparent primary quality, let alone which determinate quality. Kant's unknowable thing-in-itself provides a grimly exact illustration of the position.

Direct Realist theories, on the other hand, allow both the distinguishing of primary from secondary qualities and the discovery of real primary qualities. The criterion of neutrality with respect to perceptual mode fixes the primary determinables only, but the qualities selected are determinable qualities of *O* itself, not determinable qualities of impressions of *O*, and so can properly be considered primary. To fix the determinate quality which is the real primary quality of *O* under a given primary determinable, a further test is required. This test is:

> The real determinate primary qualities of *O* are those whose attribution to *O* will allow (in conjunction with natural laws) the most economical and comprehensive explanation of *O*'s behaviour and appearances.

In some of its primary quality appearances *O* will appear to have the quality it really has. The conditions under which this occurs are candidates for election as 'standard conditions'. The conditions elected as standard conditions are those where coincidence of apparent and real quality is regular and reliable. Our choice of standard conditions is thus fallible and improvable just as choice of natural laws and best explanations is fallible and improvable, and regular and reliable coincidences are subject to breakdowns. But this does not disable us from making a reasoned distinction between standard and non-standard conditions. By its means it is possible to distinguish veridical from erroneous perception.

A reasoned defence can thus be given of the description of the shape and constancy effects from which we began. In some perceptions the primary qualities *O* appears to have are at variance with *O*'s real qualities. These perceptions are accordingly erroneous and hence occur under non-standard conditions. In other perceptions, there is no such variance. These are veridical, and occur under standard conditions. The case of colour constancy will require more elaborate treatment in terms of qualities of *O*, imperceptible and hence neither primary nor secondary, without which *O* would not be coloured, yet which like primary qualities belong to *O* as it is in itself and do not alter under observation by different subjects. The lesson in both cases is the same, namely that the difference between the two groups of subjects is a difference sufficient to make the difference between standard and non-standard conditions of observation. The difference the experimeters hoped to isolate was knowledge of *O*'s real properties in one group of subjects and ignorance of these in the other. The moral drawn was that a lively expectation of what one will perceive, if not guarded against, is one more factor making for non-standard conditions of observation.

It has often been said that the facts of perceptual error suffice to explode all forms of Direct Realism. This claim is motivated in part by the mistaken conviction that if the immediate object of perception may be other than it seems, perception can yield no knowledge. It seems that on the contrary only a theory of the Direct Realist type can satisfactorily accommodate mistakes like those of the shape- and colour-constancy effects, and at the same time preserve the axiom that knowledge can be gained in perception. The argument here developed thus supports Direct Realist theories, and in particular versions according to which the immediate object of perception may be other than it seems (theories, it might be said, of Sophisticated Realism). This argument is not conclusive, for theories of other types may be able to accommodate what is commonly called misperception and its detection in ways not here considered (for example, by adopting some metaphysic of independent, wildly unstable, bodies, or by finding methods of detecting error which involve no appeal to the distinction between primary and secondary qualities). But plausible alternatives do not spring readily to mind. Until they are produced the argument advances considerations which ought to influence the intellect.

NOTES

1 See, for example, M. D. Vernon, *The Psychology of Perception* (Penguin, 1962), pp 66–70, 78–9.

2 What are here called the immediate data of sense are not sensory impacts of which I am not aware (e.g. changes at the inner ends of the optic nerve)—these are not *data* at all. Nor are they what is given prior to all judgment or formation of belief. If there is an awareness on the basis of which we come to form perceptual beliefs, it neither counts as knowledge nor stands in any epistemic relation to natural knowledge.

3 The connection between true and false belief gained in perception and veridical or erroneous perception is at least so strong that the former is a

sufficient condition for the latter. Some go further, and identify the two. Cf. D. M. Armstrong, *Perception and the Physical World* (London, 1961), chapter 9.

[4] In §11 of D. M. Armstrong's *A Theory of Perception,* in Nagel and Wolman (eds.), *Scientific Psychology,* Basic Books (New York, 1965), for example, the causal responsibility is said to be 'part of our concept of *veridical* perception' (italics mine). Closer to the general causal doctrine is that of R. J. Hirst, *The Problem of Perception* (London, 1959), p 287, that I cannot perceive *O* when *O* is not a cause of my perceiving, but I can be perceptually conscious of *O* under such conditions. Perception is perceptual consciousness having a particular causal history. Hirst's doctrine is, however, unsatisfactory, for in the perception of *O*, *O* may be other than it seems (witness the shape-constancy effect), whereas in perceptual consciousness of *O*, explained on p 219 as perception considered in abstraction from whether or not it is veridical, *O* may not be other than it seems.

[5] The charge that this demand for the possibility of strong explanation displays a prejudice in favour of natural science must be admitted. If explanations by real mechanism are incurably Realistic, so much the worse for Phenomenalism.

[6] The same disability afflicts many suggested criteria whereby, in Phenomenalist theories, the status of members of construct *O* as normal or abnormal is to be determined. It is, accordingly, likely that Phenomenalist theories would fail by our second touchstone also.

[7] Cf. W. C. Kneale, 'Sensation and the Physical World', *Philosophical Quarterly*, vol. I (1950–1), pp 121 f.

[8] This is not to say that any particular theory of light is incorrigible. For the definition refers to ultimately, not merely putatively, compatible data. Whether or not given conditions are standard is a question never finally closed.

PERFORMATORY SELF-REFERENCE AND THE PHILOSOPHY OF MIND

S. COVAL

IT HAS BEEN, directly and indirectly, a point of debate in the Philosophy of Mind whether our main device of self-reference, the first-person pronoun, performs a function sufficiently unique to prevent its rôle from being taken over by our impersonal referential devices. I want to argue that there are some unique features to the first person and that they are responsibly related to the troublesome asymmetry between some self-ascriptions and some other-ascriptions which is traditional to the Philosophy of Mind. I want to show, however, that these asymmetric features of the first person are due to the contingent but highly economic use we are able to make of the speech situation itself as we self-refer. Hence, I shall argue, these asymmetric features of our first-person device are not really powerful enough to be used as aids in making out the traditional asymmetries between Selves and Others and Selves and Things. Quite the reverse is the case: self-reference is so much like other-reference, except in some non-necessary but useful ways, that the topics of those sentences whose referring devices are the first person do not, on the linguistic evidence, differ from the topics of those sentences whose referring devices are other than the first person. *That* argument would seem to require that the asymmetries of our self-referential devices with respect to our other demonstratives be more than a matter of economic contingency.

I intend to proceed as follows: 1) To merely set down the special features of the first person, our (main) device of self-reference. 2) To test which of these special features we could replace and yet still achieve successful self-reference. 3) To offer an account of why we retain those particular first-person features even though they are non-necessary. 4) To see how the sceptic, who argues that self-ascription differs from other-ascription, is affected by the fact that certain key features of our device of self-reference turn out to be non-necessary. Perhaps his scepticism about persons will turn out to be non-necessary in the same way.

1. *Special features of the first person.* I take the following features of the first person, taken together, to be shared by no other demonstrative.

a) Only I may use 'I' of myself.

b) Anyone may use 'I' of himself.

c) Only the speaker may use 'I' of himself.

I want to see whether the special features of our first-person device are required for the achievement of self-reference or whether unique self-reference may be achieved without them. I shall examine three candidates for substitution of the device of the first person. Each of these candidates I think would achieve for us unique self-reference, but none of them has all the properties of the first person. We shall then want to ask what if anything is served by those special but non-necessary properties of the first person.

1. We might introduce a convention of speaker-restricted 'names'. In such a case there are 'names' which each of us uses only of himself. There will have to be individual conventions for each 'name' because there is, *ex hypothesi*, no formal general way of indicating the difference between such speaker-restricted and non-speaker-restricted 'names'. But this device of separate, speaker-restricted 'names', though it could supply us with unique self-reference, loses the economy of generality of our first-person device—that anyone may use 'I' of himself. It does not satisfy characteristic *b*). I shall expand this soon.

1.2 Instead of a convention of speaker-restricted 'names' we could use our proper names as they are now used. This, too, would achieve self-reference and with less vocabulary than the first case, but it would require that hearers 'know the name' of everyone who would successfully self-refer in their presences. This awkwardness is in contrast to the elegance and economy of the single device of the first personal pronoun wherewith *any*one may refer to himself. The use of our own names for self-reference then lacks the advantages of characteristic *b*). It also retains the ambiguity of being usable both by and of the user. In our use of the first person this ambiguity is prevented by characteristic *a*)—that only I may use 'I' of myself.

1.3 Pointing to oneself as a means of self-reference has all of the economies and features of the first person except that visual cues are not as effective as auditory cues. Visual cues, for instance, are not as attention-getting as are auditory ones. The extent to which pointing can, however, get us both reference and self-reference is the extent to which both our personal and impersonal demonstratives are basically the same operation.

1.4 Other candidates of substitution for the first person, such as special predicate inflexions or the use of the general demonstrative 'this', rather than particular demonstratives such as names, are unimportantly different from the cases already scouted.

The use of 'this' as a surrogate for 'I' differs from the use of a self-restricted proper 'name' in that while 'this' satisfies the characteristic of generality that anyone may use 'this', it does not satisfy the restrictive feature that only the speaker, or only I, may use 'this' of myself. In this respect it is no different than the use of ordinary proper names for self-reference since, like names, 'this' would with appropriate changes be usable by anyone of himself but would not be uniquely restricted to use by the speaker of himself. The speaker could still use 'this' to refer to things other than himself. But the situation in which a term, like 'this', may be used to self-identify does not differ relevantly from the situation in which 'Enos' may be used to do so.

The point, again, of all these cases is merely to show that although some surrogates may not have some of the characteristics of our self-referring device of the first person, they are nevertheless each adequate to perform the function, if not to duplicate what I shall argue is the economy, of that device. This would show that the characteristics not shared by these surrogate ways of performing the function are not essential to that function.

2. I want now to try to account for the nature and importance of those three characteristics of the first person. It remains to be seen, in 4, whether the personal paradoxes can or cannot be stated in the absence of the economics of the first-person device as it stands. Should they be incapable of statement in the absence only

of the economic aspects of the function of the first person, then their solution might just reside in that demonstration.

What, then, is the function of the first person in the light of its special features?

2.1 When we speak, it is clear, or can be, who speaks. We have no need for special monograms to mark an utterance as uniquely mine or yours; neither have we need uniquely to mark any other actions of ours to make them each discriminable as our own. Performances take place at a place, at a time and hence could be used uniquely to identify the performer.

Let us grant that the speech act itself is uniquely identifying—no one else at this time at this place could so have acted. Hence reference *via* the act itself would be unique reference. Now, if the question of concern to us is how do we achieve unique *self-reference* in speech, obviously that will be a matter of how we achieve self-reference while in the act of speaking itself. *Self*-reference *must* occur *en acte*. Since the speech I am engaged in would be uniquely and necessarily my act, we are able to exploit this unique proprietariness in the achievement of unique self-reference. This is exactly what the first-person device does capitalize upon.

No other-referring device of speech makes capital out of the proprietariness of the speech act itself, and this is exactly what our surrogate devices of self-reference failed to do also. But, then, no other-referring device can make use of the fact that the act of reference, the speech act, the utterance of 'I', is a uniquely proprietary and hence identifying event in itself. This, to project the argument again, may be much of the nature of the troublesome asymmetry between the first person and the second and third person—and, if it is, our treatment of that asymmetry and of its previous philosophical and sceptical consequences will undergo some change.

This, then, in rough, is my case for the function of those special features of the first person—that 'I' is peculiarly a device of reference whose utterance or performance itself provides, by the unique proprietariness of such performance, its own basis for that reference. Our conventions are such that to utter 'I . . .' is to refer by way of that proprietary act of utterance itself, to the speaker himself. This, I think, is unique among all expressions of speech; but, then, so are the requirements of a *general, inter*changeable, device of unique self-reference.

2.2 It must not be thought in opposition here that there is a 'self' beyond the speaker, as it were, a 'self' further related to the uniqueness-supplying act of speech to which the use of 'I' is tied by convention. We might wonder, that is, why 'I' must be merely a speaker-restricted term and is not perhaps (also) a 'self'-restricted one. Or further, why is 'speaker' not a 'self'-restricted expression rather than 'self' a speaker-restricted expression. The answer is the one already given: in the speech situation the only sufficiently unique events to serve as context for a *general convention of self-reference* are those of the acts of speech themselves, which, as acts, belong uniquely to the performer himself. None of our self-referential terms (nor any terms) is in use except as we perform; moreover, the first person, 'I', 'me', 'mine', 'myself', is limited in application *to* performers; and such bastard self-referential terms as 'a self', 'the self'; 'an I' ought, in being kept in quotes, to indicate their cashability as something like 'the speaker', which is something quite unlike 'I'. Unlike I, they are not used by the speaker of himself alone. When we are not performers the performer's words have no function for us or applicability to us, because in that we cannot, *ex hypothesi*, be self-referrers but only spoken of, or spoken to, only third or second persons.

I want to return for a look at the special features of the first person and then to question their rôle in the formulation of (some of) our personal paradoxes.

3. These features were: i) only I may use 'I' of myself; ii) anyone may use 'I' of himself; iii) only the speaker may use 'I' of himself.

i) *Only I may use 'I' of myself.* There are two facets to this. The first is the trivial and itself unimportant truth that only the self-referrer may refer to himself. This aspect of self-reference we cannot shake. The second is the construction that I may use 'I' *only* of myself; that is, the self-referential device may be used only for self-reference. This, as we saw earlier, is a non-necessary feature of self-reference: we may perform the function of the first person by pointing or by using proper names which may be used by you of me as *well* as by me of myself. The tool of self-reference needn't limit itself to just that rôle; and of course the reason it needn't be so limited is that there is not all that difference between self-reference and other-reference. But if the device of self-reference *in speech* is not restricted to that rôle alone and it is allowed to other-refer as well, we would lose the economy of having a single word with a single convention, usable by anyone to achieve self-reference. That is the generality of the first person.

ii) *Anyone may use 'I' of himself.* The *generality* of the first person is a highly economic, though still inessential, characteristic of its function. A self-restricted 'name' would achieve self-reference but would be usable only by one of us of himself, while the first person is a single device usable by any of us for self-reference.

iii) *Only the speaker may use 'I' of himself.* This feature adds that advantage has been taken of the unique proprietariness of a speech action and, by means of that proprietariness, in conjunction with the fact that the self-referrer must anyhow speak, a *general* basis of unique self-reference has been provided. One of the main differences between self-reference and other-reference is that in the latter case we do not have a single purely verbal convention of reference for diverse particulars: we must point or do something else of that sort *as well as speak*. But for self-references we needn't do more than verbalize, 'I . . .'. In our spoken use of the first person we economize by conventionalizing upon the necessary condition of spoken self-reference—the condition that the self-referrer must himself speak. We might have ignored this and set up many separate, hence uneconomical, conventions of self-reference.

It does seem that all three special features of the first-person referring device are inessential to the job of self-reference; that perhaps the first person is a specialized way, with perhaps good reason for such specialization, of achieving such results.

3.1 I began with three concurrent questions. I asked whether unique self-reference could be achieved without the use of our first-person device as it is. The answer, I think, is that it is so achievable. I asked what, then, were the nature and point of the special non-necessary features of our present self-referential conventions. My answer was that these special first-person features served as an economic function enabling us to work with a *general* and interchangeable single tool of self-reference rather than many such tools. We introduce ourselves as topics automatically, as it were, by means of a single convention based on the proprietariness of speech action and dispense with the need in speech of many single self-introductions we would have to perform as alternatives. And, as I have just suggested, if this is how 'I' functions, then, despite the asymmetries of the first person, we perform our self-introductions on the same grounds as we perform our other introductions. This does not seem to me an implication readily acceptable to most sceptics in the Philosophy of Mind. I asked also in what sense the first person was involved in the formulation of many of the problems associated with Selves and Others and Selves and Things. I want to return to that bit now and look more closely at this involvement of the first person and also to see whether our view of the first person affects the formation of the personal paradoxes.

4. Is our view of the first person relevant to the alleviation of the paradoxes? It seems to me that one important, if not the important, aspect of the personal paradoxes would surely be contained in the purported difference between self-ascription and other-ascription. The proprietariness and uniqueness of a self-ascription as opposed to an other-ascription produces the rub from which spring the sceptic's claims. These claims are of the nature that these two forms of ascription are so essentially different that though we use the same list of epithets for both selves and others, there must be some line or other drawn in principle between one use and the other.

I want to suggest that the proprietariness and uniqueness wrongly claimed to be characteristic of some self-ascriptions, and without which the personal paradoxes cannot stand, are linked to the proprietariness and uniqueness of the first-person device as it is.

We can make out the unique proprietariness of personal self-ascriptions only in link with a self-referential device which is proprietary-making: only *I* may know that I am in pain; *my* pain cannot be *your* pain; *you* cannot in principle have *my* pain, and so on. The 'parallel' between such claims to proprietariness on behalf of a certain class of personal self-ascriptions and the proprietariness afforded just by some of the non-necessary rules of the first person is too close to be ignored: only I may say 'I' of myself, we remember.

It can be argued, however, that we may insert the required asymmetric proprietariness into our personal ascriptions without using the first person or any other self-referential device. Peter cannot have Paul's pain; (in a sense), only *Paul* may say that he is in pain; (in a sense), only *Paul* may know that he is in pain, and so on.

Clearly we do not here want to discuss that form of proprietariness which is merely a recitation of the Law of Identity. Here we want before us the sense in which certain, say psychological, states are in a special proprietary fashion apparent to their owners while their, say physical, states are not. When I am in pain I am aware of myself being so in a way which, even if you truly remark it of me, you are not aware of my being so; while when I am of a certain shape I may, say see, this of myself in ways shareable exactly by you if you see it of me. There is nothing apparent to me about my shape which would not be equally apparent to you. It is the epistemological proprietariness of a certain class of cases we want before us, not the proprietariness of identity.

Then I want to ask whether this epistemological proprietariness may be stated without the use, or background presence, of a self-referential device like the first person. The counter-case before us was, Peter may not feel Paul's pain, or, Only Paul may feel Paul's pain. The proprietariness of certain of our states seems utterable with the use of only third-person indices or even person-neutral indices rather than *self*-referential ones.

But how could I know that Peter may not feel Paul's pain? After all, that is a crucial question since 'Peter' and 'Paul', being *ex hypothesi* third-person devices, must be in the mouth of another who, as he utters their names, is thus first person. Why should any of us who are not Peter and not Paul apply the operative words 'only', 'feel', and 'pain' in *such* ways to Peter and Paul? Suppose Paul tells me this of Peter and himself. What form of words, persuasive of this point, could Paul use but: 'Peter may not feel my pain'? This can't help a non-first-person formulation since we are back just with the first person. But unless I can get some such first-person information from Peter and Paul, then, *ex hypothesi*, there is no allowable basis for these proprietary other-person claims of mine about Peter and Paul.

It is part of the case, isn't it, that if we are limited solely to other-reference as in the examples before us, such evidence as *would* allow any of us to make a sufficiently proprietary other-person claim by means of 'Peter cannot feel Paul's pain' is unfortunately enclosed solely between Peter and Paul. And this, then, bars the speaker from access to what is required for the contrast between those others, those third persons, Peter and Paul. This case which claims we can get the required contrast between selves and others without the implicit force of a self-referential device would then be like solipsism in reverse: there are only others. And where 'there are only others', then Peter may feel Paul's pain. What we need in order to be allowed to enter the case, to make the troublesome contrast, is for any one of us to be able to feel pain when others of us just then do not feel pain. What we need to enter the case is at least one first-person ascription *contrasted* with an other-ascription. Contrasts among second and third persons alone cannot produce the required epistemological proprietariness: in such a case the predicate in question remains univocal, hence without contrast. The sceptic only begins, contrast starts, when equivocal senses are possible. And equivocal senses become possible only when we introduce the first-person qualification of some predicates in contrast to the other-person uses of such predicates. Neither, of course, would contrasts among first persons alone do. Both selves and others are needed, not just others and not just selves.

If both are needed to make the case for troublesome epistemological proprietariness it is yet 'the self' which is naturally vested, or expected to be, with the epistemological 'extra'. That is perhaps why Wittgenstein, just to avoid this non-transferably owned extra, is willing to say that some uses of 'I' are not (self)-referential at all. Surely it is at least partly why Descartes would settle for two disparate senses for 'I'; and possibly why Strawson feels that since criteria of self-ascription (the 'extra') do seem to differ from those of other-ascription, the concept of a Person, or 'Self-plus-Other', is implied to lend coherence to predicates used with this otherwise systematic difference. Persons are what allow the meanings of such predicates to be the same even though their criteria of ascription seem to differ from first- to other-person cases.

Surely it will be the case generally that a view which finds certain personal predicates to be, for whatever reason, type-distinct from impersonal ones will also feel the need for a type-distinct or type-proprietary personal demonstrative. It would hence be important to show whether or not our personal demonstratives are type-distinct, that is, whether or not they function differently from our impersonal demonstratives. Moreover, whatever reason is found for such a view about personal predicates, that view in its statement will still need the contrast between the first and the other persons, as I have tried to argue. And if one can show that our main tool of self-reference is only superficially a different type of index from our impersonal demonstratives, we shall perhaps have removed at least one of the bases for such stateable contrast between selves and others. *Is* the contrast between personal and impersonal predicates really separate from the contrast between selves and others? And is this separate from the contrast between 'I' and 'he' or 'I' and 'this'?

We have, then, a strong and a weak case to be made at this point for the utility of working upon our personal demonstratives, and in particular, upon the personal pronouns, which afford the crucial means of distinction between ourselves and others. The strong case would be that the first person, our means of distinction between selves and others, is as good a point to *test* the notion of a person as any, given the consistency of that set of concepts.

Should, for instance, a sceptical view be held about the possibility of knowing what other minds know, then we have in consistency a right to expect a contrast among our personal demonstratives which will reflect that epistemological scepticism. 'I' would have to be somehow systematically different from 'you' or from 'this', or both, to support the epistemological difference of the self. Hence the first-person device will have to perform its demonstrations in a manner typically different from our other-person devices or our impersonal devices of reference. How could we otherwise successfully form our sceptically-minded sentences?

Or should, for example, the view be so put that personal verbs are said to be category-different from material-object verbs, then this category difference too must be reflected among our personal demonstratives: how else could the verbs still be category-different in a way which is relevant to the problems we have had in the Philosophy of Mind? But if we could show our personal demonstratives to be not category-different or not sceptic-productive, then we show any such contrast views to be mistaken. It is this lack of contrast between our personal and impersonal demonstratives, this lack of type-proprietariness in our first-person device, its normalcy, that I hope to have suggested to this point.

The weak view about the importance of our personal demonstratives for the problem of persons is that the contrast between our use of the first person and the other persons is by itself only a single source of temptation to an asymmetric perspective between selves and others and selves and things. It would then be useful to block off that one avenue misleadingly pointed to by the actual aberrations of the special features of the first person. It would be useful to show that the first person is only apparently not a normal demonstrative: its special features are not special enough problematically to contrast selves with others. I have tried to show something of how we might take this to be the case. But to have done this is only to have closed off one misleading approach which, on the weak view, holds no implication for the success or failure of any other approach.

On the whole my leanings are, of course, in the direction of the strong view.

THE INTERCHANGEABILITY OF MACHINES

CORA DIAMOND

I

CAN A MACHINE think, choose, learn? It's sometimes said that we cannot rule out the possibility that machines will behave in ways which will give us all the evidence we need that they do such things. (I shall use 'Think' as an abbreviation for an indefinitely long list of things we, and in some cases animals as well, do, feel, and so on.) If someone refuses to regard such behaviour as evidence, this may be because he regards machines as peculiar among things behaving in these ways, peculiar in such a way as to justify his refusal to use the ordinary criteria. Two sorts of oddness sometimes mentioned are these: 1) A machine is a collection of tubes, transistors, and so on, and we cannot say of such a thing that it Thinks, any more than we can of a human body. 2) A machine does only what it is intended (programmed, designed, instructed) to do, and so resemblances to us, if any, are intended by the designer. These objections are close enough to being right to make it important to see why they are inadequate.

1) There are two reasons why it's inadequate to say that a machine is a collection of wires, etc., and can't Think any more than a body can.

a) Consider a child who believes he has hurt a doll. How can we say that that is what he believes, if it is nonsense to say a doll has been hurt? What we are saying is that he believes he has hurt what is in fact only a doll; and we know that he does not regard the doll as *only* a doll. If he is intelligent, we should not be able to convince him that there is no sense in saying that the doll is hurt by saying 'We don't say of bags of sawdust that they can be hurt'; in taking it that the doll is merely a bag of sawdust, we have begged the question.

b) Someone may say of a machine that it can Think, not because he wishes to deny that it is just an arrangement of tubes, etc.; he denies that it is nonsense to say of such a thing that it Thinks; and the reply we are considering is no more use than 'You're wrong'.

Most of this paper will be a discussion of such a view; I will say a bit more later about the possible views of someone who thinks a machine is not just a machine.

2) There are two reasons why it won't do to say that if machines behave like us, it is only because exactly that was intended by the programmer or designer.

a) It is just not true that machines do only what they are intended to do. For one thing, programs have errors, and machines don't always work properly. More important, machines can be programmed to modify their own programs in complicated ways. A machine programmed to play chess[1] may modify the program determining what moves will be made in ways the programmer could not foresee. It would be wrong to say of such a machine that the programmer intended it to castle in such and such circumstances, if that is what the machine did. It could be argued that provided there are no 'bugs' in the program or the machine, there is always some description of what the machine did under which it was intended by the programmer. But this is hardly adequate to support the claim that any behaviour like ours exhibited by a machine is exactly what is intended by the programmer.

One may wish to say that it doesn't matter whether someone did actually intend that the machine do exactly what it did: someone might just as well have. That is, there is no important difference between a case in which some behaviour like a man's is intended by the programmer, and a case in which the same behaviour is the result of a learning procedure involving random modifications, or of a mistake in the program. There is some truth in this; I shall say more about it later.

b) The basis of the objection is not clear. It has not been shown why the designer of an animal-simulating machine should not intend that it would run when large objects approach *because* it is afraid. We cannot without begging the question simply assume that this possibility is ruled out because the machine could not *be* afraid.

Having seen that we do not get very far with either of these two attempts to show that the ordinary criteria for Thinking are inapplicable to machines, one may try to avoid altogether the question whether these criteria can be used and to formulate instead a completely different procedure for settling the question. I shall consider one such suggested method.

II

'If you know that a particular machine can be counted on to give you true answers to questions, you can just ask it whether it is conscious, whether it wants this, believes that, understands some command, and so on.'

There are two distinct procedures which might be meant. First, we are imagined to have *something* out of which emerge true answers to our questions. This device is exceedingly reliable. We make assumptions neither about how the information gets there nor about whether the thing means what it says. And then we begin to ask this extremely useful truth-box questions about itself of the type mentioned. The alternative idea is that we have a machine programmed to learn a language, and trained in some way to give true answers to questions.

The idea of the truth-box seems attractive because we seem to be able to make clear sense of *both* of the answers 'the history of England' and 'you wrongly suppose this device can think' to the question 'What is the device thinking of?', and at the same time we imagine the device to be in a special position to give us *either* sort of answer. Now if the device *were* a thinking being, it would make sense to imagine that *it* is the thing to ask if you want to know what it is thinking (though not because it is going on facts inaccessible to you). But if it is not some sort of thinking being, the device is in some way dependent on facts which we might just as well dig up for ourselves. For example, the device may have been made by someone who stored the answers to all the questions he could think of, and he thought of all the ones we'd asked. He knew that the answer to 'Is the device a thinking being?' is 'No'—and so would we, if we knew what he'd done. In other words, the answer 'the device cannot think' can be justified by facts in principle available to us. And if so, we should be able to say without consulting the device what facts would, if we knew them, put us in a position to say that something can or cannot think. If we cannot say what those facts would be, the idea that the truth-box might tell us that it didn't think is no different from the idea that we might some time be able to tell whether machines could think by finding an infallible source of information, whom we could ask.

The alternative idea, of the computer that learns a language and is trained to give true answers to questions, is no better. We may think that if it understands what it is saying, it is not *just* a device out of which true answers emerge. But how could we tell that the machine understands the answers it gives? Since one question I am discussing in this article is how we should take the fact that a machine's behaviour seems to indicate it ϕs, where ϕing is something men or animals do, we cannot let the satisfaction of the criteria we use for a man's understanding some word settle the matter. (I am not taking it for granted that a machine *could* satisfy these criteria. In fact it would appear question-begging to assume it could, in at least some cases. No one could have a grasp of the use of a word like 'want' unless he had a grasp of the first-person use, and this is shown by his use of the word in connection with the things we have other reasons for thinking he wants. Something like this point is denied by Hilary Putnam;[2] I shall return to it.) And we cannot use the suggested procedure itself to settle the question whether the machine understands what it says, without its becoming apparent that this version of the procedure has collapsed into the first version. To see this, consider the answer 'No' to 'Do you mean the words you utter?' If such an answer is given, the machine cannot mean that it does not mean the words it utters; if the sounds it makes tell us anything, they have the same significance as an answer from the truth-box; that is, their coming from such a machine may be a good sign that the facts are such as to justify that answer. But the point of the second version of the procedure was that we wanted it to be the case *both* that the machine said what it did because it meant it *and* that there is some sense in its telling us that it cannot think, or that it has no intentions, or that it cannot understand the sounds it makes. To appeal to *either* of the two procedures is to answer the philosophical question 'What facts would justify us in saying that a machine cannot think?' by 'the facts that would justify an infallible source of information in saying it couldn't'.[3]

My arguments against the suggested procedure have so far rested on difficulties with answers implying that the machine can't Think, but I do not know how to take contrary answers from a machine for other reasons than that negative answers are puzzling.

I am not sure why the reliability of a machine when it comes to informing us of what the weather is going to be should suggest that we can trust it when it tells us its Thoughts. Is it that it cares for truth or that it is reliable here too, or what? The true answers we got before we started asking about its Thoughts could not show us the machine cares for truth. The questions we go on to ask about its thoughts, feelings, or intentions were meant to help us decide whether it cared for anything at all: if a love of truth could be shown by the answers to the questions about the world, we should not need to use the suggested procedure. If it is not the machine's love of truth, then, is it that we think a reliable source of general information will be reliable about its inner life, too? The idea of a reliable source of information about the source's inner life suggests a contrast with someone who exaggerates his pains, or who deceives himself about what he believes or wants or enjoys, or perhaps who says he wants this or that and is never happy when he gets it. But the reliability of the machine is not being contrasted with *such* cases. Is the point supposed to be that certain sorts of mistake are ruled out in reporting one's own Thoughts? This may be true, but is not helpful. It would enable us to say only that *if* the machine is reporting Thoughts, it is not making the sort of mistake that is ruled out.

If I am unsure what it means to speak of reliability here, this is partly because altogether I do not know how to take positive answers. My reaction might be 'How can such a thing Think?' I might just look for a way of explaining away its answer, such as 'Even a machine whose parts had *just* been put into the state that the parts of this one were in, would print out "Yes" when the input was "Were you thinking of Detroit?"' Here it may seem that I am saying 'It can't be thinking of Detroit because machines can't think' and that is no argument. *That* this may be my reaction is part of the problem.

I have pointed out difficulties in understanding what the possible results of the procedure would show. The root of the problem is this: if we are not clear about whether machines are peculiar in some way which would make the usual criteria for Thinking inapplicable to them, we cannot have a clear idea of what it is we are trying to discover by an alternative method. It is a mistake to think we can devise a procedure for dealing with the odd case without an understanding of how exactly it is odd, an understanding sufficient to show whether *any* procedure could work. I shall now return to the problem of the fundamental difference between a machine and a living being.

III

Whatever a machine is doing it is always possible in principle to stop it, and to put another machine in a state in all relevant respects the same. If one now starts both machines, there will be no difference in what they then do traceable to the difference in their histories. I am not saying that the results will be the same, because I am not making the assumption that the output of the machine can in principle be predicted. The machines I am considering may contain some element introducing unpredictable changes. But consider two machines, M_1 and M_2, each with one such element, E_1 and E_2. To simplify things, imagine that M_1 and M_2 are computers of identical type. E_1 and E_2 provide random signals, either 0 or 1, say, with the same relative frequency, but this is predictable only over the long run. We stop the operations of M_1 and duplicate its state at that time, except for the state of E_1, in M_2. Now, it does not matter which element E we have in M_2. The present state of E_1 did not determine the future operations of M_1 in any way which would not allow us to use E_2 instead. And so, although it is true that the results you will get depend on whether you use E_1 or E_2, it is not possible to give in advance any difference this would make, or to say 'M_1, because of its being the particular machine it is, with a particular history, can do such and such, which M_2 can't'.

Further, having kept a record of what M_1 has done during some period, one can duplicate in all relevant respects the operations during some part of that period; in particular, the later stages can be duplicated without the imitating machine's (M_2's) having gone through the earlier stages. This is true even if M_1 contained E_1, as above. We can regard M_1 as two machines, E_1, and the rest, R, the output of E_1 being part of the input of R, whose output is in principle predictable given its input. The relation of R to the input from E_1 is like that of any computer to input we cannot in fact predict. But there is no difference between what such a machine does with predictable input and what it does with unpredictable input. (This was implied by what I said earlier about testing a machine programmed to fly a plane by inventing data representing the information which might be available to the machine during flight.) What R does with what it gets from E_1 is thus no different from what it does when we settle in advance that the information available instead of the signal from E_1 shall be 0 at such and such times and 1 at the rest. Thus any portion of what M_1 has done during some period can be duplicated on M_2 once the signals provided by E_1 during that part of the period are known. The ways in which we can describe what M_1 is doing during that part of the period are also descriptions of what M_2 is doing in the imitation period.

In general, the ways in which we can describe what a machine is at present doing and its present states do not depend upon its having had any particular history. The fact that a particular machine has actually gone through certain procedures involving modifications (predictable or not) of the program it is following does not mean that in following that program it is doing anything different from a machine that was just put into the state the first machine had reached at the end of the program modification or learning procedure. This characteristic of machines I shall call their *interchangeability*. Someone who takes what we regard as machines as some kind of living beings might deny that machines are interchangeable. I am concerned at the moment, however, to bring out certain features of our ordinary conception of machines.

There are three respects in which what I have said so far is oversimple:

1) M_1 may be following a self-modified program, when the replacing machine, M_2, cannot be so described. This is an apparent counter-example to my claim that descriptions of what M_1 is doing apply to M_2. To say M_1 is following a self-modified program would be to say something of the following sort: it is now following a program, and that program was produced under its earlier operations. So there are present-tense predicates applicable to M_1

which are not applicable to M_2, but there are none which cannot be analysed in the way just shown: predicates in the past tense or perfect, or both, conjoined with predicates in the present tense applicable to M_2.[4]

Some events, which I shall call *R-events*,[5] make a difference to what happens later in two ways only (the second way being trivial, not really a difference at all). *a*) They may change the condition of things in describable ways, the resulting condition being one which can in principle be duplicated without the occurrence of such an event, and *b*) they may make possible certain descriptions using past- and perfect-tense predicates, and some using present- and future-tense predicates, the ascription of which to something includes as part of what is being said, that such and such happened or has been the case. (Thus breaking a pencil at *t* makes possible the description of some later events as 'sharpening the pencil broken at *t*'.) All events in the history of a machine are R-events. That a machine which has modified its program can now be described as following a self-modified program is trivially true; the only non-trivial difference made by the program-modification procedure is that the machine is now in a different condition, and its being in this condition will make a difference to what it does in future. The difference made by the procedure is given by the change effected, where the initial and subsequent stages can each be described independently of any reference to the procedure itself. That all the events in the history of something are R-events is necessary and sufficient for it to be interchangeable.

2) A machine's interchangeability depends on the possibility of duplicating the condition of the parts with which an engineer or machine designer is concerned, or of substituting parts in equivalent condition. Whenever a machine is operating, we can divide its characteristics into two sorts, according as they are relevant or not to what it is doing, from (roughly) the point of view of the machine designer, and we might call the irrelevant features decorations, relative to the present operations. Thus a computer might have a printer which would be decoration if the computer's output on some job were entirely on magnetic tape. When the printer was in use the type of print might be decoration relative to that job. Any features which are always decoration, no matter what the machine is doing (for example, its colour, or its having been built

by a man named Smith), we might say do not belong to the machine *as a machine*. I am claiming that all events in the history of the machine as a machine are R-events. This class includes not only the ordinary operations of the machine but also, for example, its breaking down. Interchangeability is then a characteristic of the machine as a machine.

3) For simplicity of exposition, I have throughout ignored the fact that parallel points can be made about the future histories of the machines we are considering.

I shall now *sketch* what I think is the significance of the interchangeability of machines.[6] The question is whether certain predicates true of living beings could be true of any future machines. I shall argue that some at least of these predicates are what I shall call *H-predicates*, that the others are applicable only if some H-predicates are, and that no H-predicate can be true of a machine as a machine. An H-predicate applies only to things with a characteristic history. I don't mean that there is some particular history essential to the applicability of all H-predicates. The history required for the application of any particular one depends on that predicate. But in all cases, we are identifying an element in a familiar temporal pattern, where the character of the particular element depends on its place in the pattern. From one point of view one might say that without this characteristic background the element is totally unchanged, 'for there is nothing different *now*'. But from another point of view, without that background we do not now have the same element, but something totally different, even though there is *nothing now* which makes the difference. An example of an H-predicate is 'asking someone something': if someone is now doing so, he must have learned to talk. Thus a newborn baby who utters coherent, grammatical English sentences cannot be said to have asked us something the moment it was born—unless at a minimum we are willing to consider it as, say, having learned to talk in some previous incarnation. Asking someone something isn't a phenomenon that as a matter of fact is found only after a period of learning. It is not that we have learned to recognize it in this context, but might find 'it' elsewhere. The ascription of this and of many other H-predicates to something does not, however, contain the assertion that the thing has had such and such a history; when I say of someone that he asked me if it was raining, I don't assert that he has learned to talk. We may contrast this case with the following: if something is being mended, some damage must have been done to it and not yet been undone. Someone who asserts that something was never damaged and is being mended is (normally) contradicting himself. On the other hand, although only someone who has learned to talk can ask someone something, the following philosophical position does not involve straightforward contradiction: 'the significance of learning to talk is merely that you then understand the language. But a child could be born with understanding of the language, and then it might ask questions and not just mysteriously utter these words'. Such a philosophical view is an attempt to turn part of the temporal background which makes the element what it is into another independent element. I shall say that x's having learned to talk *comes into* x's asking a question (and I shall use '*brings in*' for the converse). A *sufficient* condition for x's having ϕd to *come into* x's ψing is this: for x to ψ or be ψing at some time, x must have ϕd (this includes what has happened to x as well as what x has done) at some earlier time, but to assert that x ψs or is ψing is not to assert (among other things) that x ϕd. If and only if there is some ϕ such that x's having ϕd *comes into* x's ψing, 'ψ' is an H-predicate. The example I have taken is one in which what *comes into* x's ψing is distinct from what is asserted by the ascription of ψing to x (I shall call such H-predicates simple), but x's having ϕd can *come into* x's ψing even when x's having ϕd is part of what is asserted. Consider these examples: 'The comet has returned to point p' and 'A kept his promise to ξ'. In each case there is a fairly straightforward contradiction (including denials of Strawsonian presuppositions in this category) in conjoining with each of these a denial that the past has been of a certain sort, namely, in the first case, the denial that the comet has been at p before; in the second, the denial that A earlier made a promise to ξ. But in the case of A's promise, the promise-making *comes into* the promise-keeping, and this is something different from the relation specified by saying there is a contradiction in 'A kept his promise to ξ but never made a promise to ξ'. I am not suggesting that something is, as it were, impossible twice over. But rather that the act of promise-keeping is just *that* because it is an element in the familiar pattern which includes the making of the promise. Now a man can keep his promise by accident. And then, although he did what he said he would, the pattern is one which we distinguish. Here, his having promised does not *come into* what he later does; keeping a promise by accident is very different from keeping a promise, although there need be nothing different going on at the time of the act. 'Keeping his promise to ξ' is then a non-simple H-predicate. The difference between simple and non-simple H-predicates comes out in disagreements about whether such predicates are H-predicates. With simple H-predicates, disagreement may be shown simply by denying that someone who ψd need ever have ϕd. With non-simple ones, disagreement can be shown only by denying that there is any connection between ψing and ϕing other than the trivial one of the same sort as that between returning to a spot and having been there before.

There are predicates which can apply to something only if it is a subject of H-predicates, but not because, or not only because, they are themselves H-predicates. For example, if something is now beginning to learn French, it must be possible that what it is now doing should *come into* what it will be doing and its future capacities. What begins to learn French may later on still be learning French, may speak or read French or be able to understand spoken French, which would *bring in* its having begun to learn French. I shall call such predicates *I-predicates*. A further important example is 'forming an intention to ξ'.

We have seen that the only descriptions of what a machine, M_1, is doing, as a machine, are descriptions which may be applicable to a machine, M_2, which shares none of the past characteristics of M_1, or, if not possibly true of M_2, this is only because the descriptions contain assertions such as that M_1 has done such and such. The events in the history of a machine are R-events, and this means that nothing it does can *come into* anything else it does as a machine. In other words, the interchangeability of a machine means that no H-predicate or I-predicate can be true of it as a machine. Of course, if there are no H-predicates or I-predicates which are true of us, this would not mark a radical difference between machines and ourselves.

I shall defend in Section IV the view that at least some H-predicates are true of ourselves. In sketching what I think is the significance of the difference marked by the interchangeability of machines, I shall not defend my assertions that this or that predicate applicable to us is an H-predicate or an I-predicate.

Very roughly speaking, we may divide the sorts of future machines which some have held might Think into two sorts: *a*) those whose behaviour might be thought to show that they carry on intellectual activities or have intellectual capacities like our own, and *b*) highly developed animal-simulating machines.

a) These intellectual machines are envisaged as speaking to us, proving theorems (perhaps showing their understanding by discussing the proofs), playing games like chess or the Turing game, getting better at any of these. (The Turing game itself includes all the others.) I should maintain that having learned something *comes into* all such activities. Our intellectual life *brings in* past events; the learning procedures undergone by machines cannot *come into* what they do.

b) There are two important reasons for which the interchangeability of animal-simulating machines rules out the possibility that the predicates characteristically ascribable to animals and to us might hold of them. The first is more general.

1) Interchangeability rules out the possibility of ascribing voluntary action to a machine; and neither emotional states nor sensations can be ascribed to things which do not act from their emotions, or act differently on account of what they perceive or their bodily sensations. I shall not argue the second premise.[7] The reason voluntary action is ruled out is fundamentally that no account in terms of R-events can be given. While there are many patterns of voluntary action, they have in common that later stages *bring in* earlier ones, and that descriptions of the initiation of goal-directed actions, of the formation of intentions, of desires, decisions, and choices involve the use of I-predicates.

2) Some of these predicates apply literally only to beings of whose life and death it makes sense to speak, and a machine cannot die, although it can be destroyed, or for some other reason permanently cease working. Why does the interchangeability of a machine make it nonsense to speak of its death? To say of a living being that it is dead is to say it is no more. But what it is to be no more depends on the sort of thing we are talking about. A painting might cease to be when the bits of paint were removed from the canvas, a man when he is dead, a body when it is burned. If I point

to a painted man who is included in an exhibition of works of art and say 'Tomorrow *that* will no longer exist', what I am saying of 'that' depends upon whether I mean the man, the body, the work of art. Similarly, I might say of something I am pointing to, something which could be regarded both as a machine and as a work of art (it had been decorated with marvellous gargoyles), that it would not exist tomorrow; but what makes it a work of art is not what makes it a machine, and the end of the work of art need not be the end of the machine. What makes it a work of art does not belong to the machine as a machine, but what makes it a machine does. To say of the machine that it is no more is to speak of the result of an R-event, and therefore cannot be to ascribe an H-predicate. To say of a living being that it is no more, i.e. that it is dead, is to ascribe an H-predicate (a non-simple one). Having been alive and having died *come into* being dead. Death is not an R-event, and so the sort of changes undergone by what is interchangeable can't include death. I should say that the sorts of gap in the world made by a death, or by the destruction of a work of art, are different from the gap marked by 'the computer you saw yesterday is no more'. I shall discuss the significance of the difference between the death of a living being and the end of something interchangeable more fully below.

'Is afraid' is an example of a predicate which applies literally only to beings of whose life and death it makes sense to speak. There is unfortunately not space for an adequate discussion of the way in which speaking of fear is connected with the possibility of death.

If I am correct, no machine, considered as a machine, can Think. In Section I, I distinguished two views, both of which might be expressed as 'Machines can Think'. The second view, which is what I am attacking, is that what is *merely* a machine can Think. On this view, if a machine Thinks, it is because of certain of the characteristics that it has as a machine. For example, it might be held that they make it a model of a psychological theory, of which we also are models, in Fodor's sense of 'model' and 'psychological theory'.[8] On such an account, what psychology studies consists of R-events, and so no psychological theory can explain behaviour described in terms of H-predicates. If one takes the predicates with which we are concerned to be H-predicates, it follows that the fact that machines could be models of such theories is totally irrelevant to the question whether they can Think. It is in a sense possible to use these predicates in another way—I shall discuss this in Section IV—but to do so requires certain changes in the ways we think about living beings.

Failure to recognize the significance of the interchangeability of machines can be seen in Turing's argument that if it is said that machines cannot think because they have no soul, it can be replied that it is logically possible for God to give a soul to anything he chooses, including a machine. This argument suggests that Turing imagined a soul as a sort of immaterial knob that some people think one must have in order to be correctly described as thinking. This may be the way some people have conceived a soul, and indeed there is a lot wrong with the idea that we need such a thing to think. But there is a sense (or senses) in which the objection that machines have no souls is correct, and if we understand the objection in such a way it is easy to see why Turing's reply won't do. I want to explain this by comparing a way of speaking about works of art. Someone who denies that a machine can produce a poem or a symphony might want to say that a set of words is a poem only because of what has gone into it, and it might be natural for him to express this by saying that a poem has to have a soul. It would only be a misunderstanding of what he was saying to reply to him that *whatever* sort of thing a soul was, it was at least logically possible for a machine to produce a set of words which had one. This is a misunderstanding because what he was trying to do with the word 'soul' did not make it a word for *any* sort of thing (nor, for that matter, an 'expression of attitude'). If one wants to say that a thinking being has to have a soul, this, properly understood, is not a reference to an immaterial part, but to the resemblances between its life and ours. I should wish to explain this partly in terms of the applicability of H-predicates, and to show that a machine has interchangeability *instead of* a soul; but other explanations could be given. If an immaterial knob made a difference to what a machine was doing as a machine, a difference which only an angelic engineer would know of, that would not mean that the machine was not interchangeable, but only that to duplicate its condition in the relevant respects you might need a machine with a similar part.[9]

Any object whatsoever can be valued by someone in such a way that he cannot be consoled for its loss by an object just like the one lost: it was the *particular* one lost which he valued. (Similarly anything, from a coin to a man, can be valued by someone in such a way that its loss can be made up to him by something more or less like the original.) Now, part of the point of speaking about souls may be to say that to have a soul is to be irreplaceable, though *not necessarily* in this 'subjective' sense. To say that something (a living being, a work of art, a creature in the literal sense, for example) is irreplaceable but not, or not only, in the 'subjective' sense is to say that its ceasing to exist is not an R-event. If it is not an R-event, the difference it makes is not just a matter of its having such and such effects, and of the truth of certain descriptions. If *x*'s ceasing to be is an R-event, we could change the world, construct something just like *x*, and say that everything in the world is just as it would be if *x* had not ceased to exist, with the exception of the trivial point that it is true that *x* exists no longer. If it is not an R-event, it may *come into* what is true later. In that case, if we were to construct something just like *x*, there would still be the trivial point that it was true that *x* exists no longer, but this would not be the only difference. In this case 'exists no more' is a non-simple H-predicate. To say that the loss of *x* followed by the construction of something just like *x* does not leave the world just as it would be if *x* had not ceased to exist, or to say that the loss of *x* is something that cannot be made good by something just like *x*, is to try to say what is shown by the use of 'is no more' as an H-predicate.

Our conception of death as not an R-event is one element of mourning. Thus, *unless* mourning is seen this way, we must say that someone who offers a person mourning a friend a new friend just like the old is merely making the mistake you might make in offering someone sentimentally attached to a pullover he had lost a new one just like the old. To say of someone that he sees something's end as not an R-event is not, however, to say he has this or that *particular* attitude or reaction. For one thing, there may be a range of such attitudes and reactions; for example, in the case of living beings, the range might stretch from delight in killing to refusal to kill even a greenfly. More important, seeing the death of something as not an R-event makes possible the understanding of certain attitudes and reactions. I mean, for example, that we can understand someone's reluctance to destroy a fly because it is alive, in a way in which we cannot understand someone's reluctance to turn off and clear the memory of a little fly-imitating machine when he is under no misapprehension about its being a machine and there is neither pleasure nor profit for him or anyone else in allowing the machine to continue. Even if such reluctance were familiar, even if one felt it oneself, it would be an *unaccountable* reluctance.

IV

I shall turn now to the denial that any H-predicates are true of us. There may be many reasons for which one might deny this; many philosophical views imply that we might, for example, discover that a new-born baby spoke with understanding of moral and political issues. I shall discuss one such view, found in Putnam's articles;[10] much of what I say is, if true, also true of other reasons for denying the applicability of H-predicates to ourselves.

Putnam holds that there are a certain number of philosophically uninteresting analytic statements in natural languages, such as 'all bachelors are unmarried'. The denials of such statements involve plain logical inconsistencies. Also, there are sentences which any linguist can tell you are incoherent. But there are no absurdities that you need philosophers to discover; at any rate, no convincing example of one has yet been found. Philosophers have suggested, for example, that there is something radically incoherent in the following: 'Last night at midnight, everything shrank', 'There is a race of beings who have pains, yet who never show this by any of their behaviour', 'There is no past'. On Putnam's view, the mistake one is making if one says any of these is incoherent is this: one notes that no isolated experiment could establish the truth of such a 'hypothesis' but fails to see that it does not follow from this that it is incoherent. We could not discover from experiment alone that everything has shrunk; nevertheless, considerations of inductive simplicity and theoretical economy might lead us to the conclusion that the explanation of an apparent change in a number of physical constants at midnight last night was that everything had shrunk. Such an explanation does not involve a change in the meanings of words, in the following sense: linguistic habits leading to the production of such sentences, given certain 'scientific experiences' (I am not sure what these are, nor whether Putnam thinks they can be given a non-circular characterization), are general among speakers of the language, and the words are used in conformity with ordinary lexical definitions.[11]

On this view there can be no H-predicates. (I shall consider in what follows only simple H-predicates, but what is said can be applied also to non-simple ones.) If it can't be true of a thing that it is ψing unless its history has been of such and such a sort, that might be because there is an analytic connection between ψing and that sort of history. If there is no such connection, we might always have theory-based reasons for accepting that something was ψing although it did not have the right sort of history. Thus, in the present state of science we might simply be mystified by the newly born moral-judgment-uttering baby. But scientific developments might enable us to establish that the baby was in all relevant respects in the same state as a man saying the same words in all seriousness. And then we should properly conclude that the baby really knew what it was talking about.

If it is the case that any connection not trivially analytic must be revisable in the light of the best available theory, it follows that there can be no H-predicates. I want to make clear the assumption that has to be made if we are to reach the conclusion that there is always the possibility that such revision will be required (required in the sense that it would be 'irrational' or 'unscientific' not to make such a revision). I shall begin by considering what Putnam says about 'multiple sclerosis', an example he uses in defending, first, the view that we can discover the duration of dreams, and, secondly, the view that we might discover a race of beings who have pains but whose behaviour never shows this. He takes 'multiple sclerosis' as an example of a term whose use 'is based on the supposition that there is something—a "natural kind", so to speak—for which our "criteria" are *good* but not *perfect* indicators. In the case of such terms, the accepted criteria are often modified in the course of time.' Whether scientists using such a term at one time are talking about the same thing as scientists using it at another is 'to be ascertained by examining the relevant scientific theory . . . and not by linguistic investigations, whether special or general'.[12]

It is important to see that willingness to accept new criteria for multiple sclerosis is not *based on* a supposition that the original criteria are 'crude' ways of detecting a 'natural kind'. To say that 'multiple sclerosis' is a term for a 'natural kind' (in this sense) is to characterize its use as one such that new criteria based on scientific theories will be accepted as criteria for *the same thing*. This point may be obscured by the ambiguity in such statements as 'multiple sclerosis is not a "natural kind"', which could be a characterization of a use (as not including the possible modification of criteria on the basis of scientific theories) *or* a way of stating the discovery that, say, the original criteria had jumbled together two quite distinct diseases; to speak of such a discovery already characterizes the use of the word as including the willingness to accept new theory-based criteria as criteria for the same thing. If the question whether scientists at two different times are using a term to speak of the same thing is to be settled by examining the relevant scientific theory (and if it is to be 'unscientific' to deny that they are), that is only because it has already been ascertained that the term has a use like that of 'multiple sclerosis' as Putnam describes it. It certainly would not follow from the fact that a scientist used a term, that he was using it *that* way; a scientist can, say, study the correlations between pains and brain waves, between rapid eye movements and dreams, without being committed to taking 'pain' or 'dream' as words for some 'natural kind' for which our present criteria give us good but not perfect indicators and which can be improved on the basis of scientific theories. We cannot simply say 'if the scientist has a way of telling when someone is in pain, say, behaviour, *and* if to say of someone that he is in pain is not just to say "such and such criteria are fulfilled", the scientist *must* recognize that better criteria could be discovered by the use of scientific theories'. That would be to say that the use of 'pain' *must* be to designate something in a way very like 'multiple sclerosis',[13] whereas it may not be used to *designate something* at all.

That, then, is the assumption that has to be made if we are to conclude that there are no connections not trivially analytic which are not revisable in the light of the best available theories, revisable without changing the meaning of the term the criteria for whose application are modified.

To deny this assumption is not to deny that someone may use

'pain' or 'understands what he is saying' this way: he accepts modifications of his criteria and new criteria usable in circumstances in which the old could not be used, on the basis of scientific theories. The expression may be used this way either because the person is making a philosophical assumption like the one just mentioned, perhaps without realizing it, or quite simply because it does come naturally to him to use 'pain' very like the way Putnam says 'multiple sclerosis' is used.[14] If someone uses 'pain' this way, he will speak of the discovery of new criteria;[15] others, who have been taught the use of the word in the same way, may say that using those criteria would mean making a decision to use the word in new ways.[16] Such a decision need not be seen as arbitrary; this is partly because in the sort of case in which some will speak of discovery and others of decision it is often possible to think of cases intermediate between these and more familiar cases, and it is impossible to say that a decision to adopt a new use is first made at such and such a distance from the familiar case.

If I am right, Putnam's arguments do not show that there are no H-predicates, that a predicate could not be used in such a way, or that it would be unscientific or irrational to use a predicate in such a way. It is unscientific to deny what the best-established theory shows: it could, however, show that a new-born baby understands what it says about philosophy only if it has been settled that 'understands what it says' is used in something like the way Putnam says 'multiple sclerosis' is; and the theory can't show *that*.[17] If 'understands what it says about philosophy' is being used as an H-predicate, there are criteria for applying it in certain circumstances, and no criteria for applying it to new-born babies.

The use of H-predicates is a necessary condition for regarding something as irreplaceable, although not necessarily *to* anyone. So although it is possible not to use any of the predicates I have been discussing as H-predicates, that has as a consequence that certain attitudes to living beings cannot be understandable in virtue of the irreplaceability of their objects. Whether this consequence is acceptable or not is another matter.

If one understands these predicates as H-predicates, it will seem that someone willing to ascribe them to a machine must be failing to recognize genuine and important differences between machines and living beings. In what sense is this justified? Dinosaurs were in pain quite independently of our turning up later to say so. The existence of language-users is certainly not a condition of there being pain; there can be pains although no one realizes that there are. Similarly, if we imagine, along with the dinosaurs, human beings whose lives and ways of thinking are unlike ours—nothing they do could be identified as recognizing the pains of animals—we can say that here, too, the animals were in pain, although no one realized this. And also, if we imagine a situation in which we have given up using H-predicates altogether, and were therefore willing to regard machines as conceivably able to do and undergo anything we could, there would be many things we no longer realized. But this is not to give any sort of absolute justification for the use of H-predicates, or for attaching any special significance to something's being a living being.

I have been considering the views of those who say a machine might Think and who regard a machine as essentially just a complicated arrangement of switches and so on. What some would regard as evidence for a machine's Thinking—its behaviour or its 'realizing' the same psychological theory or whatever—may not strike others as evidence at all, given the interchangeability of machines. If it does not seem to one to have a sense, this will characterize one's use of the predicates I have lumped together as 'Thinking'; it does not show a failure to recognize what science might show. I have not said anything about those who might assert that a machine is Thinking because they think of it as a sort of living being. It is necessary to say a few words about this. For if someone wanted to say a machine could Think, and was convinced that a mere collection of tubes, etc., couldn't, it might seem open to him to regard it as a living being. But this is not just something one can *decide* to do. There are situations in which a man might be described so: 'He thinks the machine is alive', but not if it is a *philosophical* view that is being ascribed to him. Someone might be so described in a number of different situations.

a) People might be living on an island where an experiment is being carried out with machines that are very like animals: they eat, reproduce, and so on. The people are ignorant of the experiment and take the machines for animals. If they are told the facts, they recognize their error.

b) A child may think of a doll as a living being, and equally might think of some animal-like machines as alive. This is unlike *a*) in that, having been shown that the doll's head is full of sawdust, say, he need not recognize that he was wrong, but may say 'now you've killed her'.

c) There is the sort of view we characterize as animistic: we may say, for example, that in a certain tribe 'they believe stones are alive'; and we might in certain circumstances describe a tribe as thinking the same of certain machines. I say we might do this, but it is not altogether clear *what* we would be doing: it is certainly not clear that they have the same idea we have of living beings and just extend it further. If *we* do not take such a view of stones or machines, it is not that we reject it because it is *simpler* to deny that such things are alive.

The philosophical view that might be expressed by 'It has not been *ruled out* that this machine has a life and is not just an arrangement of tubes and so on' is not one to be set alongside *a*), *b*), and *c*), although the person who holds such a view may say 'I believe this machine *is* alive'. What his belief amounts to is that he says that sort of thing. He has not formulated what can be taken as an alternative to something others believe about machines; he has not got a hypothesis which we might reject because, we might say, it is less simple than looking at machines as just arrangements of transistors and so on.[18]

I have tried to show why it is right to reject the notion that we might discover a machine which could Think. 'It only does what it is designed to do' comes close to being a reason for rejecting it. This is because, whatever a machine does, in doing it, it is doing nothing different from what a machine designed to do just that in those ways is doing; to object that a machine is only doing what it is designed to do is to say 'What it does cannot be rooted in, or grow out of, its experiences, its wants, the conditions of a life'. And this is fundamentally because a machine is interchangeable. To say this is not to give a description which we could discover to be false of a machine.[19]

NOTES

[1] I shall not use inverted commas where there is no danger of confusion. 'Playing chess' here means doing such things as printing out 'Q-R4' in certain circumstances. Whether the machine is only as-it-were playing chess need not be settled at this stage.

[2] See 'Brains and Behaviour', in *Analytical Philosophy* (Second Series), ed. Butler.

[3] It is in any event not clear what is meant by the machine's meaning what it says. What is essential in the operations of a machine can be given a formal characterization. What I mean is illustrated by the way we can test a program for a computer that will fly a plane on an ordinary computer. We invent test data, having decided on a representation for all the results and input data we are interested in distinguishing: what is important in what the machine is doing is (in *Tractatus* language) what it has in common with all the representations which can serve the same purpose. If what a machine does is what any machine producing equivalent changes in formally similar ways on formally similar input would be doing, could it be playing chess, calculating, could it mean what it said? I shall give my reasons for answering 'No' later. (That answer does not imply that what makes what a man does different from what a machine does is some further activity, such as 'interpretation'.) On this question see Wittgenstein, *Philosophical Investigations,* §200.

[4] This is itself an oversimplification, as it includes Strawsonian presuppositions.

[5] 'R' for Russell; see *Analysis of Mind,* p 159.

[6] I have already made use of the notion several times. See pp 51, 54, and note 3 above.

[7] See Anscombe, *Intention,* p 68, for a discussion of this point.

[8] 'Explanations in Psychology', in *Philosophy in America,* ed. Max Black. See also Putnam, 'Robots: Machines or Artificially Created Life?', in *Journal of Philosophy* (November 12, 1964), and 'Brains and Behaviour', *op. cit.,* p 4.

[9] For a point similar to Turing's but more sophisticated, see Putnam, 'Brains and Behaviour', *op. cit.,* 4n.

[10] 'Brains and Behaviour', *op. cit.,* 'Dreaming and "Depth Grammar"', in *Analytical Philosophy,* ed. Butler; 'The Analytic and the Synthetic', in *Minnesota Studies in the Philosophy of Science,* vol. III, eds. Feigl and Maxwell.

[11] I have drawn especially from 'The Analytic and the Synthetic', *op. cit.,* pp 362–5; 'Brains and Behaviour', *op. cit.,* pp 5, 13–14; 'Dreaming and "Depth Grammar"', *op. cit.,* p 224.

[12] 'Dreaming and "Depth Grammar"', *op. cit.,* pp 219–20.

[13] For the only difference mentioned by Putnam see next footnote.

[14] I should say that it comes naturally to him to use it as a theoretical term of sorts. Putnam would deny that 'pain' is here being used as a theoretical term: he does not wish to accept that I might be wrong about my pain, anger, and so on. It is important to bring out the way this consequence is avoided and the reason I should say 'pain' is being used very like a theoretical term. Words like 'pain' are not logically tied, on his view, to behaviour *or* physical states. But, in addition to that part of its meaning fixed by its 'reporting' use, 'pain' has logical connections with avoidance desires, and other 'functionally' characterized states of a psychological theory. It can be well established that a certain physical system 'realizes' this theory, and that is how it is supposed to be discovered, in Putnam's example, that certain beings have pains although they don't show them in their behaviour. Such an account can include

the following logical relation: a man can't be said to be wrong about whether he is in pain. Now suppose that a man who fulfils the *behavioural* criteria for sincerity says 'I am in pain' when, on the same sort of grounds (brain waves, etc.) on which it was supposed to be established that there were pains felt by the beings who had no pain-behaviour, he is shown to be in pain. The reply to this is that sincerity is no more tied to behavioural criteria than pain is; in other words, if a theory allows us to conclude that he is in pain, it will, in such circumstances, allow us to conclude also that he is not sincere. Physicalists may take the view that we can be wrong about whether we are in pain; a consistent theory in which 'any situation that a person cannot discriminate from a situation in which he himself has a pain *counts* as a situation in which he has a pain' ('Brains and Behaviour', *op. cit.*, p. 8) will never put us into a position to say 'A wrongly thinks he is in pain': that would be an obvious inconsistency.

[15] Compare 'Brains and Behaviour', *op. cit.*, pp 7–8.

[16] See Wittgenstein, *The Blue and Brown Books*, p 58.

[17] If 'unscientific' means unlike the view which would be adopted by a large number of scientists, it may, of course, be unscientific. Wittgenstein was not entirely right in saying that you have to be calloused by doing philosophy not to notice something wrong with, for example, 'These deaf-mutes have learned only a gesture-language, but each of them talks to himself inwardly in a sound-language'; science will often do as well.

[18] There are also views we can make-believe we have, e.g., in science fiction. But there we play with uses of words akin to our own; understanding such uses is not understanding what might be.

[19] The question I was asking at the beginning seems to envisage a situation in which we might first exclaim 'Gosh! The machine did that just like a man might!' and then go on to ask whether we can regard this behaviour as we might regard such behaviour in a man. But my envisaging such a situation shows that I was in the same confusion I was trying to get clear about in Section III. There is no reason to think there are 'behavioural criteria' which are somehow neutral and which might be fulfilled by a machine *or* a man. What a machine does will not be just like what a man does; this isn't to say one could not be taken in. [This note was added at proof-stage by the author.]

MEANING, CONVENTION, AND *THE BLUE BOOK*[1]

JERRY A. FODOR

IN PART I of this paper I shall present a detailed reconstruction of an argument that I take to be central in Wittgenstein's *Blue Book*. My main concern will be to arrive at an accurate characterization of Wittgenstein's views,[2] and I shall omit criticism and commentary wherever doing so is compatible with clarity of presentation. In Part II I shall try to assess the likelihood that a central premise of Wittgenstein's argument is true. The two parts of the paper are intended to be independent in that I should want to maintain that the arguments in Part II are sound even if the reading of *The Blue Book* proposed in Part I should turn out to be untenable.

PART I

I take it that *The Blue Book* is concerned to defend four major theses. Stated very roughly these are:

t_1 The meaning of a sign cannot be an object. In particular, the meaning of a sign cannot be a mental object (e.g. a thought, image, etc.).

t_2 That a sign has the meaning it has is the result of a *convention*.

t_3 The meaning of a sign is fully explained when we have described the conventions which determine how the sign is used.

t_4 It follows from t_2 and t_3 that certain questions that philosophers ask, though apparently questions about the non-linguistic world, are, in fact, questions about linguistic conventions and that certain claims that philosophers make, though apparently claims about the non-linguistic world, are, in fact, recommendations that new linguistic conventions be adopted.

For present purposes I shall assume without discussion that t_1 is both clear and true. I shall be mainly interested in describing the form in which Wittgenstein holds t_2 and t_3 and in displaying the arguments by means of which Wittgenstein seeks to establish t_4.

Since Saussure[3] it has become commonplace in philosophy and linguistics to remark upon a certain arbitrariness that appears to attach to facts about natural languages. By this is meant not only that it is simply a matter of historical accident that a given language is spoken in one place and not in another but also that it is not possible to give any justification for persisting in particular linguistic usages other than the practical inconvenience of altering them.[4] One (slightly misleading) way of putting this is to say that we could, in principle, alter any detail of our language simply by agreeing to do so, just as children do when they agree to converse in Pig Latin. This is meant to be analogous to saying, for example, that we could alter the conventions that determine what counts as correct evening dress simply by agreeing to do so, and to be *dis*analogous to saying that we could alter the way we walk simply by all agreeing to limp. Precisely what is denied when the arbitrariness of facts about language is stressed is that anything corresponds to a natural way of talking in the way that something corresponds to a natural way of walking. In short, then, what is behind the notion that facts about language are arbitrary is the belief that they do not obtain by virtue of any logical or empirical necessity. (Wittgenstein: 'The man who is philosophically puzzled sees a law in the way a word is used . . .' (27).[5]) Hence, it is supposed that we could, in some sense, alter such facts effortlessly;[6] i.e. in precisely the sense that we could not alter the way we walk effortlessly.

Usually the theorist who claims that facts about language are arbitrary has in mind such examples as the following. We could adopt the practice of henceforth using the phonemic sequence represented by the conventional spelling 'boy' in just those cases in which the phonemic sequence represented by the conventional spelling 'girl' has hitherto been used and vice versa. Or we could adopt the practice of pronouncing every other word in a sentence backwards or of replacing it by its translation in French, etc. With such cases before him the theorist may argue that since we could alter facts about language by adopting the relevant *explicit* conventions, it is useful to think of such facts as obtaining by virtue of *tacit* conventions. He thus arrives at a 'principle of conventionality' to the following effect: *linguistic facts obtain solely by virtue of the acquiescence of speakers.* (Wittgenstein: 'I want you to remember that words have those meanings which we have given them. . . . Philosophers very often talk about investigating, analyzing, the meaning of words. But let's not forget that a word hasn't got a meaning given to it, as it were, by a power independent of us, so that there could be a kind of scientific investigation into what the word *really* means. A word has the meaning someone has given to it' (27–8).)

It will be noticed that although the examples in the last paragraph were all drawn from conventions concerning the physical representation of a word (i.e. as a series of shapes on paper or as a sequence of sounds in speech), the principle of conventionality was stated as a *general* truth about facts about language and is thus intended to cover (at least) facts about the meanings of words as well as facts about their spelling or pronunciation. That Wittgenstein holds the principle in this general form seems clear from the quotation just cited.

It is important to recognize that Wittgenstein could have consistently adopted t_2 and rejected t_3: the principle of conventionality does not *require* the use theory of meaning. To see this it is only necessary to suppose that t_1 is false, i.e. that the meaning of a word *is* some non-linguistic object, say, the object the word names.[7] In that case a consistent theory could be developed which maintains t_2 but denies t_3. Such a theory might claim that the fact that a word has the meaning it does is the result of a convention which establishes a relation between the word and the object it names (the convention perhaps being expressed or initiated by ostensive definition), but that to explain the meaning of the word requires not only that one describe the convention *but also that one exhibit the object.* Much of the criticism in *The Blue Book* is directed against the generality of that sort of position. Very often it has the form of showing that, in the case of a clearly meaningful utterance (as, e.g., 'I have an itch'), the request that the relevant object be exhibited is not logically competent, so that the question 'How could the meaning of the utterance be explained?' becomes logically unanswerable on such a theory.[8]

That Wittgenstein does, in fact, accept t_3 is perhaps the most characteristic feature of *The Blue Book*. '. . . if we had to name anything which is the life of the sign, we should have to say that it was its *use*'(4). 'The mistake we are liable to make could be expressed thus: (when we take the meaning of a sign to be an object) we are looking for the use of a sign, but we look for it as though it were an object coexisting with the sign' (5). 'The sign (the sentence) gets it significance from the system of signs, from the language to which it belongs. Roughly: understanding a sentence means understanding a language' (5). 'The use of the word *in practice* is its meaning' (69). What is less clear is what Wittgenstein takes the conventions which determine the meaning of a sign to be like. To explain this is to establish the precise form in which Wittgenstein holds t_3. I shall try to do so in the context of a discussion of Wittgenstein's technical vocabulary.

There are a number of terms in *The Blue Book* for which Wittgenstein invents neologistic employments and which must be correctly understood if his argument is to be followed. Among these is 'grammar' when it is used in the manner exemplified by the following: 'We don't say that the man who tells us he feels the visual image two inches behind the bridge of his nose is telling a lie or talking nonsense. But we say that we don't understand the meaning of such a phrase. It combines well-known words but combines them in a way we don't yet understand. The grammar of this phrase has yet to be explained to us' (10). 'When I say: "we can only *conjecture* the cause but we *know* the motive", this statement will be seen . . . to be a grammatical one. The "can" refers to a *logical* possibility' (15). '. . . it [is] a way of examining the grammar (the use) of the word "to know" to ask ourselves what, in the particular case we are examining, we should call "getting to know" '(23).

These quotations suggest what a careful perusal of *The Blue Book* will confirm: that Wittgenstein uses the term 'grammar' broadly enough to comprehend very nearly *all* the conventions which determine the rôle of a word in a language. To describe the grammar of a word is thus to enumerate the conventions in accordance with which the word is used.

Though Wittgenstein is inexplicit on this point, we must assume that such conventions are of three sorts. In the first place, there must be conventions which fix the combinatorial properties of words, i.e. which determine the sentential positions a word can occupy. Secondly, there must be conventions which determine meaning relations between words or expressions, e.g., which determine which sentences of the language are true (or false) by virtue of the meanings of their component terms. Finally, there must be conventions which fix relations between words and non-linguistic entities, objects, events, situations, etc. (In each case such terms as 'fix' and 'determine' must be understood as only figuratively characterizing the way that a convention governs the use of a word. '. . . in general, we don't use language according to strict rules—it hasn't been taught us by means of strict rules either' (25).)

It is conventions of the third sort with which Wittgenstein is mainly concerned in *The Blue Book.* Two points need to be made about them. First, it seems clear that some words are *not* governed by conventions of this sort. These include 'logical words' like 'not' and 'grammatical words' like 'to' in *I want to go home*. Secondly, the conventions which determine the relations between linguistic forms and features of the non-linguistic world are of very different kinds, depending upon the word whose use they govern. Compare the conventions governing the use of the word 'hello' with the conventions governing the use of the word 'cat'.

Among the kinds of conventions which determine the relations of some (not all) linguistic forms to features of the non-linguistic world are *criteria of application*. These are conventions which determine when a word is correctly (or truly or accurately, etc., depending upon the word and the context) applied to something non-linguistic.

To the question, 'How do you know that so-and-so is the case?', we sometimes answer by giving 'criteria' and sometimes by giving 'symptoms'. If medical science calls angina an inflammation caused by a particular bacillus and we ask in a particular case, 'Why do you say this man has got angina?', then the answer, 'I have found the bacillus so-and-so in his blood', gives us the criterion, or what we may call the defining criterion of angina. If, on the other hand, the answer was, 'His throat is inflamed', this might give us a symptom of angina. I call a 'symptom' a phenomenon of which experience has taught us that it coincided, in some way or other, with the phenomenon which is our defining criterion. Then to say 'A man has angina if this bacillus is found in him' is a tautology or it is a loose way of stating the definition of 'angina'. But to say, 'A man has angina whenever he has an inflamed throat' is to make an hypothesis (24–5).

The striking difference between a criterion and a symptom is, then, that if I know that a criterion for the application of a word is satisfied, I may justify applying the word simply by appeal to a linguistic convention. But if I know just that a symptom occurs, I may justify applying the word only by appealing to an empirical correlation. Hence applying the word is making an hypothesis in the second case, but not in the first. Briefly: criteria express grammatical norms; symptoms express nomological relations.

Though the logical differences between symptoms and criteria are thus fundamental, it would be a mistake to suppose that, for any given statement about the relation between a word and something non-linguistic, we can invariably tell whether it expresses a criterion or a symptom. 'In practice, if you were asked which phenomenon is the defining criterion and which is a symptom, you would in most cases be unable to answer this question except by making an arbitrary decision *ad hoc*' (25). 'We are unable clearly to circumscribe the concepts we use, not because we don't know their real definition but because there is no real "definition" to them' (25).

Having said this much about language, we may now consider some philosophical implications.

In philosophy arguments are often set forth to support the claim that some predicate from ordinary language can never be used to make a true (correct, warranted, etc.) statement; i.e. that the predicate in question does not have, or at least cannot be known to have, any application to the world. Much of *The Blue Book* is devoted to detailed investigations of such arguments. But what is most novel about *The Blue Book* is that it offers an analysis of the nature of the sceptical claims these arguments purport to substantiate. This analysis derives from Wittgenstein's views about language in ways that I shall now try to make clear.

Consider the following sceptical claim.[9]

C. I can never know that *S* has a pain unless I myself am *S*.

In the first place, it seems clear that a philosopher who maintains that *C* is true does not intend to deny that there are occasions on which one would, without hesitation and without apparent linguistic impropriety, claim to know that someone other than oneself is in pain. '... the man ... who says that only his own experiences are real, does not thereby disagree with us about any practical question of fact...' (59). What such a philosopher *does* wish to deny is that we have reason to believe that what we say on such occasions is true. In particular, he wishes to deny that the fact that someone exhibits pain *behavior* can ever be sufficient grounds for saying that that person is feeling pain.

I think that Wittgenstein's position in *The Blue Book* is this. For 'pain' to have a rôle in the language (e.g. for it to be possible for us to explain what 'pain' means, to argue about pains, to agree, in practical circumstances, about the occurrence of pains, etc.), it must be the case that the conventions which determine the grammar of 'pain' include criteria for the correct application of 'pain'. Such criteria, as we saw above, do not express hypotheses. In particular, they do not express hypotheses to the effect that if a certain sort of behavior is manifested, then, usually or always, a certain sort of sensation is present. Rather, they express *norms* which determine what it is for the word 'pain' to be correctly applied. Hence, in order for talk about pain to be possible at all,[10] there must be some cases (or at least there must be some imaginable cases) in which to say of a person who is behaving in a certain way that he is in pain '... is a tautology or it is a loose way of stating [a] definition'.[11] And in such cases the sceptic's doubt is *logically* misplaced; for, though it makes sense to doubt the reliability of a symptom, it is a point of logic that there is nothing corresponding to reliability in the case of a norm, hence that there is nothing to doubt.

In short, the sceptic has failed to distinguish between statements justified by appeal to symptoms (i.e. by appeal to empirical correlations) and statements justified by appeal to criteria (i.e. by appeal to linguistic conventions). His failure to appreciate the normative aspects of certain linguistic conventions has led him to treat *all* cases of justification as cases of empirical justification, and this, in turn, makes it appear inexplicable that we should know certain statements to be true that we do, in fact, know to be true.

Faced with this sort of confusion, the philosopher must seek, first, to describe the sorts of situations in which the criteria for the application of the relevant predicate are clearly satisfied, 'Philosophy really is "purely descriptive"' (18), thus recalling to the sceptic the way in which the language actually operates. Secondly, he must seek to disabuse the sceptic of a theory of meaning on which all statements which do not express truths of formal logic are taken to express empirical hypotheses (albeit hypotheses which, in some cases, are susceptible neither of confirmation nor of disconfirmation).[12]

None of this is intended to suggest, however, that no sense can be made of such claims as *C*. The sceptic doubts certain statements, the truth of which are, in fact, consequences of the linguistic conventions operative in English. But, clearly, other systems of conventions, other 'notations' are possible, and in some of them the statements the sceptic doubts need not be necessarily true. The sceptic is 'irresistibly tempted' (60) to employ such notations, and there is 'no objection to adopting a symbolism in which a certain person always or temporarily holds an exceptional place. And therefore, if I utter the sentence "Only I really see", it is conceivable that my fellow creatures thereupon will arrange their notations so as to fall in with me by saying "so-and-so is really seen" instead of "L. W. sees so-and-so", etc., etc.' (66). Indeed, since the meaning of a word is determined by the conventions which govern it and since the change in notation for which the sceptic is implicitly arguing is precisely a change in the linguistic conventions, it is not clear that the sceptic's new notation and our old one could even conflict. For it appears that if the sceptic's notation is adopted, the term whose applicability would thereby be denied would only be a homonym, not a synonym, of that term when it is governed by the conventions operative in *our* notation. In particular, the sceptic's assertion of *C* would not contradict our denial of *C* since the words in *C* differ in meaning when the sceptic utters them and when we do.

Occasionally in *The Blue Book* this sort of argument is made quite explicit.

Consider this argument: 'How can we wish that this paper were red if it isn't red? Doesn't this mean that I wish that which doesn't exist at all? Therefore, my wish can only contain something *similar* to the paper's being red. Oughtn't we, therefore, to use a different word instead of "red" when we talk of wishing that something were red? The imagery of the wish surely shows us something less definite, something hazier, than the reality of the paper being red. I should, therefore, say instead of, "I wish this paper were red," something like, "I wish a pale red for this paper." But if in the usual way of speaking he had said, "I wish a pale red for this paper," we should, in order to fulfil his wish, have painted it a pale red—and this wasn't what he wished. On the other hand, there is no objection to adopting the form of expression he suggests as long as we know that he uses the phrase, "I wish a pale x for this paper," always to mean what ordinarily we express by, "I wish this paper had the colour x." What he said really recommended his notation, in the sense in which a notation can be recommended. But he did not tell us a new truth and did not show us that what we said before was false' (60).

The sceptic is, then, not to be understood to be making claims about what sorts of things there are in the world, or even about what sorts of things can be known to be in the world. Our disagreement with the sceptic is not in that sense a substantive disagreement. The sceptic's objection is to a convention which we accept, and our resistance to the sceptic's claims is a resistance to adopting a new convention. 'By a new notation no facts . . . are changed. It is true, however, that we may be irresistibly attracted or repelled by a notation. (We easily forget how much a notation, a form of expression, may mean to us and that changing it isn't always as easy as it often is in mathematics or in the sciences. A change of clothes or of names may mean very little, and it may mean a great deal)' (57).

PART II

There are a number of *prima facie* reasons for feeling uncomfortable with this argument. These, in turn, suggest deeper difficulties which I shall pursue throughout the present section.

In the first place, the suggestion that the arguments for scepticism be treated as, in effect, analogous to arguments for the metric system, i.e. as recommending a change of notation, hardly appears to do justice to the intention of the sceptic's argument, which is to claim that some of our beliefs about the world are less well founded than we had thought them to be. Nor is it clear, if the difference between scepticism and realism is analogous to the difference between two systems of measurement, why one should be 'irresistibly tempted' to adopt the one position or the other. One may prefer the metric system to a system of inches and feet, but one is not irresistibly tempted to adopt it, nor does one find oneself tempted to say that the truth of estimates of distance given in miles is incompatible with the truth of estimates of distance given in kilometers.

Moreover (and this is a point on which *The Blue Book* is quite clear; cf. pp 61 and following), we can often give *reasons* for adopting one convention rather than another. (It is easier to calculate in meters than in feet; it is easier to learn a phonemic orthography than a hieroglyphic orthography, etc.) That is, the choice of a convention need not by any means be an arbitrary choice. But this consideration alone would appear to give the sceptic a way out of the net. For precisely the arguments that he has been accustomed to use to show that skepticism is *true* he may now employ to show that scepticism is the justifiable notation. And may he not add that the decision to call disagreements between philosophic systems, disagreements about notation and not about truth, is, by Wittgenstein's own arguments, just a decision to adopt a notation in which such words as 'true' and 'notation' are used in somewhat novel ways?

Finally, it appears that the argument that scepticism cannot be formulated without equivocations is inconclusive even on the conventionalist account of meaning. For suppose that it can be shown that what the sceptic is doing is (tantamount to) recommending a new notation in which the conventions governing the use of key terms are changed to a greater or lesser degree. It is nevertheless clear that not *every* convention governing the use of a word is *ipso facto* involved in determining the meaning of the word. (For example, it is a convention which governs the use of the word 'doctor' that it has precedence in such forms of address as 'Doctor and Mrs. Smith'. But, clearly, this is a convention that could be dropped without altering the meaning of the word 'doctor'.) From this it follows that it is not enough to show that the sceptic's notation involves some alterations in the conventions governing key words. It must also be shown that the conventions the sceptic wants to alter cannot be changed without equivocation. Now it is notorious that we are without adequate criteria for identity and difference of meaning, nor does it appear that such criteria are provided by the theoretical mechanisms of *The Blue*

Book. Some argument is thus required for the very surprising conclusion that throughout the history of philosophy, sceptics and realists have really not been in disagreement. (It might be supposed that the notion of a criterion of application provides an instrument for distinguishing those conventions whose alteration alters the meaning of a word. Thus the alteration of a criterion might be thought a sufficient condition for change of meaning.[13] This, however, merely raises the old question in a new form, for we must now have some way of distinguishing criteria both from symptoms and from other sorts of conventions. And this is, in general, not forthcoming.)

Though I do not by any means suppose that these arguments are conclusive, I think they are strong enough to suggest the advisability of a careful re-examination of the position set forth in Part I. In particular, I wish to re-examine t_2 and the principle of conventionality. If they are not true, or are not true in the sense supposed in Part I, it appears that the central argument of *The Blue Book* must be untenable, since Wittgenstein's demonstration that there is no disagreement in substance between the realist and the sceptic depends precisely on the principle that nothing firmer than convention (e.g. no logical or empirical necessity) supports our linguistic usages. In what follows, then, we shall try to discover just which properties of the usage of a word obtain by convention and in what sense of 'convention' they do so.

Since part of our problem is to find an adequate definition of 'conventional' when it is applied to language, let us begin by understanding the term in a way which makes it appear most obvious that at least some features of language are conventional. Suppose we say 'x is a conventional feature of a language just in case speakers of the language can alter x at will'. (Notice that it is sufficient for Wittgenstein's argument if the meaning of a word is conventional in this sense.) What I shall argue is that, at least in this sense of 'convention', the principle of conventionality, when applied to the meanings of words, is by no means clearly true.

What first suggests the notion that the meaning of a word is conventional is the apparent obviousness of the claim that at least some grammatical properties are. Yet even here the situation is less clear than it might be thought. The difficulty is that the grammatical properties of words are interdependent to an as yet unknown extent. Thus alterations in some such properties bring in their train quite unintended alterations in others. Such forced options are easy to find even in the case of features of the way a word is sounded, features which, at first glance, would appear most obviously to enjoy conventional status. A rather trivial example will stand for a host of more significant (but more complicated) ones. Thus suppose you intend to adopt the convention of always pronouncing the word 'toy' backwards.[14] Clearly this is a change which it is within your power to effect; what is less apparent but equally true is that by adopting this convention you have committed yourself to a change in, e.g., the plural form of the word. For where 'toy' pluralizes by the addition of a sound identical with the first sound in 'zoom', your new form, 'yot', will pluralize by adding a sound identical with the first sound in 'stop'. This is, of course, a consequence which you may avoid either by the stipulation that 'yot' is to be an exception to the pluralization rules (like 'ox' and 'fish') or by altering the pluralization rules themselves. But, in either case, something about the language which is at least not *directly* conventional has forced you to adopt *two* new conventions where you had only intended to adopt one.

Still it will be argued that even if it is not a convention but the result of some fairly general rule that 'yot' pluralizes 'yots' and not 'yotz', that that rule itself obtains is either a convention or the consequence of a convention and is thus either directly or indirectly alterable.[15] I do not wish to deny this; my example is intended only to show that, even in the case of grammar, a distinction must be made between two kinds of conventionality. Some grammatical features of language may be considered directly conventional, i.e. they do not obtain as a consequence of some general grammatical rule, and they may be altered without producing further disturbances in the linguistic system. Other grammatical features of language are conventional only in the sense that they obtain by virtue of conventional rules, rules which are not themselves consequences of still more general rules. That 'toy' is pronounced as it is is a convention of the first kind. That 'toy' pluralizes as it does is a convention of the second kind. Probably many fewer features of language are conventional in the first way than philosophers have supposed. That is another way of saying that, at least at the level of grammar, language is probably far more systematic than philosophers have supposed. How systematic it is we shall not know until linguists have concluded work now in progress on the interrelation of such features of words as stress, juncture, word-class membership, pronunciation, etc.

The claim must, then, be the following. However much particular features of language obtain by virtue of systematic features, these systematic features themselves obtain by virtue of conventions. That is, we could change them if we wished to do so; we could speak French instead of English, or we could invent a language which has vastly different syntactic and phonological properties from those of any natural language, or we could make various changes in English, granting that the changes we make may have unforeseen ramifications. I am willing to accept this claim about the grammatical features of languages, at least for purposes of the present paper.[16] But I want to investigate carefully why we feel that it is so obviously true. The lack of analogous reasons in the case of features of the meanings of words will give us grounds for doubting that they too are conventional.

Why, then, do we feel so certain that (say) phonological features are conventional? It is quite clear that our certainty derives from the knowledge that natural languages differ in phonological structure. Such variation from language to language may usually be taken as conclusive evidence that the linguistic feature involved is conventional in the required sense. For the most convincing way of showing that some feature of a natural language *could* be altered, short of actually altering it, is to exhibit a natural language in which that feature does not, in fact, obtain.[17]

It is worth describing just *how* we know that phonological structure does exhibit the required interlingual variation. Avoiding technicalities, the situation seems to be the following. First, we know what it is for a language to *have* a phonological structure: roughly speaking, the utterances of the language must be capable of a natural representation in terms of a relatively small number of discrete, recurring, minimal units. Secondly, we can say with considerable precision what it is for two languages to differ with respect to phonological structure. Thus following what currently appears to be the most promising approach, we represent a phoneme as a set of choices in a matrix of 'distinctive features'. The phonemic inventory of a language is a set of such sets of choices, and a pair of languages are phonologically distinct just in case they differ in at least one phoneme.[18] Given this conceptual background, the question whether there exists appreciable interlingual phonological variation becomes a relatively straightforward empirical question, to which the answer is decidedly 'yes'.[19]

Parity of argument demands that if we can show a similar degree of variation in the semantic structure of natural languages, we shall have to admit the claim that facts about meaning obtain by virtue of conventions. Hence we must ask whether such variation, in fact, occurs, and if so, whether it is comparable in extent to the interlingual variation displayed by phonology (and syntax).

I shall argue presently that this sort of question involves logical difficulties which do not arise when we inquire into the conventionality of grammar. For the moment, however, I want to ignore these difficulties and pretend that the question is as easy to understand as it looks. It appears, then, that what evidence there is suggests that languages do not exhibit the sort of semantic variation that the conventionalist position would lead one to expect, at least not in many of the philosophically interesting cases.

Wittgenstein says: 'What we did in these discussions was what we always do when we meet the word "can" in a metaphysical proposition. We show that this proposition hides a grammatical rule' (55). Let us suppose for the moment that this remark is intended literally so that all such statements as the following are taken to be grammatical (i.e. to express linguistic conventions):

1) I can never be wrong about whether I am in pain.
2) Nothing can be both red and green all over.
3) No effect can precede its cause.

We may ask: 'Do such conventions vary freely from language to language?' Still assuming that this is no more than a straightforward empirical question and taking into account the regrettable lack of data on the semantic properties of exotic languages, it seems fairly plausible to maintain that there do not exist languages in which such conventions are freely violated. Thus *if* such statements as 1–3 express conventions, the conventions they express differ from those which determine grammatical structure in that the former, but not the latter, appear to be interlinguistically stable.

I said that certain logical problems inhere in the question 'How similar are the semantic structures of different languages?' which do not arise in the case of the analogous question about phonology. These problems stem from the fact that the considerations relevant to decisions about the similarity and difference of semantic properties of a pair of languages are not independent of the considerations which determine what constitutes a good translation from one language to the other, for, unlike phonological and syntactic relations, semantic relations must be preserved in translation.

Hence the argument that semantic properties, if they are determined by conventions, ought to exhibit a degree of interlingual variation which they do not, in fact, exhibit, appears to be open to the following sort of parody. 'It counts against the claim that semantic features are conventional that, for example, in whatever language we investigate, the word which translates the English word "brother" always refers to a male.' Clearly this argument is ludicrous in that it takes what is no more than a requirement upon the translation of a word (no word is a translation of the English word 'brother' unless it at least refers to a male) to express a surprising correspondence between the semantic systems of different languages. But may not the conventionalist say that our whole argument reduces to this sort of mistake? May he not claim that the supposed interlingual stability of, say, conventions about 'pain' or 'color' is simply a projection of our policy of translating no word as 'pain' or 'color' that does not obey precisely the conventions that these words obey in English? 'Of course the Navajo concept of color is just like our concept of "color". If it were not, it would not be a concept of *color*.'

In the first place, we should notice that even if this argument were correct, it would be of no aid to the conventionalist, since it would do no more than shift the question from 'If semantic facts are conventional, why do they not exhibit interlingual variation?' to 'If semantic facts are conventional, how can one account for the fact that translation is possible?' That is, if the conventionalist explains the interlingual stability of semantic features by saying that we only translate by an English word a word which is governed by the corresponding conventions in the alien language, he must then explain why historically unrelated languages exhibit conventions that are sufficiently similar to permit us to establish the correspondences necessary for translation. Surely there is no logical necessity that requires that the conventions governing words in English shall have counterparts in the conventions governing words in other natural languages. If semantic features are indeed conventional, the existence of this correspondence needs to be explained.

In the second place, if we are careful, we can avoid the conventionalist's objection to our argument altogether. We do this by pointing out that many words are characterized by *clusters* of conventions, each of which contributes *part* of the delineation of the meaning of the word but which only jointly are adequate to completely determine the rôle of the words in the language. Thus it is (perhaps) one of the conventions which determine the rôle of 'pain' in English that we are never said to be mistaken about whether we are in pain. It is another and logically independent convention that pains (unlike beliefs) are said to have spatial locations. A third relates 'pain' to 'person' and 'body' by the principle that a person can only feel a pain that occurs in his own body, and so on. Now, while we cannot without absurdity ask why the word which translates 'pain' in a language other than English has *any* of these properties, we can quite reasonably ask why the word has *all* of them. That is, we can ask for an explanation of the fact that independent languages tend to develop the *same* clusters, a fact which it would seem difficult to account for on the view that the semantic features that a word has are determined simply by convention. Put it another way: if the conventionalist story were true, we would expect that there might be languages which had a word just like our word 'color' except for the omission of the convention that colors are incompatible. Or we would expect that there might be languages which had a word just like our word 'pain' except for the omission of the convention to the effect that each person has privileged access to his own pains. It is clearly an empirical question whether such languages exist. If they do not, the conventionalist owes us an explanation.

The presence of interlinguistic variation is a *sufficient* condition for the conventionality of a linguistic feature. But since it clearly is not also a logically necessary condition, it is incumbent upon us to say something about the status of the principle of conventionality in the absence of such variation. With this discussion I shall close this paper.

There appear to be only three available positions.

A. The null hypothesis: semantic features obtain by convention, and the lack of interlingual variation is simply an unexplained fact.

This position can be adopted only at the risk of circularity. For notice it was the privileged status of such statements as 1–3 which we had intended to explain by saying that they expressed grammatical conventions. But such an explanation avoids circularity only if the conventions the explanation invokes are not themselves privileged. (Otherwise, we have merely replaced the problem of the unalterability of statements like 1–3 with the completely equivalent problem of the unalterability of the grammatical norms such statements are purported to express.) We have seen that the alterability of such conventions would be sufficiently demonstrated if we could show that they exhibit interlingual variation. Failing this, it appears that we must either provide an explanation of their invariance or admit the possible vacuity of the 'grammatical' account of metaphysical statements.

One might put this argument a different way. If you understand 'Two colors cannot be in the same place at the same time' on the model of 'You cannot be in London five minutes after you've been in New York', then you are likely to suppose that because the second sentence is true by virtue of a fact, the first must be true by virtue of a sort of super-fact. Scepticism sets in when you are inclined to argue that since it makes sense to doubt that a fact obtains, it must also make sense to doubt that a super-fact does—if it makes sense to require evidence in favor of the one, it must make sense to require evidence in favor of the other. It is a way of avoiding this muddle to say that statements that seem to be true by virtue of super-facts are really true by virtue of grammatical conventions, so that to doubt a super-fact is really just to recommend a change in the conventions. This is still a way of avoiding the muddle even if you add, 'and, in fact, the conventions can't be changed', so long as you can show that this 'can't' is of a different sort from the troublesome 'can't' in 'Two colors . . . etc.'

Our argument has been that the invariance of linguistic norms appears to suggest that the relevant conventions *can't* be changed. If this is, in fact, the case, then the conventionalist's position is in danger of circularity so long as this invariance remains unexplained; i.e. so long as he has not shown that the unrevisability of the grammatical norms is a different sort of thing than the unrevisability of the metaphysical statements whose truth these norms insure.

B. Both the conventionality of semantic features and their interlingual stability are to be granted. They are to be reconciled by the supposition that the semantic features which natural languages display are determined by conventions which, for one reason or another, are so clearly justified that they have been spontaneously adopted even by language communities whose languages have developed independently. For example, the choice of a unit of weight is conventional, but no society chooses, for its daily transactions, the weight of an atom of hydrogen. Here we have universality (albeit of a negative sort), but the reasons for this universality are evident and do not constitute an argument against the conventionality of units of measure. Perhaps analogous reasons are to be brought forth in justification of whatever conventions are found to be common to the semantic systems of all languages.

C. The interlingual stability of semantic features is to be granted and is assumed to provide grounds for denying that these features are conventional. On this view some alternative account of the necessary statements will need to be provided. But it is worth emphasizing that there is no *a priori* reason for supposing that the *same* account need hold for all such statements. It is a *prima facie* argument against the grammatical account that it indiscriminately groups such statements as 1–3 with one another and with '7 + 5 = 12', with 'bachelors are unmarried' and with indefinitely many other types of necessary statements with which it is highly doubtful that they have much in common.

One could imagine a more piecemeal approach to the necessary truths proving more convincing. Among the possibilities are the following. Some such statements are perhaps to be defended by reference to their essential rôle in conceptual frameworks to which no alternative is *de facto* available and which we are therefore not prepared to abandon. (One reason why we are unwilling to admit that colors might overlap is perhaps that doing so would play havoc with the logic of the relation '*x* matches *y*', which would then be an equivalence relation when *x* and *y* are colors, but would be intransitive, irreflexive, and asymmetrical when they range over colored surfaces.) In still other cases the interlingual stability of necessary truths is perhaps to be explained as a contribution of the speaker; i.e. as the result of an innate tendency of human beings to develop certain sorts of concepts, and not to develop other sorts, even under a very wide range of experiential conditions. I suspect that this is the view toward which Wittgenstein was tending in the *Investigations*, where the 'bedrock' prerequisite to which the possibility of linguistic communication is referred is identified not with shared conventions but with shared 'ways of life' and with a tendency toward consensus in judgment which is said to be a consequence, and an expression, of our common humanity. But that is another story.

We entered upon this discussion because we wanted to know whether the principle of conventionality is sufficiently reliable to be assumed as a premise in philosophical arguments. Our results are the following. The principle of conventionality must be understood as nothing more than an empirical hypothesis about natural languages. As such it would appear to be true for certain grammatical features of language but is quite likely false for certain semantic features. If it is, in fact, false (if, for example, position C should be true), then at least one version of the attempt to argue from the possibility of language to the incoherence of scepticism would be unacceptable. The disagreement between the sceptic and the realist would then turn out to be a disagreement in substance in at least the following sense: while the sceptic may agree that the truth of 'necessary' propositions is insured by grammatical norms, he may well deny both that we can provide any justification for adopting the norms we, in fact, adopt or that we could adopt other norms were we so inclined. I do not wish to say that a sceptic who argued this way would be arguing correctly. But it seems to me that such a sceptic would have earned the right to be refuted.

NOTES

[1] I want to thank Dr. Hugh S. Chandler and Professor Charles Chihara for having read an earlier version of this paper and for having attempted to convince me of the error of my ways. I fear that their efforts deserve to have met with more success. Also, part of what is in this paper I owe to discussions on the general topic of convention and language with Dr. Jerrold J. Katz.

[2] But I shall not be particularly concerned to adhere to Wittgenstein's terminology (I propose a reconstruction, not merely a summary, of the argument in *The Blue Book*). In particular, 'convention', though it appears throughout this paper, is my word, not Wittgenstein's.

[3] Cf. F. de Saussure, *Cours de Linguistique Générale* (Paris, 1949), for a presentation and defense of the conventionalist position.

[4] That is, the inconvenience that results just from the fact that a given language is spoken by many people, so that a decision to alter the language is a decision to which many people would have to consent.

[5] Numerals in parentheses following quotations are page references to L. Wittgenstein, *The Blue and Brown Books* (Harper & Row: New York, 1958).

[6] Strictly speaking, the claim must be that it is facts about our *own* speech style that we can each alter at will. See footnote 4.

[7] This object would, of course, fail to be 'nonlinguistic' in the case of such words as 'word'. This is, however, irrelevant to our present argument.

[8] It is also possible to maintain t_3 and reject t_2. The use theory of meaning does not require the principle of conventionality. The meaning of a word might well be (or be determined by) its rôle in a language though that rôle was itself fixed by, say, a law of nature. The independence of the use theory from the principle of conventionality has not often enough been stressed; if it is not noticed, one is inclined to feel that the principle of conventionality must be true since the use theory is.

[9] As often as not in *The Blue Book*, it is the generic metaphysician rather than the generic sceptic with whom Wittgenstein is arguing. If I understand Wittgenstein correctly, this is because he takes these positions to be two sides of the same coin.

There exists a body of propositions (a sub-set of the necessary truths) about which philosophers puzzle. If one is impressed by the immunity of these propositions from revision, one may be inclined to suppose them to be metaphysical truths. If one is impressed by the fact that these propositions, though they may be denied without contradiction, do not appear to have the status of empirical generalizations, one may be inclined to doubt that there is any reason to believe them at all. In either case, what one requires is a satisfactory analysis of such propositions, and this is what *The Blue Book* seeks to provide.

[10] On this reading, the form (though not the substance) of Wittgenstein's argument is strongly reminiscent of Kant. Just as the argument of the first Critique purports to derive certain philosophically important consequences from the possibility of knowledge, so the argument of *The Blue Book* purports

to derive certain philosophically important consequences from the possibility of language.

[11] Of course we may not be certain *which* cases of saying that someone is in pain are cases of this kind, since the distinction between a criterion and a symptom is not clear-cut in ordinary language.

[12] Wittgenstein sometimes expresses this argument by saying that the sceptic is mislead by superficial grammatical similarities. Thus because *some* applications of psychological predicates have the form of inferences from (relatively) observable properties of behavior to (relatively) hidden states of feeling, belief, attitude, etc., the sceptic is led to suppose that *all* applications of psychological predicates have this form.

[13] This clearly cannot also be a necessary condition, since some words have no criteria of application ('help', 'hello', 'etc.', etc.).

[14] I identify a word with a set of conventions: phonological, syntactic, semantic, etc., not just with a sequence of phonemes. On this understanding it is possible to speak without contradiction of the same word being pronounced a different way, since sense can be assigned to the idea of altering none of the conventions with which the word is identified except those which determine pronunciation.

[15] It may also be argued that the consequences of a convention ought also to be called conventions. I have no objection to this way of talking.

[16] It would be unwise to accept it without qualification. For there appear to be very impressive arguments for the proposition that some very general (and perhaps some quite specific) grammatical features of natural languages are determined by innate human predispositions. Such features would, of course, not be conventional in *any* sense, since their occurrence would be determined by a law of nature. For a stimulating defense of the innateness hypothesis as applied to grammar cf. E. Lenneberg, 'On Language Acquisition', in J. A. Fodor and J. J. Katz, *Readings in the Philosophy of Language* (Englewood Cliffs, New Jersey, 1963).

[17] N.B. 'to exhibit a *natural* language in which that feature does not obtain'. One can, of course, describe a formal system which differs in any desired respect from, say, English. But this proves nothing unless it can be shown that the system described is a *language*: the sort of thing that human beings could learn to speak as a native tongue. (The question 'What sorts of systems are possible human languages?' is a *psychological* question and it is an *open* question.)

[18] For an account of the distinctive features approach cf. Jackobson, Fant, and Halle, *Preliminaries to Speech Analysis* (M.I.T. Press: Cambridge, 1961).

[19] Though this sort of argument justifies the claim that which phonemes a language employs is a matter of convention, it also illustrates the sorts of considerations which suggest that some grammatical features of languages are *not* conventional. For it is implicit in the distinctive-features approach that a small set of features is sufficient to characterize the phonemic population of *any* natural language. This means that, according to the distinctive-features account, all systematic phonological relations in any natural language can be specified by reference to one of a small number of properties of speech

sounds. If this is true and, particularly, if it is true of historically unrelated languages, then we must suppose that the possible phonological relations exhibited by a language are not at the arbitrary disposal of its speakers. That is, it is a matter of convention which speech sounds a language chooses. But the choice is made from a set which is very small in comparison to the number of sounds a human being is physiologically capable of making. That this fact could be in any sense the consequence of a linguistic convention appears extremely doubtful.

PLEASURE AND ENJOYMENT

J. C. GOSLING

ONE THING THAT is puzzling about pleasure is to see just how it explains our doing things. That it does is obvious enough. We play golf for pleasure, we scrimp and save for the pleasure of seeing our children given a good start in life, we read late into the night because we are enjoying the book so much, and some of us spend our lives in the pursuit of pleasure. Further, while we may be puzzled as to why anyone is interested in discovering who wrote the *Odyssey*, there is something bizarre in wondering why anyone should be interested in pleasure. Such a question seems to betray lack of understanding of the words. Yet while pleasure clearly functions as an explanation, is something for which we do things, it is difficult to see just what its relation is to the things we do for it. It is not like doing the washing-up for money. As Plato in effect points out in the *Philebus*, there is in our experience no such thing as mere pleasure, by itself, just as there is no such thing as mere knowledge. There is knowledge of mathematics, knowledge of medicine, and knowledge of music, and what knowledge is can only be discovered by examination of it in its manifestations. Similarly there is the pleasure of philosophizing, the pleasure of drinking, the pleasure of being praised in public; but these pleasures are not to be confused, and we can only discuss what pleasure is by discussing what makes these various experiences pleasures. Yet if pleasure is not something that we experience over and above the activities, how can we do things for it, and what do we mean by talking of it as something that we 'get out of' activities and experiences? This is the problem both for hedonists and their critics. Anyone who wishes to hold that we do or should act with a view to immediate or over-all pleasure, or that we do or should act 'out of pleasure', will have to give some account of the way in which pleasure functions as an explanation of action; only when we 'know what pleasure is' can we judge what any given form of hedonism amounts to, and what its plausibility is. So, first, we need an examination of why we apparently speak/think of pleasure both as something got out of activities and at the same time in some way identical with the activities. Those who criticize hedonists on the radical ground that they have all misconceived the nature of pleasure have the same work to do.

The first thing to do here is loosen up our ideas a little, by taking a look at some of the variety of ways in which pleasure does explain what we do. One of the troubles with many recent discussions has been an undue assumption that they are all equivalent, or at least not significantly different. This shows in the tendency to take a treatment of enjoyment as a treatment of the whole question or even, more blatantly, in the open treatment of 'being pleased with', 'being pleased to', 'being pleased at', 'enjoying', 'taking pleasure in', 'getting pleasure from' as all equal and indifferent examples of something called pleasure, something which falls into that intriguing class of things which may have a cause and must have an object. The consequent easy dismissals of hedonism have been altogether too easy.

ENJOYING

As has often been pointed out recently, enjoyment is closely bound to the activities or experiences enjoyed. To begin with, what I am particularly said to enjoy is some activity or experience. I may enjoy a meal, but this is to enjoy eating it, together, perhaps, with enjoying the smell and sight of it; and I may enjoy a football match, but if I neither saw it, nor heard a commentary nor played in it, nor did anything of this sort, then to say I enjoyed it is one of those tiresome 'humorous' ways of speaking by which, in this case, I may with luck make it clear that I enjoyed the peace created by everyone else's absence at the match. Further, I cannot go on enjoying the concert once the players have stopped playing, nor my meal when the last crumbs have been tucked away. Again, if I am to enjoy my meal, or my rest, or my concert, I am well advised to give myself up to eating, resting, or listening to the music; the more I attend to the question of how much I am enjoying it, the more clear it becomes that I am not enjoying it. If I am to enjoy the music, I must listen to it. My enjoying it is not something to which I can attend over and above the music; to say that I enjoy the music is, it seems, to comment on the circumstances or the manner of my listening. It would follow that 'because I enjoy it' must explain my doing things on a model different from that of 'because it brings in money'; that enjoyment is not separable even logically from its object; and this has seemed a good stick with which to beat the hedonist. For on accounts of this type there are not two objects of experience: the activity and the pleasure. The pleasure *is* the activity, but calling the activity a pleasure is saying something about the way it is performed or engaged in. Anyone who thinks of pleasure as an experientially isolable item which might be either the cause or goal of action has made a conceptual mistake. Pleasure is not something experienced over and above what it is pleasure in: cessation of the object entails cessation of the pleasure.

BEING PLEASED

Suppose we now turn to being pleased. A conference has been in progress to negotiate a pay-rise for the academic profession. The union bargainer leaves the conference table for his lunch looking, as the press reports, 'obviously pleased—indeed pleasure showed in every line of Mr. X's face, in every gesture, even in the jaunty angle of his hat'. The negotiations have been going well and Mr. X is pleased. At lunch he treats his colleagues to a bottle of champagne, because he is so pleased with the turn things have taken. Here pleasure has got disturbingly loosened from its moorings. First of all, while Mr. X no doubt does enjoy his meal, that is not what is being said; the meal is not even the 'object of his pleasure'. The object of his pleasure (i.e. what he is pleased about)[1] is the turn things have taken, and he is clearly not enjoying or disenjoying that. He may not even be thinking of it: perhaps he likes a change of subject; so it is not even being said that he is enjoying thinking of it. Still, he is pleased with the turn the negotiations have taken, and his pleasure is clear for all to see. It is, in fact, so easy to separate, in this sort of case, the pleasure from what gives rise to it, that we are even prepared to talk of the occurrence of the pleasure in the absence of anything that it is with or about. True, so heavy is the weight of usage that some grammatical object must be supplied, the usual one being 'life' or 'things'; but being pleased with life is very different from being pleased with the turn negotiations have taken. The word 'life' does not here indicate the circumstances which give rise to the pleasure, but the fact that the man is 'just pleased', that he is ebullient, takes things easily in his stride, is hard to put out, and such-like. When a person is pleased, whether with life or with something in particular, one may expect exceptional gestures of glee, whether they take the form of smiles and hand-rubbing, or the more acceptable form of champagne. Such occurrences are what we are led to expect in being told he is pleased, and it is in this way that our negotiator's pleasure explains his extravagance. It is analogous to: 'because he is in a good mood as a result of . . .' This is not, perhaps, a very typical hedonistic example of pleasure-explaining activities, for pleasure is not here what the man aims at but what stimulates him to his activity, and most, though not all, hedonists have treated pleasure as a goal rather than as a cause. It does no harm, however, to see how variously pleasure may enter into explanations of behaviour, and it is worth noting how the notion is sometimes connected with extra vitality and enthusiasm.

FOR THE PLEASURE OF . . .

A more convincingly hedonistic example is found in cases of doing things for the pleasure of something or another. Grown-ups can often be observed in strange antics before small babies for the pleasure, apparently, of seeing them smile. In this sort of case it is often indistinguishable from doing these things because they enjoy seeing the baby smile; but this equivalence does not hold in the case where I deny myself and save money for the pleasure of knowing that my wife, when a widow, will be better off than my neighbour's. I do not do this because, or just because, I enjoy, or think I shall enjoy, thinking about it. If only I can get this money saved the galling picture of my neighbour's wife scorning my impoverished widow will be punctured; I shall be able to replace it, if not with the reverse picture, at least with a different and more satisfactory one. I do, no doubt, enjoy this prospect, and look forward to being able to enjoy this picture in the assurance that it will come true. That, however, is a mere part of the pleasure. Just as important is the hoped-for condition of being cheered by this assurance, of being more pleased with life once this aim has been accomplished. I shall at last be able to go about my ordinary tasks with contentment. Between these two examples is that of the man who does the antics before the baby for the pleasure not just of seeing the child smile but of having the child smile at him. Clearly, he would normally do it because he enjoyed being smiled at; but also the pleasure stays with him through the day: if only he can get a smile he will go happy to his work and so on; and it is just because he knows it gives him such pleasure that he consents to the humiliating introductory performance. In short, pleasure here again shows its liability to become separated from that which gives rise to it. Explanations of behaviour done 'for the pleasure of . . .' may amount to no more than 'because X enjoys it'. But sometimes what is aimed at is an improvement of mood: the pleasure for which the act is done is not simply, if at all, the enjoyment of some state of affairs—a well-off wife or a baby's smile—but a general improvement of spirits resultant on the assurance or attainment of this state of affairs. Here we have a motivational example where the pleasure aimed at may be described as a state separable, except causally, from the state of affairs for the pleasure of which the action is done.

FOR PLEASURE

'For pleasure' is perhaps the most obvious expression to select in treating of pleasure as a motive, and yet, strangely, is one which is among the least easy to dress up as a motive, and one which it is unfortunate to concentrate on, if motives are one's interest. To say that something is done for pleasure does, of course, in some way explain the doing of it, but it is, first, usually the explanation of a regular doing; it usually explains why I do something, not why I am doing it. I read novels for pleasure, works on logic for serious reading, as part of my job. 'For pleasure' places the activity as one that is done when I have only myself to please; if I play golf for pleasure, this is not to say that whenever I pick up my clubs I have in mind the end of making myself pleased or achieving pleasure; it is just to say that golf is not my job or something I play because of some duty I am under, but something I do when I am off work, and only have to consider myself. This may be brought out by contrasting 'for pleasure' with 'because I enjoy it' or 'because I find it pleasant'. If I only teach logic as part of my job it would also be rather misleading to say that I teach it because I enjoy it—though not so misleading if in fact I do enjoy it and that is why I chose the job; but 'for pleasure' cannot come to explain my taking the job, nor my continuing with it. I may take up teaching logic for a career because I enjoy it or find it pleasant, but I cannot choose a career for pleasure, although I may, no doubt, do for pleasure anything that I can do for a career. If, however, I teach logic both as part of my job and for pleasure, I must be a glutton for work and teach it not only in official hours but also in my spare time, just for the fun of it.

Allied to this use of 'for pleasure' is that sense of the noun 'pleasures' by which to list a person's pleasures is to give a list of his favourite pastimes; and to say that man's only pleasure is his work is a way of saying that he has no pleasures, however much he enjoys himself—just as to say that a man's only job is following his pleasures is just a way of saying that he has no job, however earnest he may be in his pursuits. In these cases 'pleasure' covers an area of activities where only my own desires are involved, and where the requirement that they are done simply from choice and not from obligation, etc., is essential for their being pleasures. This tie between pleasure and choice used to be more widespread. Fowler thought it worth warning people not to answer invitations by saying 'It is my pleasure to accept . . .', and we still talk of prisoners being detained at the Queen's pleasure, without attributing to her an arbitrary sadism. The split in the notion of pleasure between 'doing as I please' and 'being pleased with what I do' no doubt springs from an underlying assumption that in general people want to do things which will leave them pleased and are pleased when they get what they want. At any rate, both halves of the split are preserved in 'for pleasure' and the use of the noun 'pleasures' mentioned above. For if my pleasures are what I do when I have only myself to please, they would be bizarre pleasures that I did not in general enjoy. The things that I do for pleasure have achieved that status because I enjoy them; but to say that I do them for pleasure is to give their status, not my motive either on each occasion or in general.

The outcome of this is that 'for pleasure' explains my doings in ways analogous to 'for a hobby' 'for a job', rather than in the normal motive way. This may seem niggling, but I suspect that this common form of pleasure explanation has been largely responsible for the persistent feeling that any form of hedonism must be a frivolous doctrine: for surely it is frivolous to urge us to abandon ourselves to our pleasures, and to live lives where all we do we do for pleasure and for no other reason. If 'for pleasure' remains undistinguished from 'for the pleasure of . . .' and other cases, it can be allowed to infect the whole range with its frivolity.

THE PURSUIT OF PLEASURE

If 'for pleasure' accounts for the feeling that any hedonism must be frivolous, idioms such as 'the pursuit of pleasure' must be largely responsible for the feeling that it is incorrigibly selfish. A man who devotes his life to delighting his wife has, indeed, somebody's pleasure as his objective, but to spend his life in the pursuit of pleasure he needs to turn to his own pleasure. At the very least he must make 'what shall I enjoy?' the basic question; preferably, his enjoyments should not be enjoyments of the welfare or pleasure of others; ideally they should be as near as possible sensual. To complain that all a person does he does for pleasure would be making a charge of frivolity: when people complained that Don Juan spent his life in the pursuit of pleasure, they were not, however, complaining that he did not make a job of whatever he did. The charge is, first, that he never considered anyone but himself, and, secondly, that some or all of the activities or experiences he pursued were pursued for the more or less physical sensations that they supply. This explanation falls fairly easily into the normal motivational pattern, but it has implications of selfishness, and usually imposes some limitations on the type of activity or experience pursued in a way in which none of the other pleasure explanations that I have considered does.

So far, then, we have four kinds of pleasure explanation, leaving aside enjoyment for the moment. First, there is the pleasure I feel explaining my buoyancy and acts of generosity. Here pleasure is well independent of its object. Secondly, there is the pleasure of, say, knowing something for which I may pursue certain courses. Here, too, the pleasure can be distinguished often from enjoyments. This case, as distinct from the first, gives a motive explanation. Thirdly, there is doing things for pleasure, which is a way of giving the status of those activities in a person's life. Fourthly, there is doing things in pursuit of pleasure, which is doing them with a view to certain sensual enjoyments.

BECAUSE I GET SUCH PLEASURE

These explanations are so varied in style that it may well be asked how the same word comes to be connected with them all. Before considering that, I propose to take one further example. This will not make the list complete, but will give sufficient variety for my purposes. Suppose someone who is very active in support of slum-clearance, and spends many exhausting hours each week visiting slum-dwellers to arouse their enthusiasm for a change, arguing with authorities to get them to take steps, canvassing for interest among the ratepayers, and so on. Amazed at his perseverance in such trying circumstances, we ask why he keeps on. 'Often I am down-hearted, but I get such pleasure from the idea of all these children in decent comfortable homes and pleasant, healthy surroundings that I cannot give up.' He is not, of course, saying that he gets pleasure from the mere picture of it as a pleasant fiction, but as something to be aimed at. Nor is the point that he is after the pleasure he will get from success. The point is rather that it is the picture of these children in happy circumstances that appeals to him, that is his inspiration. When he gets down-hearted he remembers what he is aiming at and this gives him renewed enthusiasm, for the prospect pleases him, gives him pleasure.

Now in some ways this explanation is like the union boss giving round drinks because of his pleasure at his success. We have again the notions of eagerness and vitality connected with pleasure. Here, however, the vitality is directed towards what gives rise to it. In fact, the man is explaining why he goes on with the work, not by giving an objective but by asserting that the objective is one which arouses his enthusiasm in some way: it is not pursued from a grim sense of duty, or a dull, unthinking devotion to the daily round, nor even in pursuit of pleasure, but because the thought of the children's changed condition gives him pleasure, inspires him.

So wavery are the lines between some of the pleasure idioms that the same sort of explanation can be provided by the expression 'for the pleasure of knowing'. Thus the man in question might be described as doing what he does for the pleasure of knowing or thinking that the condition of these children will be improved. This is of importance because this style of explanation is one whose prevalence accounts to a large extent for the plausibility of some forms of hedonism. One slips from the openly motivational expressions to asserting that there must surely be something attractive, something that pleases us or gives us pleasure, about any course of action that we embark upon, and this is why we embark upon it. Now clearly this is very different from saying that we do it for pleasure, or in the pursuit of pleasure, or because we think we shall enjoy it; but the recurrence of the word 'pleasure' has still a magic about it. This shift serves Mill well, for instance, when in trying to show that men 'do desire nothing for itself but that which is a pleasure to them' he observes that 'to desire anything, except in proportion as the idea of it is pleasant, is a physical and metaphysical impossibility' (*Utilitarianism*, Chapter iv).

ENJOYMENT

So far I have been dealing with explanations involving some part of the word 'pleasure'. It will help the final purpose of bringing some order into the chaos to make a few observations on enjoyment. For while it is not true that all pleasure explanations are explanations in terms of enjoyment, it is true, I think, that any explanation in terms of enjoyment at the least *implies* some pleasure explanation, and perhaps in context amounts to the same.

It is normal, when discussing enjoyment, to concentrate on that form of which 'because he enjoys it' is a typical specimen. It is, of course, true that this is more fundamental—that is to say, the present-tense explanation—than, say, 'because he hopes to enjoy *X*'. It has, however, been an unfortunate choice. For the present here is the habitual present, and it typically explains habitual actions. As many of these are ones in which we indulge of set policy, one is in danger of thinking of enjoyment as primarily a final explanation, in some sense, of desire. Thus if we want the sort of question to which 'because he enjoys it' is a typical answer, cases that spring to mind are such ones as 'Why does he play golf?' 'Why does he read Jane Austen?' 'Why does he beat his wife?' 'Because he enjoys it', explains a regular activity, explains why he goes in for whatever it is. This leads one to overlook the continuous present 'because he is enjoying it'; and yet only if this is understood will the former be.

Even 'because he enjoys it' may explain either something which I regularly do of set purpose or just something that I regularly do. If I play golf because I enjoy it, this is no doubt explaining why I go to all that trouble and expense, why I want to play golf. Suppose, however, that on warm summer afternoons I habitually linger on in my deck-chair for an hour and then two hours. It is not that I am asleep, but there is the soothing sensation of the sun penetrating every limb, the nostalgic sounds of mowing or hedge-clipping or bees, and it is all so enjoyable that somehow I stay there and suddenly the afternoon is gone. Now I might, of course, settle down to all this of set purpose; put aside the afternoon to snoozing, because I enjoy it. Yet it might also be that all I mean to do is take forty winks to recover from lunch, but once I have got into the chair my resolution is forgotten. It is not that I deliberately dally, but I so enjoy it that I lose all sense of time.

Now there is a difference between 'because I enjoy it' here and in the golf case. For while both explain habitual performances, in this case each performance is to be explained by reference to my actually enjoying it. I may play golf because I enjoy it, and this explains why I play it today, but 'because I am enjoying it' does not explain why I play it today, nor need it explain why I am persisting with the game I have started. If, by contrast, it is true that I linger on in my deck-chair because I enjoy it, in the sort of case considered, then it must hold of each occasion that if someone asks 'why is he idling on out there?' you must be able to say 'because he's enjoying it'. It is my enjoyment of it that accounts for my staying there. In other words, 'because I enjoy it' here directly presupposes 'because I am enjoying it'.

When one takes cases like golf, 'because I enjoy it' typically explains why I go in for it. Once started on this road the natural further examples to think of are hobbies, the sort of absorbing activities a person chooses in his spare time. This has two results. First, it concentrates attention on cases where enjoyment explains why I want to do *X*, or why I go in for it, and so leads to overlooking cases where it explains continuance in an activity, not of set purpose. This leads to uneasy analyses of 'because he enjoys it', since in fact this may cover either sort of case. Secondly, the sorts of example that come to mind are relatively special cases of enjoyments which make it attractive to adopt a special analysis of enjoyment in general. For hobbies and their like are characteristically activities which engage one's attention, and which, as one's chosen leisure activity, one enters on with gusto. Concentration on these examples makes it tempting to say that what is being said when I am said to enjoy something is something about my mode of attention to the activity, or the enthusiastic way in which I go about it. My enjoyments are what I go in for because I enjoy it, and they usually fit these analyses. It is one of the joys of deck-chairs that they demand neither vigour of performance nor attention to what is going on, but encourage, on the contrary, a state of semi-conscious drift. Gusto and attention analyses seem very plausible so long as one confines oneself either to such muscular activities as golf or such intellectual entertainments as concerts or chess; but they falter when they come to the enjoyments of the idle man. In short, 'because he enjoys it' can cover two quite different sorts of explanation, one of which demands reference to the more basic 'because he is enjoying it'. This last sort of case raises doubts about two popular types of analysis of enjoyment as it draws attention to cases for which they are unplausible. Indeed, it is the vast variety of cases that enjoyment can explain that is really bewildering, and suggests that any adequate account of enjoyment is going to be very complex.

TYPES OF ENJOYMENT

That this is so becomes clear if we consider ways in which 'because he enjoys it' can be filled out in face of 'but why does he enjoy it?' This sort of question is susceptible of two kinds of answer, one dull, one illuminating. The dull one, which really tells what the person enjoys about it, just specifies the feature enjoyed. Thus if asked why I enjoy watching cricket I might say that I enjoyed seeing the men in the middle trying to run with funny things on their legs. This specifies the particular feature of the general spectacle that I enjoy. The second kind of answer specifies the type of enjoyment, and is what such questions are usually after. 'Why do you enjoy reading Jane Austen? Do you find her amusing, or do you find that confined and cosy world soothing after a day of real life?' 'No, I find her exciting, my heart is always in my mouth in case Fanny or Emma should at the last not quite win home.' Now these are various ways in which Jane Austen may be enjoyed, but while some of them may on occasion be combined, they are clearly quite different. Few people take to their deck-chairs for excitement, or go to a bull-fight because they find it soothing, though they may do either because they enjoy it.

The first point that emerges from this is that one reason why 'because he enjoys it' and 'because he is enjoying it' are puzzling is that as they stand they are hopelessly unspecific. The next thing, therefore, is to consider some of the specifications. The first point that strikes one here, once one has got over the variety, is that the verbs used to explain enjoyment tend to be active verbs which attribute some sort of influence to the object of my enjoyment. Thus enjoyment is typically explained by saying that I find the activity amusing, exhilarating, interesting, soothing (and so on): 'nostalgic', another possibility, also suggests the way I am affected. Not all forms of enjoyment, of course, have ready-made verbs, but the search for an explanation does seem to be a search for ways of specifying how we are affected, and such terms as we have already are terms for doing just this. So the continuous present 'because he is enjoying it' always amounts to saying that in one way or another what the agent is doing wins his ungrudging performance. We do not have to look beyond what is being done or experienced, but to inquire about the way in which it affects him.

It is difficult to say anything which will cover all cases of this. To say, with Professor Ryle, that enjoying something consists in doing it with your heart in it, and other such things, goes very well for things we enjoy because we find them interesting or exhilarating—but what of things we find soothing? A similar point holds against attention analyses.[2] All that can be said is that in all cases where 'because he is enjoying it' is the explanation, the subject has in one way or another been inveigled by some feature of what he is enjoying to continue whatever it is, and that it is a willing surrender.

WHY DO WE WANT TO DO ENJOYABLE THINGS?

All this may be true about 'because he is enjoying it' and also about 'because he enjoys it' where this relies on the habitual applicability of the former. But we have already seen that 'because he enjoys it' may well explain why a person wants to go in for a certain activity, so we still have to see what is happening in these cases. It has sometimes been suggested that 'because he enjoys it' is here a terminating answer, that it functions to put an end to a series of questions, 'Why?' This can be seen by noting the absurdity of asking 'Why do people do things just because they enjoy them?' This question, however, is puzzling in rather different ways, according to the interpretation put on it. Suppose, first, we take it as applying to cases where a person's doing or persisting in doing something is explained by saying that he *is* enjoying it. Now the question would be puzzling because it is tantamount to saying: 'Granted that he finds the book interesting, still, how does that account for the fact that he goes on reading it?' or 'Granted that he finds lying in a deck-chair soothing, still, how does that explain his lying on out there?' The question is puzzling just because words such as 'interesting', 'soothing', and their like seem devised to describe ways in which certain objects or experiences charm people into continued performance of some sort, so that to admit their applicability seems to involve accepting an explanation of the performance.

The peculiarity is the same where 'because he enjoys it' covers a series of cases to each of which 'because he is/was enjoying it' applies. It is different, however, when 'because he enjoys it' explains why a person goes in for or pursues a certain type of activity, of set policy. Further, it is only in this case that it functions to terminate a series of the form 'Why do you want *X*?' For this word 'want', which was out of place in situations of lingering, comes into play when it is a matter of intentionally setting about an activity. To see how 'because he enjoys it' explains differently here, an example might help. Suppose I am a golf player. I explain my early breakfast by saying that I want to get the clubs in the car by 8.30 a.m., because I want to get started by 8.35 a.m., because I want to get to the Golf Club by 9 a.m., because I want a game of golf. Why? Because I enjoy it.

The first thing to note is that 'because I enjoy it' does not really answer the question at all. You might reply that you know I enjoy golf, but the question is: do I think I shall enjoy a game this morning? My answer must be taken elliptically to contain this point, while at the same time making it clear that this is not a freakish flash in the pan, but an activity that I commonly enjoy. There is, however, a further way of expounding my answer, which might hold in certain contexts. It might be that I take the question to have shifted from interest in my activities this morning to interest in why, in general, I go in for golf: why do you want to play golf anyway? Because I enjoy it.

Now here both question and answer can be taken in at least two ways. First, the question might amount to: 'Why do you give golf this place in your life?' In this case, the answer 'because I enjoy it' gives the consideration which determined the selection of golf, but not, of course, any reason why that consideration should weigh. Consequently, the original question is not fully answered, and the question 'Why do you want to play golf just because you enjoy it?' makes perfectly good sense, and might be answered, say, by pointing out how important some enjoyment is for a balanced, useful life, thus showing why I consider that the fact that I enjoy it should have weight. 'Because I enjoy it' is by no means the last word on this interpretation.

Alternatively, the word 'want' might be italicized: 'Why do you *want* to play golf?' When so emphasized, the question carries the force 'What attracts you about it? What is it that gives you pleasure in the idea of playing golf?' Here the answer might be that while I do not enjoy it, I get a great kick out of the idea of playing the game the great Hogan played and so on. 'Because I enjoy it', on the other hand, would specify that it is something actually about the game itself that attracts me: I find it a challenge to get the ball off the ground, and it presents a number of other intriguing problems. Thus the fact of my previous experience of its attractions is brought in to explain why the prospect of the game is liable to attract me, and so why it should occur to me to set aside time for it. The further question 'Why?' is odd here, because the form of attraction was being asked, and this is just what 'because I enjoy it' specifies.

Pleasure and enjoyment connect here, as explanatory concepts, in two ways. First, 'because he is enjoying it' is analogous to 'because the idea gives him pleasure' in that both explain by reference to a charm, as it were, exercised over the subject. (A further analogy will be mentioned below.) Secondly, 'because he enjoys it' functions as a specification, at a fairly general level, within the reasons for which a prospect might give pleasure, in that it indicates that we should look to the way in which the actual performance or experience is known by the agent to influence him.

PLEASURE AND ENJOYMENT

The upshot of what has gone so far is that expressions using the words 'pleasure' and 'enjoyment' do not explain behaviour according to a uniform pattern. Central to the idea of pleasure are the complementary notions of pleasing and being pleased. To be pleased is not, indeed, to have any particular sensation, nor to attend to anything, to do anything with one's heart in it, but in one way or another to be in a good mood. 'In one way or another' because according to what, if anything, gives rise to it, and according to the temperament of the person concerned, it is liable to take very varied forms—though the most favoured sign is some indication of relative geniality. Still, 'being pleased' is something of a rainbow concept. The connection with fulfilled desire often holds, and if a person gets what he wants we expect him to be pleased. Yet it is not necessary either that all cases of being pleased are cases where a desire has been fulfilled, nor do all fulfilled desires give pleasure. Again, especially in cases of being pleased at prospects and so on, we expect the pleased person's pleasure to show itself in his enthusiasm about its object, but again, not always. When we move to expressions like 'for pleasure' there are still connections: we expect that in general a person will be pleased at the prospect of doing any of the things he does for pleasure, and will enjoy doing them and so forth. When we get to cases, such as the great pleasure of eating a banana, the connection has grown dimmer. A person experiencing this pleasure is not thereby rendered pleased, he is enjoying it. There are still, however, connections and analogies. First, many enjoyments do involve a heightened vigour of pursuit analogous to the ebullience of the man who is pleased. Secondly, many enjoyments in fact serve the function of rendering a person more pleased with life. Being soothed is appreciated when our nerves are jangled, excitement when our circumstances are dull, and so on. Commonly enjoyments restore us to a happier state of mind, and give a pleasure that lasts beyond the experience.

None of this, however, avoids the point that pleasure explains our doings in a variety of ways: sometimes some pleasant experience is the goal, sometimes the goal inspires us, sometimes we are pleased and so act, and so on. Those who hold that consideration of the concept of pleasure will serve to show any form of hedonism untenable may therefore take heart. Maybe it is too simple to equate pleasure and enjoyment and conclude that there is no element in experience, pleasure, which could be the goal or cause of all actions. Still, what has been said above at least constitutes a challenge to any hedonist, for I) he can no longer rely on the fact that over a wide area some pleasure explanation or another is applicable, to show anything about the actual or possible applicability of a single type of explanation to all our actions; for the various pleasure explanations differ in form. He will have, therefore, either to choose one as his protégé or else argue that in some complex way these various types of explanation form a coherent unity making possible a single ethical position. To hold that all actions either are or should be performed according to just one of these explanations seems unplausible, and I have no idea how the second alternative can be worked out. II) It still remains that with each form of explanation the terms 'pleasure' and 'enjoyment' are very general. Once we come to be more specific as to what it amounts to in any given case, it becomes increasingly difficult to see how the notion of pleasure can be made to yield any precise rules of conduct: pleasures are notable for their incomparability, and the same goes for the ways in which goals attract us, so that the idea of ordering them in terms of pleasure seems senseless. In short, the prospect of any useful form of hedonism grows dim.

For all this, distinguishing the various forms pleasure-explanations take makes it possible to appreciate better at least one point which makes some form of hedonism attractive to many philosophers and non-philosophers alike. For a common step, in face of cases where something is desired, but apparently what is desired is not one's pleasure, is to insist that still the agent must get pleasure at the idea of achieving it. As an attempt to preserve the same explanation this fails. But the point, insisted on by Mill, and common enough, betrays a feeling that there is a close tie between wanting something and taking pleasure in the idea of it, and that this makes some form of hedonism essential. If we set aside arguments about doing things for pleasure and in pursuit of pleasure and so on, and concentrate on people's goals in life, the considerations they hold most important, the things they set their hearts on, then it seems very strange to suggest that the idea of success in these areas need give them no pleasure, that there is no problem in their remaining quite unmoved. A sense of this is part, I think, of what makes it attractive to cling to some form of hedonism even in face of all the particular critical arguments marshalled against it.

At this point someone might hold that all this can be easily explained. For there is a noticeable bias about the word 'want' such that we are happiest to say that a person really wants something when he is eager about it, sets his heart on it, when the idea of accomplishment obviously gives him pleasure. Failing this, he does not really want it. In this sense of 'want', pleasure is indeed necessary to explain the desire and consequent pursuit, but this is because this notion of pleasure is a necessary part of the explication of this sense of 'want'. That is to say, it is only wanting in this sense if in fact the idea gives pleasure to the agent, so it is hardly surprising to find that all such desires are 'explained' by the fact that the agent gets pleasure from the idea. It is not, however, the only sense of 'want', and once this is realized we can see how naïve even this prop of hedonism is.

Such a dismissal is, however, rather too quick. Talk of different senses suggests a case of simple ambiguity, so that when we recognize the two senses our problems are over. It seems, however, that the fact that an agent is quite unmoved at the prospect of attaining his goal is sufficient to warn us that this is not a full-blooded case of wanting. Such a case has some features of wanting, but falls short. The 'not really' suggests that the one case has some primacy over the other, and that they are not related as two essentially different words with the same sound. So someone like Mill might claim that while it is possible to describe a case of an agent wanting something but getting no pleasure from the idea of what he wants, still such cases must be secondary. For an agent in such circumstances is only described as wanting his goal by analogy, and because the usual condition with him is the more full-blooded case. If he were always unmoved, he could not be described as really wanting anything at all, and he can only be described in any sense as wanting anything in virtue of sharing some features of the central case.

The difficulty here, of course, is to see just what this talk of primary and secondary amounts to. It is fairly clear that there is some idiomatic bias in favour of the pleasure case, but is there anything more? For the proposed secondary sense of 'want' to be applicable, it is sufficient to be able to single out a goal which explains the agent's activities. The agent's attitude to the goal is immaterial. In what sense, if any, does the description of an agent break down to whom only the secondary sense of 'want' is applicable? It is not clear how one could argue that such a description ends, say, in self-contradiction. Suppose we describe someone who never has any enthusiasm about any of his pursuits, but stolidly, unemotionally, calculatingly just pursues the things he pursues. Such a being seems quite describable, but a fish of such frigidity becomes progressively unintelligible to us as the temperature drops. But unintelligible to us in what way? After all, his actions are explicable and predictable by reference to various goals. The peculiarity about such an agent lies in his unemotional character. The supposed total lack of enthusiasm about his ends makes it hard to see what place there could be for his feeling grateful to anyone who helped him, angry with anyone who frustrated him, jealous of anyone who did better. What place is there for friendship in an agent incapable of being pleased at the prospect of helping or sharing interests? In short, it is not that it is inconceivable that an agent should pursue goals bereft of pleasure, but that such an agent, first, does not pursue them in a way typical of human beings, and, secondly, is incapable of a range of feelings characteristic of human beings. These two points are important. For the feelings excluded are the common material of inter-personal understanding. An agent without enthusiasms, incapable of affection, anger, gratitude, and the rest is beyond the range of human sympathy. So while it may be that the secondary sense of 'want' might be applicable without presupposing the applicability of the primary sense, the general applicability of the latter is presupposed when the subject of discussion is human beings, and those capable of inter-personal contact with them. It is no accident that cold fish are felt to be inhuman. So far as men are concerned there is truth in the dictum that 'to desire anything, except in proportion as the idea of it is pleasant, is a physical and metaphysical impossibility'.

To sum up: consideration of the concept of pleasure and the ways in which pleasure explanations function render it very improbable that any form of hedonism can be made to stand up, and quite certain that any such position would be very complex and in need of a good deal of clever argument. Most hedonists have felt, however, more or less explicitly, that the notion of pleasure is somehow inextricably tied up with that of desire, so that to talk of desire apart from pleasure is some sort of absurdity. On this it seems to me that there is no essential connection between the ideas of pleasure and intelligent pursuit, but that there is one between the ideas of pleasure and human pursuits; that if one went ultra-Kantian and sternly advocated the complete exclusion of pleasure from one's desires, one would be advocating the general incapacitation of human beings for human intercourse, which would, I suppose, be dubiously universalizable. So perhaps pleasure is essential to morality. The common insistence by hedonistically inclined writers on the relation of pleasure to desire is thus worth exploring, and it would be sad to dismiss examination of such authors on the basis of an ill-conceived equation of pleasure and enjoyment.

NOTES

1 I say 'i.e.', but the vocabulary of 'objects' here and in talk of feelings generally seems to me highly confused.

2 For such analyses cf., e.g., Ryle and Gallie, *Proc. Arist. Soc.* (1954), and Ryle, *Concept of Mind*, pp 107–9.

OBJECTS OF AESTHETIC COMMENT AND PERSUASION

ANDREW HARRISON

CERTAIN TYPES OF modern painting and sculpture are often attacked on the grounds that the objects might just as well have been picked up on a beach or found on the floors of box-rooms as have been made in an artist's studio. By what right, it is often asked, do artists foist such things on us when the contribution they make to them seems to amount to little more than putting the things in frames or on plinths? To these philistine objections the reply is inevitably that though maybe anyone could have picked such things up, anyone didn't. It is precisely the merit of *objets trouvés* that they have been found. Finding and isolating such things is the essence of aesthetic insight, and responding to them the mark of one who is aesthetically aware.

Both sides of this debate are shallow, but also of interest, particularly when the debate is set against the equally common objections that are made to art critics and writers when they attempt to convert us to their own way of looking. It is often objected that their language collapses under the weight of its own verbiage into a mass of metaphor and obscurity. Why can't they say what they mean?

For this reason I want to consider some examples of attempts at such persuasive talk. I shall refer first to natural-object situations. It is surely remarkable if there really does turn out to be an area of talk indulged in by intelligent people where they are forced to babble in metaphors. How does one persuade others to respond with one?

Suppose we see a large rock on the sea-shore and, mysteriously, we respond to it aesthetically. A friend, however, fails to 'get it' at all. To him it is merely a rock.

'Look at that magnificent rock!'

'Well?'

'Well, don't you think it's wonderful?'

'It doesn't look very beautiful to me. What's so splendid about a rock?'

'Yes, but can't you *see* it? Doesn't it look awe-inspiring, as if it had a looming presence, a personality?'

'How do you mean?'

'Look at the way it hunches itself forward into the sea as if doggedly defying the wind and the waves: it looks as if it's been there for ever and is determined to go on!'

'It certainly hasn't been there for ever, and it isn't going to last very long either. It's the softest of all the rocks hereabouts and geologically the most transient: still, I see what you mean now, there *is* something about it. Not that it's beautiful of course. . . .'

'I never said it was beautiful; I said it had a presence.'

'Yes, all right. I do see what you mean.'

What has one's friend been persuaded to see? Does it matter that we have given the rock a personality? Suppose we show him an old man a little farther on. We would be less likely to call the old man magnificent, though we might; a more likely beginning might be to call him quaint, even funny. 'Why, he looks as if he was a piece of jetsam himself, half-blown against the cliff edge there!' 'Or a ship—look at that—sheer harmony of line!'

Clearly a number of words that indicate aesthetic, or quasi-aesthetic, comment do not seem to presuppose any such justification. To call something dumpy or clumsy, magnificent, sublime, pretty, majestic, and so on, quite apart from calling it beautiful or ugly, does not force anything more on us than the simple comment. Such words, however, have the function of *announcing*, rather than *arguing for*, an aesthetic reaction. To say to someone who trusts my judgment in aesthetic matters that I think any object is any of these things may well be good enough to persuade him to try to see them my way. But this is very much because he does not need telling 'the trick of it', and the question is whether there is indeed a specific 'trick of' seeing something aesthetically or not.

One attempt to answer such a question affirmatively is well represented by Hampshire's suggestion that amounts to the thesis that the specially aesthetic way of looking at something is to see it 'bracketed off' from the normal stream of everyday assumptions, presuppositions, and perceptual categories. In this neo-Kantian tradition it is a characteristic of aesthetic response to objects that the perceiver 'takes a holiday' from his normal strenuous categorizing of experience. Let us look at this sort of claim against the background of aesthetic persuasive talk.

Stuart Hampshire (*Thought and Action*, p 244) remarks:

> . . . Experience of arts is by definition an experience in which practical interests, and the ordinary classifications that reflect them, are for a time suspended in an impractical enjoyment of the arrangement of something perceived. Any strong aesthetic experience is necessarily an interruption of normal habits of recognition, a relaxing of the usual practical stance in the face of anything external. It is, therefore, a disturbance, because it is a temporary refusal to classify usefully, and to consider possibilities of action.

But is to see something aesthetically to relax the practical stance always? It is of course trivial that 'contemplation' is not 'action', and accordingly to be concerned merely to contemplate, aesthetically or otherwise, is 'by definition' not to act, but is Hampshire saying anything more than that? Earlier he says:

> . . . we can sometimes contemplate reality, in perception and introspection, without any kind of comment, and even, with rather greater difficulty, without in any way acting or intending action, and without even an apparent shadow of a practical interest. We are then deliberately enjoying moments of pure aesthetic experience. When we are not deliberately inhibiting action, as in aesthetic experience, and are fully conscious, our intentions are always focused on some objects to the exclusion of others. . . .

Which again seems merely to be saying that in 'pure' contemplation, that is, contemplation which does not result in any action or decision, here defined as aesthetic experience, there is no question of action; which is true by definition. This may seem a brutal way with the argument, but alternative interpretations seem to lead to falsehoods. It is simply not true that aesthetic contemplation excludes comment; the conversation exhibited above is such comment. Equally, there seems to be something very odd about saying that in an aesthetic experience we are 'deliberately inhibiting action' (presumably with respect to the object of the experience). Such experience might well lead directly to the action of painting a picture or writing a poem, to telling others of the experience, or of trying to avoid its occurring again or of trying to make it more likely to occur again. To insist that these are not actions of a normal or utilitarian kind simply begs the question, by assuming that there is a clear distinction between practical and aesthetic activity.

Even if it were pure contemplation of an object would it necessarily be aesthetic contemplation? It is arguable that when the mystic talks of pure passive contemplation of the object of his mystical experiences that what he is really talking about is an aesthetic experience. Arguable, but also by that token, deniable.

What I want to maintain, in contrast to Hampshire's suggestion that 'experience of art is . . . an experience in which . . . the ordinary classifications . . . are for a time suspended', is that in fact an aesthetic reaction to an object, or certainly the discussion of such reactions, presupposes simply that the ordinary classifications are *not* suspended, and that were they suspended such discussions would be impossible. Something very like a suspension goes on, but it is not a suspension in the sense that the normal everyday classification of things are, as it were, thrown overboard or are ignored. Indeed, quite the reverse.

I am not, however, sure how radically I am in disagreement with Hampshire's account of the nature of aesthetic experience, for it is essential for him that such experience does in some way, broadly speaking, challenge and modify our hidebound classifications of things. The difference is, very likely, merely one of emphasis, though emphasis is usually crucial in philosophy. For there is a perfectly proper sense in which to regard something as an aesthetic object contrasts with regarding it as, say, a saleable commodity. Also, it may well appear that I am at cross-purposes with Hampshire in that, whereas I am concerned primarily with arguments and persuasive conversation that follows our aesthetic experiences, with a view to getting others to experience them also, he is concerned to ask in general what an aesthetic experience is, how it contrasts with, say, a moral experience. But even if one could answer such a question and even if one could recognize a distinct aesthetic experience whenever it occurred (and it might even be so), the interesting consideration is, surely, what one has to say to someone else in order to get him to sympathize with one's responses. And it is quite possible to discuss that without reference to the nature of the feeling at all.

Of course, to see something aesthetically may be to have a feeling of its being in some way 'bracketed off' from the mainstream of everyday dull conglomerations of things. It may be to regard it as something to which the attitudes of buying and selling or of improving the lot of mankind is inappropriate. It may well be that in contrast to the utilitarian world of the stockbroker's office the world of art is pleasantly gratuitous, and aesthetic objects are perfect in their own right and not instruments in commercial strategy. One may quite rightly have all these feelings about art, but to say so is neither a necessary nor sufficient foundation for a philosophical account.

Just as the attitude of regarding a piece of sculpture 'for itself' is contrasted with that of regarding the same as a non-perishable asset—the former being an aesthetic attitude—so similar contrasts are often offered in other directions. To regard a road accident aesthetically is sheer irresponsibility, since such things have to be regarded practically, whereas only the most naïve regard plays practically. The difference is that to regard anything aesthetically is to regard it as part of an isolated context. Hamlet's troubles happen within the play, despite the fact that the sort of troubles they are happen anywhere, and only a fool would ask to how many children Lady Macbeth had given suck. On the other hand, to regard a road accident as an aesthetic object is equally irresponsible; the thing is 'too real' for that.

Difficulties arise, however, when one looks at the words used about such things. What words does one use to express having seen an accident which one regards aesthetically? To say it was beautiful would normally be regarded as evidence either of perversity or an attempt at paradox (but because in this case 'beautiful', like 'nice' or 'good', expresses approval, not because of some aesthetic impropriety). Suppose one said that it was elegant, or exciting, ugly, hideous, clumsy, etc.? These are all words that can be used in avowedly aesthetic contexts: in talking about pictures, or plays, and so on. They may also be used in avowedly moral contexts. For instance, an action may well be called beautiful on moral grounds; we may regard the behaviour of someone as morally ugly, or his ineptitude as clumsy. Equally, one may describe works of art in terms normally associated with moral judgments, such as 'sentimental' or 'cruel'. The use of these words does not distinguish the two attitudes. Can they be distinguished other than by introspection? Is there a distinction beyond that of merely feeling that in aesthetic contexts we are bracketing the object off from the stream of normal classifications?

Of course there are some practical differences: those remarked above. One does not gaze at, or feast one's eyes on, a thing if all one is interested in about it is selling it to someone else. There are a number of words that we use when contemplating rather than acting or manipulating things, the above list, for example, but these things are only indications.

There are, in fact, very few, if any, adjectives the use of which as such distinguishes aesthetic, as opposed to 'practical', moral contexts, and this in itself is significant. When, however, we are asked to justify our judgment a difference does appear. The same adjectives are used whether we call a building or an act of courage magnificent, or a tree or an example of tact graceful. Whether the words are being used in a moral sense or an aesthetic one depends on the context; one cannot identify the type of justification offered for the judgment merely on the presence or absence of certain words. For example:

A. 'I simply cannot see that that building is magnificent.'
'But look at the proportions, look at those massive pillars!'
'Oh, I can see it is a magnificent piece of successful engineering, but I can't see the building as such in that light. It simply looks clumsy to me.'
'Oh no! . . . How can I put it? Look at the way the weight of the roof thrusts against the pillars and is resisted by them . . .'
'Seems to be staggering under its own weight to me.'

B. 'What magnificent courage!'
'Why? I think the man was simply showing off to himself.'
'How could he have been? He had no need to prove to himself that he had courage. There was no self-deception about the action. He no doubt knew very well how frightened he was and simply accepted his own fear.'
'Well, we can't know that, and I suspect the contrary, though, of course, I agree that if you are right it would have been a magnificent action.'

In each of these conversations the basic assumptions of what in general is to be called magnificent morally or aesthetically are shared by the speakers. There is no question of disagreement about fundamentals. Secondly, it should be noted that 'magnificent' is not merely a 'pro' word; to say that something is magnificent is to say something a lot more specific than 'I like it very much, don't you?' That which is graceful is not magnificent, though it could be 'magnificently graceful' in some contexts, usually aesthetic ones, though not necessarily. The difference between the two cases lies in the fact that whereas in the moral case, having granted general agreement about what would be a magnificent act of courage, the argument then turns on supposed facts, in the former case while equally granting that a certain kind of way a building looks would be magnificent, the disputants are debating how in fact the building does look.

But what sort of debate is it? How a thing looks is quite another matter from how it is; to say something looks like something surely contrasts specifically with saying that it is, or even that it is like, that something. We want to say that how a thing looks is essentially a matter of how it looks to me; is subjective. 'It looks to me as if . . .', whether said of arguments or things, means at least that there is no question of my being proved wrong by your assertion of how it looks to you. 'It looks to me as if . . .' countered by 'And it looks to *me* as if . . .' represents not so much argument as agreement to differ. (Though of course the reply 'Yes, but you are wrong; it is . . .' is a retort in an argument.) So what sort of debate can there be which starts off on the basis of completely agreeing to differ?

It might be maintained that the reply 'It looks to me as if . . .' simply represents a person's report on the aesthetic features of an object; that is, that he is reporting on the data provided by his aesthetic sense'. It is worth seeing how such a position might be argued for.

An object may or may not have an aesthetic quality, the argument might run. If it does it produces one kind of reaction (a 'private experience') in a person, and if it does not it produces another. The reaction may be different for any two people (owing to temperamental variations, perhaps, which 'screen' the response differently), or it might be the same. It might be that each person 'really felt' the same thing before the same aesthetic quality—for example, that possessed by the building—only he put it differently. The debate about whether the building really possessed these aesthetic qualities would then be factual, but a factual debate against, as it were, heavy odds.

Whereas we have words like 'yellow', 'red', 'gritty', etc., which are fairly precise descriptions of qualities, we have no such simple precise description for the subtle aesthetic quality that the building possesses. We accordingly have to make do with elliptical and long-winded comparisons—'the roof thrusts, the pillars crouch'. Each object, in fact, possesses its own aesthetic quality: aesthetically the world is very various, which is why we do not have such simple words, and this quality is something over and above the other more commonplace characteristic it may have. Owing to their complexity, we do not spend our energies all the while attending to the aesthetic qualities of objects, with the results that, in the first place, our aesthetic senses become dull, and for some people much duller than others, while, in the second place, we have to be called on to attend to the qualities present—'wake up, look, and see!' One could imagine a group of people some of whom were quite conscious of the voices of bats, others so habituated that they only heard them when they attended carefully, and yet others who had lost all ability to hear them at all. To those who heard bats' voices each one was different, as different in fact as human voices are, yet there were no words to describe the difference exactly; since the bats had no names, one could only say that one was more excited than another, or more like the voice of an old woman or an emperor—wavering or firm bat voices.

Similarly the question of whether anything possessed or did not possess an aesthetic quality would be like the question of whether a particular bat were calling. Some people are more sensitive to beauty than others; they have to describe what they see elliptically, since there is no other way; they have to call their duller fellow men to pay attention to what is around them and to suffer the contempt of the rest of the common herd who can hear and see nothing. Are not artists more sensitive people, and is not their fate just this—to be the 'antennae of the race', perceiving a world that others do not see, or not so clearly?

Such a view is likely to arouse the disgust of all those who have a preference for economy of ontological categories: there is something peculiarly distasteful about the kind of intellectual ham-fistedness which having postulated a special faculty continues by creating a special world of a special type of thing as the object of such perception. Such distaste should be sufficient to warrant a lie direct to the theory of aesthetic facts, but in this case the lie direct can be reinforced by a stronger argument. For if such facts exist, it is still difficult to know whether a particular aesthetic discussion is about them or not. In the case of bats' voices we have other means than unaided hearing of verifying what the acute listeners are talking about. Nowadays electronic instruments can assist us greatly in the investigation of what is after all only acute hearing, and we could always have imagined such aids in the past (crudely, perhaps, but it was not beyond the invention of Swift). This is because what is in question is simply ordinary hearing, only more sensitive ordinary hearing, and that is by no means a different faculty from hearing. Aesthetic perception would have to be, however, not more acute normal perception but a different faculty altogether, and moreover one the information from which has to be 'translated' into terms of other faculties, much as the sighted man 'translates' an account of seeing into purely auditory verbal formula for the congenitally blind.

Of course it does not follow from this that there is no aesthetic perception of aesthetic facts. If, however, one returns to consider the raw material of the question, it soon becomes apparent how bizarre the suggestion that there should be such facts is. For the debaters are not divided on whether *anything* can be aesthetically beautiful, magnificent, or ugly; it is not the case that one of them had *never* responded aesthetically to an object before, that one was congenitally 'aesthetically blind', or even that one had acute aesthetic perception while the other had very little; they differ simply in 'how the building looks'. The reason why all concepts of sight have to be explained to the congenitally blind in terms of the other senses is simply that he *is* congenitally blind, and if we did suppose an aesthetic faculty it would not be because all discussions between people on matters of aesthetics are cases where one party is congenitally aesthetically blind or nearly so (unless, of course, one wishes to suppose a separate faculty for the object of every disputed aesthetic comment!). Is it therefore plausible that with a large number of people sharing the aesthetic faculty there has not developed a whole range of purely aesthetic adjectives that did not have to be reinforced by adjectives drawn from the departments of the other senses? And this is just what is not the case.

There are in fact no adjectives that are used specifically in aesthetic contexts. The notorious 'beautiful' and 'ugly' I have already insisted are equally words of moral appraisal. Austin's suggestion that one should turn instead to words like 'dainty' and 'dumpy' is illuminating, but not because these are aesthetic adjectives in all contexts. 'Dainty' and 'dumpy', 'pretty', 'ungainly', and so on are certainly words used to introduce an aesthetic discussion or evaluation (which are, incidentally, two different things), but the former pair may be used of non-aesthetic description—'Pass me the dumpy candlestick over there' does not necessarily presuppose an aesthetic appraisal of the candlestick in all contexts. It may simply mean the squat, short candlestick, squat and short, that is, as candlesticks go—a straightforwardly non-aesthetic description. It is the *context*, not the word itself, which indicates the aesthetic use of a word. By the same token there are no *sui generis* aesthetic objects: there are only objects of peculiarly aesthetic talk, or 'context of judgment'.

Then what is the context? The context is, I have suggested, indicated by a readiness to apply to the object a description which would normally not be applied to objects of the type in question. A candlestick is aesthetically 'dumpy' if we are prepared to justify our description of it as such, not merely by referring to candlesticks in general—'dumpy as candlesticks go', 'one squat and short for a candlestick'—but by referring to objects which are in fact very unlike candlesticks, in extreme cases to fat old women, for example, and in less extreme cases to any material object that could not under any circumstances be mistaken for a candlestick. 'Well, it's shaped like a cottage loaf.'

This last description is in fact only minimally an aesthetic one. The candlestick might well look very like a cottage loaf in that its outline and proportions were in fact describable in the same way. If that is being understood, then no aesthetic description is intended or can be expressed in such a context. If, however, the likeness is held to be in terms of its homely associations, its edibility—'the thing looks good enough to eat', and so on—then the aesthetic element is, I suggest, increased. It is, I suggest, a necessary and sufficient condition of an aesthetic description, or the justification of an aesthetic description, that some comparison is finally called for to a characteristic that both parties to the discussion know could not in fact *be* characteristic of the object in question. *How* they 'know' it is unimportant; they may assume it, perhaps falsely; *that* they should is all important.

There are two obvious difficulties for such a view, however, though not, I think, insuperable ones. In the first place, there is the fact that we frequently do say of sunsets or girls that they are beautiful and, while meaning an aesthetic comment, are not concerned to offer a justification for it on the lines suggested.

One reason for this, however, is that we have for such things a set of conventional standards of beauty. This is one of the reasons why 'beautiful' is such a notoriously difficult word to define. (Because philosophers try to look behind the conventions and find that there is little or nothing there.) On the one hand, we want to understand it as an adjective of aesthetic appraisal, while, on the other, we find that its meaning is inextricably bound up with conventions of taste that have at most a derivatively aesthetic value, conventions of fashion, of the picturesque, and so on. It is only when we come to question these conventions, 'Why are such women beautiful, as opposed to being sexually desirable?' (the opposition has to be mentioned precisely because the adjective 'beautiful' does not in itself make the distinction—'She gave me a beautiful kiss'), 'Why are such views beautiful—what is it about that one that is so beautiful?', and so on, that we are forced to consider purely aesthetic justifications, and these too are of the kind I have suggested for other cases. 'She looks as if she floats on air; her face looks as if it were a delicate carving; her complexion looks like a succulent peach' and so on are only the beginnings of such justifications because still highly conventional, and by that token tending very much towards simple non-aesthetic description. 'Shall I compare thee to a summer's day. . .?', however, is closer to being a fully fledged aesthetic justification simply because it is less conventionally descriptive. Similarly, to compare a landscape to a painting 'It's like a Constable' is to go some way, though not very far, towards a justification of an aesthetic comment. To say that the landscape looks like two contending armies of sun and shadow crashing together is to go much further, and not because the notion of contending armies is a more exciting or emotional one. Exciting to whom, one might ask. The comparison might equally have been to a geometrician's projection.

The fact that we can use such words like 'beautiful' as predominantly aesthetic terms, more specifically than general words of approval, 'I enjoy looking at that landscape', is owing to the possibility of there being some aesthetic justification for their use at some point in a discussion of the remarks containing them ('I enjoy looking at that landscape' might equally be said on aesthetic grounds, of course). It does not matter what the particular aesthetic justification is.

The second objection is this. If to justify seeing any object aesthetically is always to be willing to ascribe a description to it that would not normally be applied to things of its type, then does this not present difficulties when the aesthetic object in question is a work of art? For though some works of art do invite such comparisons—representational art, for example—others, tunes, for example, do not.

But this is to miss the point that the sense in which a block of stone or a painted surface 'looks like' something utterly different; a man, or a three-dimensional landscape, is surely different from the sense in which a boulder may have a brooding or lowering look. The boulder is not a representation of someone brooding.

In fact the opposition between paintings which are paintings *of* something, represent something, and 'abstract' paintings or melodies which are not *of* anything is a totally different contrast from that between a boulder seen simply as a boulder and a boulder seen as something brooding, as 'having a presence'. Indeed, one may even wish to go further and point out that the relations, *a representing b,* and *a* being viewable as *b*, or *a* having a look of *b* have almost nothing to do with each other: Peter may have a look of Paul without in the least *representing* or being a picture of Paul, and a Viceroy may represent the Queen without being the least little bit like her or even having a look of her in half-light. I should wish to argue elsewhere that the sense in which a picture represents its subject is fundamentally the same as that in which any proxy may represent a principal: suffice here that it is a totally different matter from hearing, seeing, tasting, etc., *a*'s as if they were *b*'s. We can talk of sad or happy tunes or of paintings of cheerful landscapes without this implying that the tunes *represent* sad or happy situations or that the landscapes *represent* cheerful states of mind. I do not propose to consider questions as to whether we tend to associate landscapes with moods simply because of learnt associations, or for other reasons. That we do is sufficient here.

It follows that simply to see a representational painting as a picture of something is not necessarily to regard it as an aesthetic object. To this extent the question of pictorial representation is irrelevant to questions about the nature of seeing something as an aesthetic object. To look at a picture of 'where I spent the summer holidays' is not necessarily to look at anything aesthetically. The major aesthetic function of purely representational art—pure *trompe d'œil* painting—where it has one, is simply to point out objects for attention as one might point out boulders on a beach. The method is the semi-conventional one of pointing to an object by exhibiting it in an unusual context, within a picture-frame, for example, much as an *objet trouvé* may be exhibited, but such exhibiting is at best only the first stage in the aesthetic process, since merely to look at something with peculiar attention is not to regard it as an aesthetic object. When in a fit of distraction I idly watch a fly crawling across a ceiling; merely noticing it in detail, I have not yet adopted an aesthetic attitude to it: it is not yet an aesthetic object for me. For this to be so, it is necessary that I see it *as* something—as if it were a minute personality, for instance. Of course the tendency to regard the object of such detached contemplation as an aesthetic object is very strong in us. It can, however, be resisted.

A work of art may be defined as an object so made that it may be easily seen as an aesthetic object. (There are techniques for achieving this that it would be in place to consider were this an essay on artistic methods.) The essentially aesthetic characteristic of a work of art is its ambivalence, that is to say, we are inclined when presented with works of art to see them, on the one hand, as things of one kind, and, on the other, as things of quite another kind. A painting may be both a representation of a natural object that itself may be seen aesthetically as well as an abstract mathematical exercise and a pleasing mosaic of particles of paint. (It cannot be too strongly emphasized again that merely to enjoy looking at something, to enjoy the sight of yellow paint, for example, or for that matter to enjoy the sound of a note on an instrument, is not to view the object of such enjoyment aesthetically: it is merely the first stage in such a process.) A full aesthetic response takes into account all these elements together. One may, for example, hear a passage of music both as a mathematical construction of intervals and as if it were the proposition and counter-proposition in an argument. It is, of course, neither a mathematical construction nor a series of sentences: it may be 'heard as' both. The sounds the instruments make are not words, they are not conventional signs that stand for anything, neither are they mathematical symbols, which is why simply listening to the noises made by the instrument as an electronic technician might, or understanding a sentence, are not in themselves aesthetic responses to objects in the way that listening to music in any full sense certainly is.

So-called abstract painting shares in just this ambivalence. On the one hand, for instance, we may see the painting as having a mysterious presence, a personality, and on the other, perhaps, as a balanced geometrical arrangement of colours. Yet again we may see it as well as a mass of delightful colour and paint. To respond fully to the painting as a work of art is to see it at once in all these ways.

Aesthetic contemplation may be disinterested in the sense that it does not lead directly to moral conclusions (though it may do so indirectly), and the object of such contemplation may be isolated from its relations with other objects in the sense that aesthetic contemplation does not specifically consider the place of the object in terms of its causal relations with other objects. But the idea that in seeing an object aesthetically one is seeing it entirely for itself and in isolation from other objects can become highly misleading. It is rather that it is considered as if it were a member of quite another type of objects than it is in fact understood to be. Contrary to at least the letter of Hampshire's view, this presupposes both that the normal classifications of things is borne in mind in aesthetic contexts and that the object concerned is by no means seen, or even enjoyed simply for itself.

So, in conclusion: I do want to say that there is indeed an area of rational human talk where metaphors are inevitable. Aesthetic comments can't be tidied up to get rid of the metaphors because it is just the presence of the metaphors that makes the comments aesthetic. This need not make attempts at aesthetic conversion absurd; simply, the ultimate thing one has to say is not literal. A fuller consideration of what is going on will have to await a separate treatment of the logic of metaphors, but it is worth pointing out that one of the many ways in which language changes is by the birth and death of metaphors. Aesthetic comment may well be called the growing-point of language.

INTENTION AND INTENTIONAL ACTION

DON LOCKE

THERE IS OBVIOUSLY a connection between intention and action. If we could not intend, then we could not act in the way that we do, and if we could not act in the way that we do, then we could not intend. Nevertheless it is a mistake to forge too close a connection between intention and intentional action. One cannot perform an intentional action without intending to be doing something, but one can intend to be doing something without performing an intentional action, either because what one actually does is some other (unintentional) action or because one does not actually succeed in doing anything (one might, for example, be paralysed). This means we must carefully distinguish the two related questions 'What is it to intend to do something?' and 'What is it to do something intentionally?' The failure to do this seems to me to have affected two well-known discussions of intention, that of Stuart Hampshire in *Thought and Action*,[1] which I have not space to consider here, and that of Miss Anscombe in *Intention*.[2] Miss Anscombe, for example, distinguishes only three topics for discussion: expression of future intention, intentional action, and intention in action. She thus fails to take account of the case where, without expressing the intention, one intends to do something but does not succeed in performing an intentional action. It is just this possibility which has led philosophers to speak about hidden volitions and occult mental causes.

I

Miss Anscombe's account of intentional action (for, despite its title, her book is not about intention as such at all) turns on what she calls 'a special sense' of the question 'Why did you do that?'

She says that if this question, in its special sense, is refused application, then the action in question is not intentional, i.e. an intentional action is one to which the question, in its special sense, applies. When does the question have this special sense? When it receives a certain sort of answer. Yet it's odd to think of the answer a question gets as determining the question's sense; presumably what Miss Anscombe means is that if the question gets one sort of answer this shows that the action was intentional, while if it does not get this sort of answer this shows that the action was not intentional. And this has nothing to do with any 'special sense' of the question.

Miss Anscombe mentions three kinds of answer to the question 'Why did you do that?' which, as she puts it, refuse application to that question in her special sense, or, as I would prefer to put it, which indicate that the action was not intentional. These are answers which 1) state or imply that the agent did not know that he was performing the action in question, 2) state or imply that the agent knew this by observation only, or 3) state or imply that the action was caused rather than done for reasons. This third alternative is never stated in these words by Miss Anscombe, but it is the only interpretation I can put on what she says. She does say 'The question has not that sense if the answer is evidence or states a cause, including a mental cause',[3] but on the following page she says that the question is refused application in its special sense if 'the action is somehow characterized as one in which there is no room for what I called mental causality'. These two statements seem contradictory. I think that what Miss Anscombe must mean is that both reasons and mental causes are to be considered as instances of mental causality (and I leave to one side the question of what precisely 'mental causality' is), so that an action will be intentional (her question 'Why?', in its special sense, will have application) if the action is brought about by mental causality but not by a mental cause, i.e. if it is not caused at all, but done for reasons.

So, ignoring the peculiar way in which she approaches her problem, it seems that Miss Anscombe's position can be stated as follows: an intentional action is one where 1) the agent knows he is performing it, 2) this knowledge is 'non-observational knowledge', and 3) the action is done for reasons and not merely caused.

Of these three conditions, the second is the one that comes in for most discussion. Miss Anscombe holds that a man normally knows the position and movement of his limbs 'non-observationally', and obviously it follows from her account of intentional action that this is necessarily, and not just normally, true of our intentional movements. Now the natural view to take is that a man knows where his limbs are and what they are doing because he sees or feels (via the kinaesthetic or the tactual sense) them. Does Miss Anscombe wish to deny this? What is this non-observational knowledge?

From what is said on pp 13–14 and 49–50 of *Intention* it seems that non-observational knowledge is marked by two important, and related, features. First, when I know something non-observationally there is nothing that acts as a sign telling me that this is so. 'Where we can speak of separately describable sensations, having which is in some sense our criterion for saying something, then we can speak of observing that thing; but this is not generally so when we know the position of our limbs.'[4] At first sight this suggests that my knowledge that there is cheese in the cupboard, knowledge which I acquire by looking and seeing what is there, is non-observational! There do not seem to be any sensations—certainly not separately describable sensations—which are my criterion for saying that there is cheese in the cupboard. However, I think this would be a mistaken inference from the misleading terminology; presumably what Miss Anscombe meant to say is that knowledge is observational where I acquire it by identifying something (not necessarily a sensation) which I perceive or observe.

The second feature of non-observational knowledge is that when a person makes a mistake we do not say that he has misjudged an appearance. 'If a man says that his leg is bent when it is lying straight out, it would appear to be incorrect to say that he has misjudged an inner kinaesthetic appearance as an appearance of his leg bent, when in fact what was appearing to him was his leg stretched out. . . . This consideration, assuming its correctness, is enough to justify saying that normally one does not know the position or movement of one's limbs "by observation".'[5] Now certainly if a person did make such a mistake we would not normally say 'He has misjudged a kinaesthetic appearance', but similarly we would not normally say 'He has misjudged a visual appearance' if he made a mistake about what is in the cupboard. These are technical expressions, and as good a case could be made out for talking about misjudging kinaesthetic appearances as can for talking about misjudging visual ones. If a person has a feeling in his knee which he normally gets when his legs are stretched out, and takes it to be the feeling he gets when his legs are bent, and so thinks that his leg is bent, then surely we can say that he has misjudged a kinaesthetic appearance, if we feel so inclined.

I think that the basic point which lies behind what Miss Anscombe is saying here is that although I discover what is in the cupboard by noticing the cheese which I see, I do not have to notice what I feel in order to know where my limbs are and what they are doing. As Miss Anscombe says,[6] 'It may indeed be that it is because one has sensations that one knows this (that one's leg is bent); but that does not mean that one knows it by identifying the sensations one has.' So perhaps we should say that this non-observational knowledge is knowledge which, although it involves various sensory cues, is not acquired by conscious attention, noticing, identification, of the sense-given data which in some way or another is responsible for the knowledge. And it does seem correct to say that our knowledge of the position and movement of our limbs is normally non-observational in this sense. Normally we do not have to notice or identify the kinaesthetic sensations we feel in order to know where our limbs are or what they are doing.

There are three points to notice about this. First of all, if this is what Miss Anscombe means by 'non-observational knowledge'—and I shall suggest in a moment that perhaps it is not—then this name is rather misleading, suggesting as it does some intuitive or completely non-sensory way of knowing. I will prefer to use the label 'subliminal knowledge', though even that is not entirely satisfactory. Secondly, this subliminal or non-observational knowledge is much more common than perhaps we realize. A good example is our knowledge of the direction from which a sound comes. Psychologists have shown that we know this by using such cues as the difference in volume between the sound as heard in one ear and the sound as heard in the other, or the time-lag between the two ears, although, of course, I never consciously notice or identify these slight differences. Another example would be when I know there is someone in the room, because of some very slight sound which I do not consciously hear, without knowing how I know it (the so-called sixth sense); or when I notice a clock chiming and realize that this is the tenth stroke, even though I did not consciously notice, and cannot remember, the previous nine. Thirdly, there is an important difference between our knowledge of the direction from which the sound comes and our knowledge of the position and movement of our limbs, in that in the latter case we can, but in the former case we cannot, notice and identify the sensory cues on which our knowledge is based. I can notice the slight sensation in my elbow which, subliminally, tells me that my elbow is bent, but no matter how I try I cannot notice the difference in volume between the left ear and the right ear.

I want now to consider a line of argument which may well lie behind what Miss Anscombe has to say (cf. her reference to 'separately describable sensations' on p 13), and which might be taken to show that kinaesthetic sensations cannot, either consciously or unconsciously (subliminally), provide us with knowledge of the position and movement of our limbs. I doubt whether Miss Anscombe does want to accept this argument (cf. the passage quoted from p 49), but it may nevertheless be one of the factors which leads her to talk of 'non-observational' knowledge in the first place. The argument comes from Wittgenstein,[7] and has been elaborated by Melden.[8] It involves two points.

The first is rhetorical. Let your finger make a small pendulum movement, says Wittgenstein, notice the kinaesthetic sensation, and then try to tell yourself that this slight sensation—if indeed you feel anything at all—gives you that precise knowledge of what your finger is doing which you undoubtedly do have. We might reply to this that it proves nothing (except perhaps that our unconscious is cleverer than we thought it was) for even if we try we cannot detect the cues which inform us of the direction from which a sound comes, and yet, as experiment shows, there are cues which do this. But there is more to be said than this, and we will come back to it in a moment.

Wittgenstein's second point is that the kinaesthetic sensations cannot provide us with knowledge of what our limbs are doing because we cannot offer an independent description of those sensations. But, for a start, it is not even true that we cannot describe a kinaesthetic sensation except as the sensation of, e.g., my hand waggling. The sensation I get when my hand waggles is a sensation of strain and tension in my wrist. In some cases I cannot offer an independent description, but this seems to be little more than a, perfectly understandable, gap in the language; we have no name for the sensation we get when our eyebrow twitches other than 'the sensation of an eyebrow twitching'. But even if this were true universally it would not mean that the sensations cannot inform us about the movements. It seems that the smell of coffee cannot be described or identified except as the smell of coffee, but that does not mean that the smell of coffee cannot be a sign of the presence of coffee. The very most—and I am not even convinced of this—that seems to be necessary if *A* is to be a sign of *B* is that *A* and *B* be distinct items, and this condition is certainly satisfied with kinaesthetic sensations and bodily movements. For it is possible to have the sensation without the movement (this would be a kinaesthetic 'hallucination', such as one gets when drunk), and it is possible to have the movement without the sensation (as when one is anaesthetized). The fact that often, though not always, we do not describe or identify a kinaesthetic sensation other than as the sensation of a part of our body being in a certain position, or making a certain movement, may prove something—that we don't have to identify the sensations before we can make the movements, for example—but I see no reason for thinking it shows that kinaesthetic sensations cannot provide us with what I am calling 'subliminal' knowledge of where our limbs are and what they are doing. Indeed, in view of the physiological evidence, it would be surprising if it did.

Let us go back to the first point, that it is odd to suggest that such a slight sensation can provide us with such detailed knowledge. Now it seems to me that Wittgenstein is right about this; I do not think that the slight sensation does provide us with the knowledge. For the pendulum movement of the finger is an intentional movement, and there is a difference between our knowledge of intentional movements and our knowledge of non-intentional movements. The failure to notice this difference complicates and confuses Miss Anscombe's account of non-observational knowledge. Suppose I am blindfolded and someone forces my hand through the movements it would make if I were signing my name. I would very likely not know what movements my hand had performed and if I did I would, I think, know this only because I had paid special attention to the kinaesthetic and tactual sensations I felt—which means this would not be subliminal knowledge. But if, when blindfolded, I intentionally move my hand as I would when signing my name, I know precisely what I have done without, apparently, any need of kinaesthetic or tactual sensations at all. This is, of course, because I know what I intend to do. Nevertheless knowledge of intention does not *constitute* knowledge of intentional action since, as we have seen, I may intend to do something without actually succeeding in doing it, or anything. Sometimes my intentions are not fulfilled, and what I succeed in doing is something which I can learn only by means of my senses, visual, tactual, or kinaesthetic. I may intend to push a button but succeed only in pushing a wall decoration, because what I thought was a button was only a wall decoration; or I may intend to push a button but succeed in doing nothing at all, because I am paralysed. But at most moments when I come to act I have been observing the world around me and my situation in it, and 99 times out of a 100, at the very least, I know that I will succeed in doing what I intend to do once I try to do it. I can be perfectly sure that if I now try to move my finger in a slight pendulum motion I will succeed in doing it. So I can shut my eyes, forget about kinaesthetic sensations, and yet know precisely what I am doing. But if I tried to do something more difficult, like drawing a map of Europe blindfold, I would very likely have little idea of what I had succeeded in doing, and that only because I paid special attention to kinaesthetic and tactual sensations in order to discover whether my hand was in fact moving as I intended it to.

So although I would reject the suggestion that kinaesthetic sensations do not and cannot provide us with knowledge of where our limbs are and what they are doing, I would agree that the knowledge they give us is far from precise: my kinaesthetic sensations advise me, normally subliminally or unconsciously, where roughly speaking my limbs are and what roughly speaking they are doing. But where the movement is intentional there is often no need to rely, consciously or unconsciously, on these sensations; where the action is of a kind which I know I can do if I want to, and I have no reason for thinking I will fail on this occasion, then I can know that I am doing it without any conscious or unconscious reference to the kinaesthetic sense, let alone vision or touch. This is obviously true where the action in question is some simple bodily movement, like waving a finger or lifting a hand. But where the action is more difficult, like drawing a map of Europe blindfold, or something that we are not sure we can do, like waggling our ears, then observation, or at the very least the unconscious, subliminal registering of kinaesthetic sensations, is necessary if we are to know whether we have done what we intended to do.

There is, then, this difference between our knowledge of the position and the non-intentional movement of our limbs, and our knowledge of intentional actions. Is this knowledge of our intentional actions 'non-observational' in any sense? We have seen that my knowledge that my finger is moving as I intend it to is derived from the prior knowledge that I can wave my finger if I want to, that there is nothing in my present situation to prevent me from waving it, and that I am, here and now, intending, trying to wave it. This prior knowledge is, for the most part, observational knowledge. I know that I can wave my finger if I want to because I have observed that my finger, unlike the tips of my hair, waves when I try to wave it. But my knowledge that I am, here and now, intending, trying to wave my finger is not observational knowledge. Nor is it subliminal knowledge. So to the extent that my knowledge of my intentional actions is based on my knowledge of what I intend to be doing, to that extent my knowledge of my intentional actions will be non-observational knowledge, though in a sense different from that so far considered. This knowledge that I intend to do such and such is an example of what is often called 'introspective knowledge', and I will use this term to distinguish it from subliminal knowledge, although I wouldn't want to be committed to any theory of a faculty of introspection or inner sense (indeed, if there were such a faculty the knowledge would be observational!).

Let us agree that knowledge of the position and movements of one's limbs is normally non-observational, in the sense of subliminal, knowledge, although without the help of observation this subliminal knowledge is usually not very precise. And let us also agree that knowledge of one's intentions, of what one intends to do or be doing, is also non-observational, in the sense of introspective, knowledge. The question was whether it is a necessary condition of an action's being intentional that the agent knows non-observationally that he is doing it. For this, as we have seen, seems to be what Miss Anscombe is saying.

If by 'non-observational knowledge' we mean what I am calling introspective knowledge, then it is clearly false to say that our knowledge of what we are intentionally doing is, and must be, non-observational. This introspective knowledge cannot extend to knowledge of what is actually happening, as opposed to knowledge of what we intend to happen. I know that I am writing my name not just because I know that I intend to do so but also because I know that this is something I can do, and that there is nothing in my present situation to prevent me from doing it. These last two facts are facts I learn from experience, from observation; if I had nothing but my intention to go on I could no more know that I am writing my name than I can know, without looking in the mirror or paying special attention to what I feel in my ears and temples, that I have at last succeeded in waggling my ears. My non-observational, introspective knowledge of what I intend to do is a partial source of my knowledge of what I am doing, but it does not by itself constitute that knowledge.

So the claim must be that when someone performs an intentional action, he always knows subliminally that he is, in fact, doing what he intends to do. This might seem obviously false, in that more often than not we happen to see what we are doing, and so more often than not know observationally that we are doing what we intend to do. But this misses the important point, which is that even where we do see what we are doing, and so know it as, in whole or in part, a result of observation, nevertheless it is often the case that we would still know we were doing it even if we hadn't seen it. Miss Anscombe's claim that our knowledge of intentional actions is always non-observational is not that we never observe what we are doing but that we would know what we were doing even if we didn't observe it.

However, we have seen that this subliminal knowledge is not very precise, whereas our knowledge of our intentional actions is, for reasons already given, often much more detailed than would be possible if the kinaesthetic sensations were all we had to go on. My knowledge that I have drawn a map of Europe blindfold, or even my knowledge that I am waving my hand, is not subliminal knowledge in so far as it is based on prior, observational knowledge of my abilities and capacities, and of the circumstances in which I now find myself. I doubt whether any action which involves more than some simple movement of part of the body—and normally when we intend to do something we intend to do more than move some part of the body—can be known non-observationally in the sense of subliminally. Miss Anscombe's second condition for an action's being intentional is not a necessary condition after all.

Nor, for that matter, is the first. It is logically and even empirically possible for a person to perform some intentional action, and not know whether he has performed it (although, of course, he will know whether he intended to perform it). A student may intend to do better in an examination than his friend, and never know whether he has. If someone rubs out my attempted map of Europe before I see it, and no one lets on how well I did, I may think I have not succeeded when in fact I have. The paralysed man may not believe the doctor when the doctor tells him that he has moved his finger as he intended to. It is possible, though uncommon, for a person not to know that he has performed a particular intentional action. What is necessary for the action's being intentional is not that the agent knows that he is doing it but that he knows that he intends to be doing it. This is because, first, an action cannot be intentional unless the agent intends to be doing it, and second, an agent cannot intend to be doing it unless he knows that he so intends. But this tells us virtually nothing about intention or intentional action.

How does Miss Anscombe come to think that we always have non-observational knowledge of our intentional actions? Part of the explanation is that she does not distinguish the two types of non-observational knowledge. Indeed, her discussion seems to shift from one sense to other: at first, around Section 8, where she is concerned with knowledge of the position and movement of our limbs, she seems to be thinking of what I called subliminal knowledge; but when she comes back to the topic, around Sections 28–30, and discusses our knowledge of intentional actions, she seems to have switched to what I called introspective knowledge. But this is not the full explanation, since we have seen that we often lack non-observational knowledge, of either kind, of our intentional actions. The fundamental source of error is the ambiguity of the phrase 'knowledge of our intentional actions'. To perform an intentional action *x*, I have both to do *x* and to have intended to do *x*; I might intend to do *x* without succeeding in doing it, or I might do *x* without intending to, but in neither case have I performed the intentional action *x*. Now, by 'knowledge of my intentional action *x*', I might mean my knowledge that I intended to do *x*, or I might mean my knowledge that I did *x*, as I intended to (actually I am more likely to be referring indiscriminately to both, but for our present purposes the distinction is important). In the former case the knowledge is non-observational, i.e. introspective, knowledge; it is knowledge of my intentions. But in the latter case my knowledge can be non-observational only in the sense of subliminal knowledge; I cannot know introspectively that I have succeeded in performing a certain action. And it is fairly clear that in Sections 28–30 Miss Anscombe is interpreting 'knowledge of intentional actions' in the first and not the second way, i.e. to mean knowledge of what one intends to do or be doing, rather than knowledge that one is actually doing what one intends to do. This is why she holds that knowledge of intentional actions is necessarily non-observational.

Naturally I am perfectly prepared to accept that, interpreted in this way, knowledge of intentional actions is non-observational, i.e. introspective, knowledge. But this can scarcely be what Miss Anscombe wants to mean when she says that when one performs an intentional action one knows non-observationally what one is doing. For two reasons. First, this introspective knowledge is not knowledge at all, as Miss Anscombe uses the term, since we cannot be mistaken about it (this is not to say that I personally accept this odd restriction on the use of the term 'know'). And second, Miss Anscombe wants to say that our knowledge of the position and non-intentional movements of our limbs is normally non-observational in the same way that our knowledge of our intentional actions is necessarily non-observational. But it is absolutely clear that although we can have this sort of non-observational knowledge of our intentions, and hence, in the sense explained of our intentional actions, we cannot have this sort of non-observational knowledge of the position and non-intentional movements of our limbs, i.e. they cannot be known by introspection.

So much for Miss Anscombe's first two conditions for an action's being intentional. This leaves us with the third condition, that an action is intentional when it is done for reasons, and not merely caused. Now this seems to be not only a necessary but also a sufficient condition, as I think Miss Anscombe would agree (she says, for example, that the sense of the question 'Why?' with which she is concerned is 'Of course that in which the answer, if positive, gives a reason for acting'[9]). But she would also agree that this analysis of an intentional action, however accurate, is not at all illuminating until the distinction between reasons and causes is itself clarified. And although she has some interesting things to say, she would not claim to have given an adequate account of the distinction, nor would she want to base her analysis of intentional action on it. My conclusion is, therefore, that Miss Anscombe's account of intentional action is not accurate, so far as the first two conditions are concerned, and not informative, so far as the third condition is concerned.

II

What, then, is an intentional action? I will say that it is an action where the agent acts in order to realize a certain state of affairs. This state of affairs need not be something which is resultant upon or produced by my action; it may simply be the state of affairs which is constituted by my so acting. If I intend to raise my hand the state of affairs I act in order to realize is the state of affairs in which my hand is rising (or has risen).

This is reminiscent of Professor Melden's talk about acting in order to make a proposition true,[10] though personally I find this misleading. For, first of all, although I may act in order to realize a certain state of affairs, I need not and usually do not think of or formulate any proposition which describes that state of affairs, and which will be true when that state of affairs is realized. And, secondly, it seems odd to suggest that one reason why I act as I do is that I want to make a certain proposition come true ('Why did you do that?'—'Because I wanted to make "My hand is above my head" a true proposition'!). But although I do not always formulate such a proposition, much less always act with the purpose of making it true, I do know what the proposition is, at least in the sense that I know what state of affairs it is that I am acting in order to realize. That is, if the action is intentional I know what I am trying, aiming, intending, to do, although, as we have seen, I may not know that I have succeeded in doing it. And this does not mean that I must consciously formulate or consider some proposition which states what I am doing, any more than it is necessary, if I am to know what I am seeing, that I consciously formulate or consider some proposition which describes what I see.

Thus an intentional action is one where the agent acts in order to realize a certain state of affairs, knowing what state of affairs it is that he is acting in order to realize (the second clause may well be contained within the first). There is then the question of what precisely an action is. Not all actions are intentional—if I wave my hands or finger my watch as I talk it is unlikely that I am doing these things intentionally, although they do seem to count as voluntary actions. Fundamentally I would say that an action involves some self-caused bodily movement,[11] although there is obviously more to most actions than the mere bodily movement. The fact that human beings possess the power, capacity, ability, of initiating movement, of doing things as opposed to having things done to them, of moving their bodies as opposed to having their bodies moved, I take to be basic and undeniable. I don't see how this fact can be reduced to any other, e.g. analysed in terms of 'volitions', and even if it can be we are still, as Melden[12] has argued, left with the fact that human beings have the capacity or ability to produce something, even if that something is now supposed to be a volition rather than a bodily movement. It is by reference to this basic ability, I think, that the notion of an action is to be explained, but there is not space to go into details here; I take the notion of action pretty much for granted. There is, however, the point that the one action may be described in many different ways, and the question of whether the action is intentional is really the question of whether it is intentional under a particular description. The answer will depend on whether that description is a description of a state of affairs which I am, knowingly, acting in order to realize.

It might be said that my account of intentional action amounts to no more than: an intentional action is an action which the agent intends to perform. I would accept this criticism. It seems more sensible to analyse intentional action by reference to intention than to analyse intention by reference to intentional action, as Anscombe appears to do, for the simple reason that there is a logical connection from intentional action to intention (if there is an intentional action x, then the agent intended to do x), but not *vice versa*. However, there is the fact that with the greater majority of our intentional actions, the things we intend to do, there is no mental or physical process which we can identify as the intention, nothing except the action itself for us to refer to. If someone asks me whether I intended to open the door as I came into this room the answer is obviously that I did, but I did not form any such intention, or even consider the action, before or even while I performed that action. There are, of course, cases where we do make a decision and explicitly form an intention before acting, but not all cases of intending like that. It is a mistake to identify intending with making an explicit decision or to identify intentions with explicitly formulated thoughts of the form 'I intend to do x'. This is what makes it tempting to analyse intention in terms of intentional action, rather than the other way around.

Now I would agree with Miss Anscombe that 'we do not add anything attaching to the action at the time it is done by describing it as intentional. . . . An action is not called "intentional" in virtue of any extra feature which exists when it is performed.' 'To call it intentional is to assign it to the class of intentional actions.'[13] But to say that an intentional action is an action which the agent intends to perform is not to say that an intentional action is an action accompanied by some internal mental event, called intending. Miss Anscombe hopes to explain intentional action without reference to intending, in order to avoid the error of thinking of an intentional act as what Professor Ryle would call a tandem event—an overt physical act accompanied by an internal mental act. But if we can analyse intending without reference to hidden mental events, we will not only fill out the analysis of intentional action given above but also show that analysing intentional action by reference to intention need not lead us into the pitfall Miss Anscombe is so keen to avoid.

The crucial point is that I can intend to do something without thinking about that action at all. I opened the door as I came into this room. It is certainly true that I intended to do so, but it is equally certain that I did not think to myself 'I will open the door', or come to any specific decision to do so. I just did it. So to ask whether I intended to open the door is not to ask what I thought about before or while I did it. Rather it is to ask whether 'opening the door' describes a state of affairs which I acted in order to bring about. So to say that someone intends to be doing x (whether he is actually doing it or not) is to say that there is some state of affairs which he is acting, or at least trying to act, in order to bring about—this involving, as we have seen, his knowing what that state of affairs is.

But this does not tell us what it is to intend to do something in the future, as when I now intend to go to France for my holidays. This is where it seems difficult to eliminate all reference to mental events. Miss Anscombe simply dodges the issue, by talking solely about *expressions* of intention for the future. Hampshire holds that 'My intention to do something is a settled belief about my future action',[14] 'An intention may be represented as a belief or as knowledge that I am going to do something'.[15] I am not sure whether this is meant as an analysis of intention, but in any case it is mistaken. Hampshire holds that although I can predict whether I will succeed or not, I cannot genuinely predict whether I will try, make the attempt. All I can do is decide, and if I decide to do it I know I will try. 'To intend to do something in the future is necessarily to believe that I shall in fact try to do it.'[16] But first, I may intend to ring my bank manager in the morning, and know from experience that I will conveniently (though not deliberately) forget to do so. And second, I can believe I will do something intentionally and yet, at the present moment, not intend to do it. A young boy observes the behaviour of his elder brothers and confidently predicts that he too will, around the age of sixteen, acquire a girl friend (or at any rate try to), even though at the present moment he can imagine nothing more horrible. He may even be determined to try as hard as he can not to fall into the same disgusting ways, and yet, reviewing the cases of brothers who have expressed similar intentions but have failed to carry them out when the time comes, he knows all the time that he too will follow suit.[17]

Perhaps Hampshire takes account of this sort of example when he says that predictions of future actions may not be equivalent to statements of intention 'when the situation envisaged is fairly remote from the actual situation of the person'.[18] But suppose I live in a country where four jazz records are released each month, and I make a practice of buying one, the best one, each month. As I go into the record shop to see the latest selection I meet a friend of very similar tastes who shows me what he has bought, which looks very interesting to me, and tells me that the other three new releases are terrible. I naturally predict that I too will buy that record, but this is scarcely a statement of intention, for I will not make up my mind until I have seen the other three records. On the evidence available I predict, and so believe, that I will do the same as my friend, but I have not formed the intention of buying that particular record. So Hampshire is mistaken when he holds 'There seems . . . an absurdity in behaviour—an absurdity that is more than the infringement of a convention of language—in trying to find grounds for predicting what I myself will do'.[19] The point is, I think, that if the factors which will influence my decision weigh with me now, then to predict the decision is to decide which factors weigh the most, and so, in effect, to decide here and now. But if it is a question of predicting which factors will weigh with me, and how much, then this counts as predicting my future decision (and intention) rather than making one now. But in any event there is a difference between intending to do something and believing that I will try to do it.

Now it seems to me that, in such a case as my intending to go to France, my intention to do so consists in the fact that I have decided to do it.[20] This means that *if* deciding is or involves something that might be called a mental act (and I am not going to go into this question), then the analysis of intending to do something in the future does involve a reference to internal mental events. Of course this does not mean that *all* cases of intending involve mental acts, such as deciding might be held to be. And even in those cases where intending does involve such a mental act, the intention (or my having the intention) is not to be identified with the mental event. I cannot be said to intend to go to France for my holidays unless I have decided to do so, which means that I must have explicitly thought about it (as I did not think about opening the door). But this thinking or deciding that I will go to France is not the intention to do so. The intention consists not in my deciding to go, nor in my thinking that I will go, but in the fact that I have decided to go. Thus even if intending to do something in the future does involve a mental act, it is not itself to be identified with that mental act.

So to intend to be doing something is to be performing or trying to perform some action in order to realize some state of affairs. And to intend to do something in the future is to have decided to perform or try to perform some action in order to realize some state of affairs. The point of this analysis is that it enables us to define an intentional action as one which the agent intends to do, without committing ourselves to saying that an intentional action is an action accompanied by some private mental event. It may be that in some cases, where we intend to do something in the future, having an intention involves having decided, and therefore (if deciding is a mental event) involves a mental event. But the intention, or the having of the intention, is not to be identified with any such mental event. So it is possible to analyse intentional action by reference to intention, while still agreeing with Miss Anscombe that 'we do not add anything attaching to the action at the time it is done by describing it as intentional. . . . An action is not called "intentional" in virtue of any extra feature which exists when it is performed.'

There is one further borderline case, where we may speak of intentions for the future even though the person in question cannot be said to have decided. If someone asks me 'Do you intend to get up tomorrow morning?' I will answer that I do, but I have not decided to get up tomorrow morning, or thought about it at all until now, and it seems odd to suggest that my answer constitutes a decision to get up. Similarly I can say that yesterday I intended to get up this morning, even though the thought of doing so never crossed my mind. Again a bachelor may say 'Of course I intend to get married some day', without it being true that he has decided to get married. These cannot be explained by saying that I believe, on inductive grounds, that I will perform that action intentionally, for we have seen that a person can know that he will do something intentionally and yet, at the time in question, intend not to do it. Rather I think we should say that if I am prepared to do something intentionally (get out of bed, or marry someone) when the occasion arises, and I believe[21] that such an occasion will arise, then we can say that I intend to do it, even though I have not decided to do it, even if the action in question has not been explicitly considered at all.

Nevertheless, these are borderline cases of intending. The bachelor says 'I intend to get married some day', but if he does not get married we do not ask when and why he changed his mind. These questions apply only if it is a case of deliberate decision, and these questions would apply if it were a clear-cut case of intending to do something. I intend to get up tomorrow, the bachelor intends to get married, only in a rather vague and weak sense of 'intend'.

III

Several of the terms used in this account of intention and intentional action are themselves badly in need of analysis, e.g. 'decide' and 'action' itself. But the one that most needs explanation, if the analysis is to be at all informative, is the notion of trying.

It seems that 'try' can be used in a weak and a strong sense, roughly equivalent to 'attempt' and 'make an effort' respectively. We might say that to try, in the strong sense, is to keep on doing something, or at any rate trying in the weak sense to do it, even though there are good reasons for stopping: exhaustion, pain, consumption of time, etc. But although the strong sense may be important in discussions of responsibility, freedom of the will, etc., it is the weak sense that interests us here.

What is it to try to do something? It is not only possible to fail to do what we intend to do but even possible to intend to do something, try to do it, and yet fail to do anything at all, even to move part of our body, as happens when we are paralysed. Such cases as this naturally lead us to think that in trying to move the person performs some inner task, which unfortunately does not produce its normal effect. We soon find ourselves talking about volitions, acts of will, 'setting oneself', and so on. If we are to avoid this we should analyse 'He tries to move and fails' not as 'He does what he normally does when he wants to move, but it does not have its usual effect' but as 'He loses his ability to move'. When I move my arm there is nothing I do in order to move it (there are internal events which must occur if the arm is to move, e.g. the excitation of various nerve cells, but it is false to say that I perform these events; these events are not prior actions of mine), so, *a fortiori,* if I fail to move it there is nothing which I have done in order to move it, but which has not had its expected effect. What do you do when you try to do something but fail even to move part of your body? The correct answer is: Nothing. The man who tries to move and fails does nothing; what has happened is that he has lost his basic power of action, of moving himself.

We might put this by saying that to try is to do what you can, which means, of course, that if you cannot do anything, then you can try without anything happening. But the paralysis example still presents a difficulty. If to try is to do what you can, and a paralysed man cannot do anything, this means not only that a paralysed man can try to move without anything happening but also that there is no difference between a paralysed man who is trying to move and one who is not! It even seems to mean that any paralysed man is, *ipso facto*, trying to move, since he is doing what he can, viz. nothing! What are we to say here?

It won't do to say, as Richard Taylor does,[22] that the completely paralysed man cannot even try. According to Taylor, trying consists in doing something physical, like tensing a muscle or bending a joint. So since the paralysed man cannot move anything, cannot tense a single muscle or bend a single joint, he cannot be said to be trying to move. But if this were so the way to tell whether the paralysed man was trying to move would be to examine his muscles and joints, and see whether anything in fact was moving. If nothing was moving, then we could say to the poor unfortunate 'We told you to try to move your finger but (as we have discovered by looking at it) you were not trying at all'. Clearly this is not how we would tell whether the paralysed man was trying; in this case the only way to tell would be to ask him.

So what does distinguish the paralysed man who is trying to move from the paralysed man who has stopped trying? The answer lies in a fuller specification of our account of trying as doing what you can. After all, it would be odd to say that in moving my arm I am trying to climb Mount Everest, since in moving my arm I am doing something I can do. Rather, to try to do x is to do what you can in order to bring it about that x has happened.

We might say that to try to do x is to do what you can in order to do x, but this is not quite accurate. I can try to raise my arm even though there is nothing I do in order to raise my arm. What is true is that there is something I do in order to bring it about that my arm has risen—I raise my arm.

Now if the paralysed man cannot tense his biceps or bend his elbow there are some things he can do in order to raise his arm. He can grit his teeth, and knit his eyebrows. Or if he cannot do even that much he can concentrate on his arm and think about bending his elbow, just as I can try to influence the dice by concentrating on the number 6. The trouble with this sort of trying, however, is that it is always futile; concentrating on the dice, or on my arm, will not influence their behaviour in the least. But equally the trouble with the paralysed man is that, *ex hypothesi,* his trying always will be futile. He can try as hard as he likes, but, if he is completely paralysed, nothing that he does in order to move his arm will have the slightest effect.

The point is that in some special cases, such as that of the paralysed man, or trying to influence the dice without touching them, all that you can do is think about it, concentrate on what you want to happen (or, in the case of the dice, make mystic signs at them). So in these special cases merely thinking (or making mystic signs) can count as trying. But merely thinking about it (or making mystic signs) does not count as trying if there is something more effective which I can do. Taylor holds that trying is making various physical movements because he wants to reject the idea that trying consists in some internal volition or act of will. I would agree with him in this. But what he does not see is that in some special cases, where there is nothing physical that we can do, we may still try (though vainly) by doing something mental, such as thinking about it or concentrating on it.

One final point: I have analysed intention, intentional action, and trying, all with reference to doing something in order to bring something about. It might be held that this talk of acting 'in order to bring something about' simply reproduces the special features of talk about intention and intentional action. I accept the criticism; indeed, in a way, this has to be so if my analysis is to be accurate in the first place. What I have tried to do is trace some interconnections between intending, acting intentionally, and trying, and to analyse these notions by reference to acting in a certain sort of way. It would be a fascinating, but difficult and perhaps impossible, task to analyse and explain all these things without reference to purposes, reasons, and actions at all. But that is a task which I do not intend to try to perform now.

NOTES

1 Chatto and Windus, 1959.
2 Blackwell, 1958.
3 *Intention,* p 24.
4 *Intention,* p 13.
5 *Intention,* p 50.
6 *Intention,* p 49.
7 *Philosophical Investigations,* vol. II, (Blackwell, 1953), p viii.
8 'My Kinaesthetic Sensations Advise Me . . .', *Analysis* (1957).
9 *Intention,* p 9.
10 *Free Action* (Routledge and Kegan Paul, 1961), pp 39 ff.
11 cf. R. Taylor, *Action and Purpose* (Prentice Hall, 1966), Chapter 8.
12 *Free Action,* Chapter 5.
13 *Intention,* p 28.
14 *Thought and Action,* p 123.
15 *Thought and Action,* p 145.
16 *Thought and Action,* p 134; cf. also *Mind* (1958), p 11.
17 I owe this example to Mr. S. Byers.
18 *Thought and Action,* p 108.
19 *Thought and Action,* p 110.
20 It is sometimes said that decision necessarily involves the consideration of alternatives, so that I cannot be said to have decided unless I have considered some alternative. But there is always the alternative of not doing anything at all.
21 'Believe', not 'know'. The fact that I don't get out of bed does not mean that I didn't intend to, but it does mean that I didn't know that I would.
22 *Action and Purpose,* pp 82 ff.

MEMORY AND PERSONAL IDENTITY

J. J. MACINTOSH

IN THE FIRST half of this paper I shall attempt a brief and sketchy derivation of some conditions for personal identity which will show, I hope, the importance of memory in establishing personal identity. Following this, since one is sometimes so carried away by the importance of memory as to consider it all-important, I shall attempt, by developing some general considerations about 'remembering' and kindred concepts, to establish some very old-fashioned and heretical results which may be used to undermine one main argument in favour of the view that memory is *all-important* for the establishment of personal identity.

It is an interesting fact that we talk about the identity of persons rather than about the identity of human beings. It may, of course, be largely a matter of euphony: 'personal identity' flows trippingly on the tongue, but even the best of players could only mouth 'human being-al identity'. But I should like to think that there were additional, philosophically more interesting, reasons for doing this. It is possible, without too much difficulty, to drive a wedge between the notions of 'person' and 'human being'. A 'human being' is a member of a particular biological species; a 'person' is a rational and accountable agent to whom personality traits can meaningfully be assigned. There are, of course, difficulties, both biological and philosophical, in deciding whether or not a given entity is a member of a particular biological species or, come to that, what constitutes *a* biological species, but these I propose not to go into at the moment. Further, if anyone objects to this distinction on the grounds that he or she uses the term 'human being' to refer to such agents they may treat this distinction as a suggested, rather than an actual, one. Following in the footsteps of Bishop Berkeley, 'I will not quibble with you about a word'. Again, the suggestion, if it is a suggestion, has a point. It is clear that there is no *a priori* reason for thinking that every member of the species *Homo sapiens* is an agent to whom personality traits can be meaningfully assigned, or that every rational and accountable agent is a member of the species *Homo sapiens*. Indeed, the first of these propositions is contingently false, the second probably so. So, if you like, I *choose,* but choose justifiably, 'person' to refer to the class of rational and accountable agents to whom personality traits can be assigned, and it is the identity of such beings that I intend to discuss.

All the questions that philosophers have wanted to raise about the identity of persons may be raised about rational, accountable members of species other than *Homo sapiens*; conversely, the questions of identity which can be raised about members of the species *Homo sapiens* apart from the rationality, accountability, and personality traits which may be ascribed to them could equally well be raised about cows, lizards, and earthworms. I don't say that these aren't interesting questions; they are. I say only that they aren't the questions one raises about the identity of persons. For the discussion of these latter questions it is the possession of a range of what we have learned to call P-predicates that is important, and the biological status of the possessor of these predicates is, by comparison, unimportant. Finally, for the benefit of anyone who is still worried about possible violence to the language (because 'person' just *means* 'human being' and really how *can* one pretend it doesn't?), it might be worth reminding ourselves that when, in the past, people thought it worth while to talk about three persons in one substance they did not, I believe, conceive themselves to be talking about Siamese triplets, not even divine ones.

To begin this brief investigation of the identity of persons I want to look at three conditions, each of which is often held to be necessary if personal identity is to be established and which, conjointly, are almost inevitably held to be sufficient. To give them labels, these are: bodily continuity, continuity of memory, and continuity of personality traits.

Perhaps the most cogent argument in favour of the necessity of bodily continuity has been put forward by Bernard Williams. The argument goes as follows: suppose that bodily continuity were not a necessary condition of personal identity. It would follow that we could correctly identify as the same person two different human beings (at, of course, two different times). The grounds upon which we would, or would be tempted to, do this would be the displaying of memory claims by the supposedly second person which revealed knowledge only available to the first and supposedly different person, and the exhibition of personality traits by the second person which had formerly not been exhibited by the person to whom we pointed when we pointed to the second human being, but which had been exhibited by the person to whom we pointed when we pointed to the first human being. To see how real a possibility this is, Williams suggests, let us construct a case, avoiding question-begging language, and see what comes out of it. The case he in fact chooses involves a dead man, which raises additional difficulties that are, in this context, red herrings, so I shall substitute a case in which we may suppose both the contracting parties to be alive. Descriptions of such cases abound, both in fiction and in philosophical fictions, so a sketch will suffice. Let us imagine two typical dons: quiet, elderly, unmarried, unassuming, courteous, intelligent, knowledgeable, and withdrawn. Call them S and D. S, let us imagine further, is an expert—if that's not too ponderous a term—on the philosophy of F. C. S. Schiller; D, in turn, is an expert on cetacea generally, specializing on the subject of dolphins. They are members of two different colleges, let us say O and T, and are awakened in the morning by two gentlemen rejoicing in the names A and B. One morning A, the awakener of S, the member of O, comes in, saying, as usual,

> Awake! for Morning in the Bowl of Night
> Has flung the Stone that puts the Stars to Flight

and is greeted not by the usual inarticulate snarl but by the puzzled and querulous question 'What has happened to B, and what are you doing here?' To cut what could obviously become an interminably long story to the quick, although A identifies the man he has awakened as S, the member of O, the man he has awakened displays the memories, interests, and professional knowledge of D, the member of T. Or rather, to avoid begging the question, not 'of D' but 'which D, until today, has always displayed'. And let us suppose that a scene similar in the relevant respects is simultaneously enacted at T college. Well, Williams points out, we all know what the newspapers would say, but then, as he reminds us, the newspapers are *so* sensational. What conclusion ought philosophers, ignoring headlines such as 'Body Switch at Oxford, Secret Vice Among Dons Revealed' to draw from the story in *The Times*, headed 'University News'?

The story we have indicated simply reveals that a man, identified as S, now claims to be D, and displays interests and knowledge relevant to this claim. This is clearly possible. But if it is possible in the case of S, then equally it is possible for some third party M, a member of Q, awakened by C, to make the same claims and display the same interests. And if the awakening of the man identified as S in this state is enough to allow him to be identified as being *really* D, then the awakening of M in this state is enough to allow him to be identified as D as well. But this, since identity is transitive, won't do, for we would then have the man identified as S identical with D, and D identical with the man identified as M, and the man identified as S not identical with the man identified as M. Therefore, the evidence can never be sufficient to allow us to conclude, different body, but same person. That is, bodily continuity is a necessary condition of personal identity.

This argument appeals to me, partly because I find it intrinsically pleasing, and partly because I should like—mainly, I suspect, for reasons of temperament—its conclusion to be true. But 'logically impeccable' has never yet entailed 'philosophically satisfactory' and I, for one, can see no way around an objection pointed out by Penelhum.

Penelhum's objection begins, disarmingly enough, by admitting the force of the above argument, but asking us simply to imagine that the second case envisaged, namely, of *two* people awakening in this state, never in fact occurs. Suppose, he suggests, that such happenings became rather more frequent than their present zero rate, and that, in fact, at most one person at a time awoke in this state; that there was, in fact, never a case of two people making such identical claims. Would we not then be inclined to admit the claims of the awakener? And, more to the point, wouldn't we be right to do so? We might decide, for example, although it is not clear that we need do so, that, although the case of *two* people waking up and making the same claims was logically possible, it was causally impossible. We might, that is, let the man who claimed to be D *continue* as a Professor of Marine Biology, in spite of the fact that he had the same fingerprints as the man who read such a charming paper at the Joint Session only last year. And clearly, it seems, we would be right to do this; to do anything else would be immoral. Of course, the universe, having surprised us once, might, as Williams rightly points out, surprise us again. Equally, though, it might not. And if we reached the point where we had inductive or theoretical evidence, or both, that it would not, then we would *rightly* decide to identify the man who claimed to be D with D. And if we could be right to do so, it follows that bodily continuity is not and cannot be a necessary condition for personal identity.

But we should not here, as Penelhum reminds us, forget that though this might well be a correct decision, it would none the less be a *decision*. In the absence of a body there is no way of distinguishing between veridical memories and what might be called accurate retro-cognition. It would be a decision, and it would be one which, in the situation envisaged—at most one D-claimant in the world at any one time—would be philosophically respectable.

I conclude, on the basis of this, that bodily identity, in any normal sense of 'body', is not a necessary condition of personal identity.

I turn now to the question of personality traits. One of the difficulties in the past has been that it has often been far from clear what exactly is meant by the term 'personality traits'. However, this has changed somewhat in the recent past, and psychologists have made what is to my mind a most exciting start on the task of imposing clarity in this field. I shan't try to give here anything more than the briefest possible sketch of what they are up to (the job is anyway beautifully done in Cattell's *The Scientific Analysis of Personality*). What they have done is, by a technique of gradual refinement, to sort out the correlated variables in the behavioural capacities and abilities of large numbers of people. With the introduction of computers to do the multivariate analysis this has become a possibility. Among some of these capacities and abilities, as well as in answers to questionnaires, there are very strong correlations. Thus, to take a familiar one, there is a strong positive correlation between ability to find synonyms, match patterns, and continue number series, among other things. In this way some twenty-odd personality factors have been sorted out and isolated. Once this has been done there still remains the question of how to interpret (or label) these factors. For example, the factor partially characterized above is commonly referred to as intelligence. It is, of course, open to anyone to remark that this is not what he means by intelligence. But this, I think, need not worry the psychologist. All he need remark is that he has, at least, isolated a unitary factor which can be measured by standardized and trustworthy means. Whether or not the label he chooses comes close to our intuitive notions need not be his concern. And, in fact, just because our intuitive notions do not always square with psychological results, the psychologists sometimes purposely eschew familiar terms when labelling these factors and invent technical labels. So, then, we are armed nowadays, if need be, with a fairly precise set of quantitative personality factors. Apart from the comfort of having an underlying foundation on which philosophers themselves need not work, there is a point of further interest to our topic which has emerged from this work. If we take any collection of measurable factors we can plot them against one another to notice whether any significant clusterings occur. This is familiar enough in the two-variable case, e.g. when we plot frequency of automobile accidents against age of drivers. But there is no reason to limit the number of variables to two. We can always plot n variables against one another in an n-dimensional space. When this is done with the results of personality factor tests it is discovered that individuals are not uniformly distributed throughout the space in question but form quite definite clusters. No doubt a good deal of this clustering is due to the directions imposed by actual societies, but it is at least an open possibility that some of the clustering is due to not yet explained relations between the factors themselves. It is already established, that is, that people fall into types; it may be that this is more than a merely contingent matter. It will suffice for our purposes, I think, to concentrate on some of the more important personality factors. Suppose we have a man who is reserved, highly intelligent, and assertive. Then, whether as the result of an accident causing brain damage or a lobotomy, or what have you, he becomes a man who is outgoing, stupid, and humble. And, let us suppose, there is a large change in these three areas. Would we be justified in holding the man who is now outgoing, stupid, and humble responsible for the actions of the man who was reserved, intelligent, and assertive? Ought we, e.g., to punish the second man for the illegal financial manœuvres of the first, or praise him for the scientific discoveries of the first? I cannot see that we ought. But if we have two persons, P_1, who is fully responsible (in the sense of praiseworthy or blameworthy) for a large number and range of actions A_1 to A_n, and P_2, who is not at all responsible for these actions, then P_1 and P_2 are two different persons. They are not, that is, the same accountable agent, though they may well be the same human being. Clearly there are going to be large numbers of borderline cases here. This is what one should expect: persons are, after all, extremely complex. But the fact that there are borderline cases does not mean that it is impossible to come to a decision in the extreme cases; and where we are imagining the case of a human being moving between two *widely* separated clusters, then, I suggest, we have an example of same human being, different person. That is, continuity of some subset of personality factors is a necessary condition of personal identity. And conversely, change of some reasonably large subset of personality factors is enough to yield a different person, a different rational and accountable agent.

And, really, it is the remark prefaced by 'conversely' that is important here. For, in a way, the phrase 'continuity of personality traits' begs the question: of course, one might say, if they *continue* the person is the same: what else would they continue in? Perhaps one should say, more precisely, that if a person P_2 has personality traits, a large number of which are quantitatively identical with those of P_1, then, given other factors, identity may be established, but if a person P_2 has personality traits, a large number of which are quantitively highly dissimilar to those of P_1, then P_1 and P_2 are not identical.

Perhaps at this point something further should be said about the notion of responsibility. Responsibility cannot be used as a criterion, of course, for if we were to try to so use it circularity would result. Before P_1 can be praised or blamed for the acts of P_2 it must be granted that P_1 and P_2 are the same person (apart, that is, from the derivative cases of causal responsibility: blaming the parent for the child's behaviour, praising the piano teacher for his pupil's fine recital, and so on). Still, the notion of responsibility, though certainly not a criterion, may yet be a very useful guide: if we decide, on whatever grounds, that P_1 and P_2 are not the same accountable agent, then there must be reasons independent of our intuitive feelings about responsibility which justify this. And a sufficient change in personality traits, I suggest, would provide just such a justification.

This brings us to the third of the three traditional factors, viz. memory. From what has just been said, it follows that memory is anyway not a sufficient condition for establishing identity. It remains to be seen whether it is a necessary condition. And then, since many people have seemed to think it a sufficient condition, an analysis of memory is required which will show why the apparently strong reasoning by which this position is supported is incorrect.

The standard sort of case which is considered here is that of the amnesiac. Total amnesia is rare, but not, so far as I am aware, non-existent. Let us define it to include, among other things, loss of language. This has certainly happened. Let us, in addition, broaden our scope to include the following non-existent but clearly allowable possibility. Suppose that medical men discovered that it was possible by independent means to distinguish two different sorts of amnesia: the one, where the patient sometimes regained his or her memories; the other, where he or she did not. Let us restrict ourselves to this imaginary second case and consider someone suffering from it. Applying once more the loose and intuitive, but highly useful, criterion of responsibility, we ask ourselves whether or not the amnesiac victim should be held responsible for the actions performed before the commencement of the amnesia.

In such a case it seems clear that it would be wrong to hold the man in question responsible for the actions committed before the onslaught of amnesia. But if this would be wrong it once again follows that he is not the same responsible agent, i.e. not the same person.

From this introductory sketch I conclude that something like exact similarity of a large number of personality traits and continuity of a body of memories are both necessary conditions for personal identity, but that neither is sufficient by itself. However, the two taken together may be sufficient, as we saw, and if bodily continuity is conjoined we have a set which is logically and not just empirically sufficient.

But now, if this is the case, how are we to answer the objection that if A remembers how a certain event, say E, appeared from a particular point of view, say V, at a particular time, say T, then A is identical with the person who witnessed E from V at T? This, it may be said, is not only true but analytic. But it is incompatible with the conclusions just derived. Therefore these conclusions are either invalidly derived or based on false premises.

In an attempt to get around this I should like to make a few general remarks about memory, and to begin *this* endeavour I should like to make a few even more general remarks.

'Remember' is one of a large group of words which display certain common features. Some others are 'believe', 'love', 'doubt', 'like', 'want', 'intend', 'sympathize', 'understand', 'hope', 'know', and 'worship', as well as 'feels guilty about', 'feels happy about', and so on.

One feature that all of these have in common is that they are functionless in the imperative form, unless the form 'ϕ' is elliptical for 'pretend to ϕ' or 'try to ϕ'. That this is so is not just a grammatical accident, however. It follows from the philosophically more interesting common feature which they share. This is the fact that they are all capable of being looked at from three quite different points of view in respect of their correct or incorrect application. On reflection, this is perhaps an obvious consequence of the job we want these words to do, viz. reporting our own mental states, and commenting on those of others.

The first point of view I label, for convenience, the logical one: we impose certain restrictions on the use of these words. Thus, we cannot *know* or *remember* anything false, what is *remembered* must be a *past* action or event, or something with which one became acquainted in the past or which was acquired in the past (e.g. events, propositions, persons, skills), we cannot now *want* some known past event not to have happened (although we can wish that it had not), we cannot *understand* anything which is not complex, and so on. From this point of view we acquire a necessary but not sufficient condition for the use of these words: we acquire restrictions which will let us disallow a given use, but are insufficient to characterize true as opposed to false remarks in which they occur.

The other two points of view arise out of the fact that there are two (connected) jobs for these words to do. From the fact that we can and do use them to comment on other people, it follows that we can have what we might call behavioural evidence for deciding whether or not, in a given situation, one of these words is correctly or incorrectly applied. The term 'behavioural evidence' is to be taken in what is almost a ludicrously wide sense here, however. For example, we might let in facial expressions; we might even let in facial expressions of which we are not consciously aware. In a recent widely reported experiment conducted at the University of Chicago it was discovered that there is a correlation between liking someone and the amount of dilation of one's pupils when looking at the person in question or a photograph of that person. Further, there was evidence that this dilation or contraction in fact influences (correctly) an observer's belief about this attitude even when he is unaware consciously of the state of the pupils of the person he is observing. It may be that 'with pupils dilated' will never replace 'dewy-eyed' in romantic fiction, but it none the less appears to be of greater practical value. And it seems likely that it is often by just such unconsciously perceived cues that we decide whether, e.g. someone is lying, pretending, or being deceitful in one way or another. All this, however, is only one side of the story.

The other side results from the fact that we use these terms not only to comment on other people but also to report on ourselves. That is, while it is certainly not the case that we are always the best judges of our own likes, wants, beliefs, and sympathies, we are often good enough judges of these things. And, in the nature of things, we are seldom in a position to observe our facial features when we are disposed to report on, or make a claim about, these matters. Our knowledge of these matters, that is, is not based on behavioural evidence, not even 'behavioural evidence' in the very wide sense just outlined. It follows, as I hardly need remind you, that not only may these terms be applied to others on the basis of their behaviour or physical and physiological states but also to oneself on the basis of one's own mental states.

It follows, in particular, that we can and do decide that something is a piece of knowledge, or a memory, or a belief without either having or needing any supporting evidence other than our own state of mind. And it is, of course, doubtful whether this latter ought to be called *evidence* at all. To do so sounds suspiciously like the thin end of a clarion call which would usher a ghostly theatre on to the philosophical stage.

It does not follow from the fact that we do not in general need supporting evidence for our memory and knowledge claims that we always get them right. Nor does this follow for any of the other members of the class we have singled out, though this is sometimes harder to see than in the cases of knowledge and memory. To pursue this further here would, however, be beside the point; consequently, even though what is beside the point may be more interesting than the point, I propose not to go into any detail about these others here.

It has even been argued, for the particular case of remembering, that it is something more than a contingent matter that we do not, in general, need supporting evidence. For, it is argued, if it were not the case that we do not, in general, need supporting evidence here, we could not have the segment of our language that deals with memory operating in the way that it does. But I do not propose to pursue this more fully here. I do not, I think, fully appreciate the strength of the argument in favour of this claim, and I am uncertain of the force of the conclusion. Further, it is not a claim which will be necessary for what follows; I therefore leave it, having drawn it to your attention or, more likely, reminded you of it.

Having reminded ourselves of these three general avenues of approach, let us look more closely at the case of remembering. 'Remember', as has often been noted, is closely connected with 'know'; I can remember that such and such only if the such and such is in fact the case; if a person remembers that such and such or remembers how to so and so, then it follows that he knows that such and such or knows how to so and so, although of course the converse does not hold. It is not, however, these obvious similarities that are the most important feature of memory here, but an equally obvious dissimilarity, namely that memory can be memory of events. I can remember *that* my breakfast coffee cup was white and smooth but I can also remember the whiteness and smoothness of the cup. And it is this sort of memory, memory of events or of my own actions, which philosophers have often and understandably concentrated on. It is this sort of memory, too, which is concerned in the putative tautology which began this section of our discussion, namely that if A remembers how E appeared from V at T, then A is identical with the person who observed E from V at T. I shall therefore talk now exclusively about this type of memory, event memory, and not about propositional or habit memory.

One of the striking features of certain past philosophers, as opposed to more recent writers on the subject of memory, is that they give full weight to what I have labelled the psychological facet of remembering. (It's only a label, by the way. 'Experiential facet' might be better.) This led at least some of them into suggesting that to remember is to have a mental image of a distinctive type. In saying what it was that made this distinctive type distinctive they differed, but agreed anyway that the image itself was essential. In this they have not been followed by contemporary philosophers, who are more interested in what we have here called the logical facet of 'remembering'. And, indeed, that mental images are not an essential feature of remembering is something which, nowadays, we all know. Only, I wonder if it is true.

It is sometimes suggested that one of the reasons which led these philosophers to suggest that mental images were essential was that they fell into the familiar philosophical trap of concentrating too exclusively on visual cases and generalizing illegitimately from these. This trap, although well known, is a trap into which it is perilously easy to fall. Let us therefore avoid it by concentrating initially on kinaesthetic sensations, which are suitably far removed from the visual field. We have all of us had, I suspect, the not very exhilarating experience of saying or doing something which embarrassed us acutely. Clearly this sort of experience is likely to stay with us for a fair while, and we may easily remember it without difficulty a day or a week or a year after it has occurred. Indeed, the difficulty is not with remembering but with forgetting. However, it is not only that we can remember easily enough *that* we were embarrassed; we sometimes have the unpleasant experience, usually in the insomniac early hours of the morning, of, as it were, reliving the experience, or remembering not only that we were embarrassed but that *just this* was how it was. I'm not sure how to put this into words, but I trust this is not too important, since I am trying not to describe the type of experience, but to remind you of it.

That is, in cases like this we distinguish between remembering *that* I was ϕ and *how it was* to be ϕ, i.e. being ϕ. And the memory image in this particular case is essential. This is true equally for certain tactile memories. And the same is true for visual memories: if I remember the whiteness of my coffee cup, as opposed to remembering that the cup was white, then a memory image is essential. The question 'Do you remember the actual whiteness and smoothness of your cup, or do you just remember that it was white and smooth?' seems to me to be perfectly understandable. This is, of course, a digression, but it might show that concentrating on the actual memory experience, as opposed to memory claims (i.e. the linguistic behaviour by which we judge the remembering of others) or the logic of remembering, does not necessarily lead us into error.

Now, given that we have these three distinct standards by means of which we may decide that a given member of our group of what we might call psychological verbs is or is not being correctly applied, it is not surprising to find that they sometimes come into conflict. For example, if someone says that he understands an individual flower, or wants the well-known saucer of mud for its own sake, or believes that God is a perfect number, we may well be uncertain what to say. We can, of course, *decide* to say that, e.g., the man who claims to want a saucer of mud as an end in itself is making a mistake about himself, that, *really*, there must be an end to which this is, for him, consciously or unconsciously, the means. We may even brainwash him into agreement. But the job our *really* is doing here is a job of decision: we are playing down the mental criterion at the expense of one or both of the others.

Sometimes, as in the case of 'know', we will be fairly clear about our priorities, about certain fundamental demands we are prepared to make: what's known must be true. But sometimes, as in the case of 'belief', conflicts may leave us genuinely undecided. If the man who professes to believe a category mistake behaves *as if* this was one of his beliefs, and is evidently sincere when professing it, ought we none the less to disallow his claim on the grounds that only what could be true or false is believable, and conclude perhaps that he didn't *really* believe it, that for him as for us it was at best a metaphor? There is, I think, no clear answer to this question. If it ever arose—it may, for all I know, in mental hospitals—we would probably decide that this was a case where, having seen the race, we could dispense with the shouting. The difficulty with this, though, is that in this, as in similar cases, it is not just that we decide to dispense with the shouting: we might want to shout, all right, only we don't know who to shout for.

That is, with this sort of term, there is always a possibility that, judged by one standard which the circumstances of the particular case make it tempting to apply, the term is being used perfectly appropriately, while, judged by one of our other two standards, the term is being used inappropriately, or misused.

With that particular sort of memory we are now keeping in mind there is not the possibility of conflict among all three standards, but only between two. This arises from the fact that there is no distinctive evidence for such remembering apart from communicative behaviour. This is, of course, sufficient; but it is important here that all non-linguistic behaviour which is evidence for A's remembering the ϕ-ness of X is also evidence for A's remembering that X is ϕ. But since, as we said, there is in general no need for external justification of such claims and often in particular cases no possibility of such justification, it follows that in the case of this sort of remembering a good deal is going to rest on the justification of the word's use in terms of the criterion of mental experiences.

What are we to say about this criterion? It would seem (another unfashionable view coming up, I'm afraid) that since we can and do get our remembering right, there must be some intrinsic characteristic (to use a very bad term for lack of a better one) in virtue of which we identify our experience as a memory experience. Russell's 'feeling of familiarity' was an ingenious but not wholly felicitous attempt to isolate this intrinsic characteristic; Hume had a less successful shot still. I don't think it's important that we can't say what it is about the memory experience that allows us to describe it as such. We can't do this—or at least, I can't—for itches, tickles, burns, and aches, either, but we manage all right.

We might note in passing that it is not being claimed that we can *define* this sort of experience without referring to, for example, veridical and non-veridical memories: but what can be done is to call our attention to its existence as a recognizable class, by means of, as it were, a quasi-ostensive definition.

So far, then, it has been argued that there is a recognizable class of mental experiences, of which genuine memories are a subspecies, the members of which serve as the basis of our memory claims.

On the other hand, not all our memory claims are allowable. How does this come about? Surely—privileged access and all that—either the thing is recognized as a member of the class or it is not. And if it is so recognized it is a member; if not, not. Well, first of all there is the point that we can be wrong about our mental experiences as we can about anything else: the concept of incorrigible knowledge is a bogus one. But this is a debatable or anyway a debated point and I don't propose to pursue it here. The point is that even if we get the mental status of the thing right, it may still not count as a memory. Why not? The answer is, in terms of the distinctions we have been setting up, that we set up additional restrictions on the use of 'remember'. This is where what I have tentatively dubbed the logical criterion cuts in.

There obviously are a number of such restrictions. The point to bear in mind is that they are *restrictions* upon a class which may be independently picked out, and, as restrictions, they must be justified. There is no question of such a restriction being true or false: it must be useful or otherwise, and if it is not useful, there is no need for us to accept it.

Let us now look at some of the restrictions we place on the notion of 'memory'. First and most obvious is the restriction that the memory be of an actual event. It is interesting at this point to note the existence of the word 'misremember', which begins with a bow to the logical criterion and ends with a curtsy to the psychological one. 'Mis' because I got it wrong, but 'remember' because it's that sort of thing all right. And clearly, this sort of restriction is not only justifiable but desirable. If we are to have a language that enables us to separate appearance from reality, a full-blown public language, we need this sort of distinction.

The next restriction that comes to mind is, I suppose, the restriction to the past: if I remember at some time, say, t_2, the ϕ-ness of X, then there is a time t_1 such that X was ϕ at t_1 and t_1 is earlier than t_2. Notice that we must here distinguish two cases: first, the case where we *restrict* our use of the term to past events, and second, the case where we don't so restrict our term, but in fact only past events are the subject of the class of mental experiences we are considering. That is, this reference to the past may be a fact about human beings, *or* a fact about our word 'remember'. At the moment, of course, cases of precognition are extremely uncommon, perhaps so uncommon as to be non-existent. This means that we don't find ourselves faced with any practical problem here. It may even be that we shall convince ourselves that precognition is logically impossible. And then, of course, everything would be straightforward and we could happily accept the restriction to pastness. But since it is not completely clear that precognition is logically impossible, let us indulge ourselves and imagine that precognition either begins to occur or (if one thinks it does occur, though rarely) becomes more common. If we allow this possibility, what would we, or rather what *ought* we to, say when we find ourselves in the position of Alice, faced with the White Queen's charge, 'It's a poor sort of memory that only works one way'? How could we justify this restriction to *past* events, given that the mental experiences on which the precognitive claims are based resemble the mental experiences on which memory claims are based in all respects save that one refers to the past and the other to the future? We might decide in such a case to speak only of remembering the past and never of remembering the future. Probably we should do so, if for no other reason than the historical one: that people have always remembered past events, and the supposedly substantial segment of people in our imaginary case who have begun to have non-inductive knowledge of the future are comparative latecomers. On the other hand, it would simply be a case for decision, and I cannot see any philosophical reason for choosing either possibility over the other.

There is, though, a third restriction we impose which might lead us indirectly to decide the precognition case in favour of remembering (only) the past. We are all familiar with cases where we are just not sure whether what we have is a memory or not, although it refers to an actual past event all right. The sort of case I have in mind is the type induced by constant repetition of family anecdotes concerning events which occurred when one was a young child. We are inclined to say, about such putative memories, perhaps they are, perhaps they aren't. Now since the first two conditions are clearly present, what is it that we suspect to be lacking? The answer seems to be that the event E, of which this experience is a memory or putative memory, must be causally related to the memory experience. And when there is reason to suspect that the causal antecedents of the memory experience are other than E, we feel hesitant about calling it a memory of E. I must confess myself quite unclear about the justification of this particular restriction. I content myself here merely with pointing out that it does seem to be a restriction we impose. But we might notice that if it is justifiable, that is, if memories must be causally tied to events, then we may decide that precognitions ought not to be assimilated to memories on the grounds that the future cannot bring about the past. But this claim is itself a long, difficult, and entirely different story about which I shall say nothing further here.

I hope by now we have familiarized ourselves with, or bored ourselves into accepting, the notion that what we call memories are precipitated out of a wider class of mental experiences by the addition of restrictions which must themselves be justified. Let us now, therefore, return to the professed tautology which was to show that memory is a sufficient condition of personal identity and (consequently) that continuity of personality traits could not be a necessary condition.

The tautology, or apparent tautology, that if A remembers how E appeared from V at T then A is identical with the person who perceived E from V at T now appears as a recommendation for an additional restriction on the class of memories. Our test case, you remember, was of a man whose personality traits were so changed by an accident, or lobotomy, or what have you that we would feel it wrong to blame him for the production of past events or inconsequent to praise him, and thus, in spite of his retention of memories, it would be a mistake to call him the same person.

What are we to do with this case in the light of the suggested new restriction? The restriction might be applied in one of two ways. First, it might be a recommendation that we should refer to the memories of the accident or lobotomy victim as being 'apparent memories', not memories at all. But why on earth should we accept this? There is, so far as I can see, no reason to do so and every reason not to. The only justification for imposing such a restriction would be in terms of the restriction itself, which is to say there is no justification. Second, it might be a recommendation that we *insist* that this person, after the lobotomy, was the same person as we pointed to when we pointed to this body *before* the lobotomy. But again, what would be the justification for this insistence? That this is what we *mean* by memory? How do we know, until we look at such a case? Even if this is our current use of 'memory' (which I doubt), mightn't we decide (or, more strongly, *ought* we not to decide) that in this area our use of 'memory' was therefore misleading, inconsistent with our other views, and hence to be altered? For, after all, this insistence would force us to adopt as morally correct a position which can be seen to be morally incorrect. But when putative linguistic niceties begin to impose on moral rightness, the time has come to revise language, not morality. I conclude, therefore, that this objection has no weight, that this restriction cannot be justified, and that memory is a necessary but not a sufficient condition of personal identity. I have suggested that, in addition, the continuity of some substantial set of personality factors is a necessary though not sufficient condition, and that bodily continuity, while necessary for strict certainty, for logical correctness, might be such that it would be, empirically, unnecessary. With which distressing conclusion I end.

MATERIALISM AND THE ARGUMENT FROM DISTINCT EXISTENCES[1]

BRIAN MEDLIN

I WISH TO discuss in this paper an argument which I believe to have done considerable damage in recent British and American philosophy. The argument seems to involve a confusion of two principles.

I. If two things are numerically distinct, then it is possible that one should exist without the other.

II. If two things are numerically distinct, then there can be no logical connections between them.

The first principle is perhaps a plausible one as long as it is not applied to abstract entities. It is not obvious how we could ever be certain that it is true; yet in the absence of clear counter-examples it may seem fair enough to adopt it as a working rule in philosophy. The trouble is that it is easy to suppose that I is equivalent to II. But then it is not clear exactly what II means. To discover this we need only try to translate II into the formal mode. It is not difficult to produce translations of II into the formal mode that are clearly false.

Shortly, I shall present instances of the argument from distinct existences which seem to turn upon principle II. Before doing so, I wish to declare my polemical motives for discussing this argument. My purpose is to defend central-state materialism.[2] Very briefly, this is the doctrine that states of mind are states of the body. I shall not try here to expound fully my version of this doctrine. But I shall say what is necessary for the purposes of this paper. When I say of somebody, perhaps myself, that he is in a certain state of mind, I say of him that he is in a certain causal condition, that there is operating within him a cause which tends to produce behaviour falling within a certain range.[3] What makes this causal condition so special is that in talking about it *as a mental state* I do not commit myself to the view that it is a physical condition. This does not mean that I commit myself to the view that it is a non-physical condition. I claim that mental states are almost certainly states of the body; that, as a matter of fact, being in such and such a mental state consists in having this and that process occurring in one's central nervous system. (If it should be claimed that 'mental' means at least 'non-physical', then the reply is that materialism implies at least that there are no such mental states.)

Such a brief statement of the doctrine will hardly render it plausible to an unsympathetic reader. But my purpose here is a limited one—to show that a certain pattern of argumentation is unsound and in doing so to defend materialism against a certain objection. In addition, I shall suggest that there is no general reason for accepting behaviourism, which is the only serious physicalistic rival to central-state materialism. I shall point out also that certain kinds of dualism are proof against the objection I rebut. I shall not attempt to do more. General objections to central-state materialism, sound or otherwise, will be irrelevant as objections to this paper, though they will have some relevance to my philosophical motives. Objections to my proposed account of intention that do not establish the validity of the argument from distinct existences will also be irrelevant: it is useless to say that my complaints against that argument are ineffectual because my account of intention is false. For what I show is that a certain argument against my account of intention is unsound. To do this it is not necessary for me to establish my account of intention. It is not necessary either that my account should be correct.

Now let us look at a few arguments which seem to turn on principle II. My first source is from Professor Melden's *Free Action* (London, 1961, pp 52–3).

This then is the logical incoherence involved in the doctrine of acts of volition: Acts of volition are alleged to be direct causes of certain bodily phenomena (whether these be brain occurrences, as Pritchard supposed them to be, or muscle movements, as we have been assuming for the sake of argument, is of no matter), just as the latter are causes of the raising of one's arm. For it is alleged, just as we raise our arms by moving our muscles, so we move our muscles by willing them to move. But no account of the alleged volitions is intelligible that does not involve a reference to the relevant bodily phenomena. And no interior cause, mental or physiological, can have this logical feature of acts of volition. Let the interior event which we call 'the act of volition' be mental or physical (*which* it is will make no difference at all), it must be logically distinct from the alleged effect—this surely is one lesson we can derive from a reading of Hume's discussion of causation. Yet nothing can be an act of volition that is not logically connected with that which is willed—the act of willing is intelligible only as the act of willing whatever it is that is willed. In short, there could not be such an interior event like an act of volition since (here one is reminded of Wittgenstein's famous remark about meaning) nothing of that sort could have the required logical consequences.

The fact that I criticize this argument does not mean that I believe that there are acts of volition.

Again in *Free Action* (pp 32–3) we find Melden discussing kinaesthetic sensations in the same way—this time with a sceptical twist. Kinaesthetic sensations are, supposedly, those feelings by which we are able to tell the position of our limbs. But, says Melden, they can only be described in terms of the position of our limbs. Quoting Wittgenstein, he says:

> His reply in the *Investigations* is decisive:
>
> 'Suppose I want to describe a feeling to someone and I tell him, "Do *this* and then you'll get it" and I hold my arm or head in a particular way. Now is this a description of a feeling? And when shall I say that he has understood what feeling I meant?—He will have to give a *further* description of the feeling afterwards.
>
> ' "Do *this,* and you'll get it." Can't there be a doubt here? Mustn't there be one, if it is a feeling that is meant?' (pp 185e–186e).

Then Melden continues:

> If all we can say about our alleged kinaesthetic sensations is that they are the ones one gets when one moves one's arm, there must be a doubt that anyone has understood what it means to say that one tells from one's kinaesthetic sensations that one moves one's arm; . . . In short, unless the alleged kinaesthetic sensations can be described, we have no way of understanding what anyone means when he says that he can tell from his kinaesthetic sensations that his arm is moving.

It is claimed here that the kinaesthetic sensations cannot be described independently of what they are supposed to 'tell us'. (They are supposed to tell us the disposition of our limbs.) To complete the argument: if they could be independently described, then they would not be kinaesthetic sensations, for then they would be logically distinct from the disposition of our limbs and could not *tell* us what it was. If the argument is not to be completed thus, then we have been given no reason to suppose that kinaesthetic sensations may not be characterized as, say, brain-processes.

Melden is not arguing here that there are no bodily sensations. He admits that there are, and that if a man were anaesthetized so that his sensations were blotted out he might well be unable to tell the disposition of his limbs. He is maintaining that there are no kinaesthetic sensations—that is, no sensations which serve to inform us of the disposition of our bodies. A little thought should show us, however, that we can use Melden's argument to get rid of any sensation at all. At least this argument will obliterate sensations if we grant the assumption that to characterize a state of mind *as a state of mind* is to characterize it in terms of its behavioural manifestations. I would want to argue for a thesis rather like this assumption so that I am obliged to meet Melden's argument. Further, such a thesis seems to be implied by the weakest possible interpretation of Wittgenstein's slogan, 'An "inner process" stands in need of outward criteria' (*Philosophical Investigations*, G. E. M. Anscombe (tr.) (Oxford, 1953), par. 580).

I think a similar argument is to be found in Miss Anscombe's excellent monograph, *Intention* (Oxford, 1961, pp 28–9).

That an action is not called 'intentional' in virtue of any extra feature which exists when it is performed, is clear from the following: Let us suppose that there is such a feature, and let us call it '*I*'. Now the intentional character of the action cannot be asserted without giving the description under which it is intentional, since the same action can be intentional under one description and unintentional under another. It is however something actually done that is intentional, if there is an intentional action at all. A man no doubt contracts certain muscles in picking up a hammer; but it would generally be false to call his contraction of muscles the intentional act that he performed. This does not mean that his contraction of muscles was unintentional. Let us call it 'preintentional'. Are we to say that *I*, which is supposed to be the feature in virtue of which what he does is an intentional action, is something which accompanies a preintentional action, or movement of his body? If so, then the preintentional movement + *I* guarantees that *an* intentional action is performed: but which one? Clearly our symbol '*I*' must be interpreted as a description, or as having an internal relation to a description, of an action. But nothing about the man considered by himself in the moment of contracting his muscles, and nothing in the contraction of the muscles, can possibly determine the content of that description; which therefore may be *any* one, if we are merely considering what can be determined about the man by himself in the moment. Then it is a mere happy accident that an *I* relevant to the wider context and further consequences *ever* accompanies the preintentional movements in which a man performs a given intentional action.

There are two ways of interpreting this passage. Under the first interpretation the argument seeks to establish the conclusion that to say that an action is intentional is to classify it as an action of a certain kind and not to say anything about the 'mental' causes of the action. This conclusion is a linguistic thesis. On the hypothesis that the events we call intentional actions are produced by intentions, which are mental states, this linguistic thesis would not be a very interesting one. Under the second interpretation the argument seeks to confound the hypothesis I have just mentioned.

If we wish to interpret the argument in the second way, the important thing to remember about our supposed intentions is that the description 'the intention to do *A*' does have 'an internal relation to a description of an action'. It has an internal relation to the description of the action *A as* the action *A*. Miss Anscombe may be interpreted as arguing that the intention to do *A* cannot be an 'extra feature which exists when *A* is performed'—that the intention cannot be, for example, some causal condition producing those events which constitutes the agent's doing *A*. Her reason would be that 'nothing about the man considered by himself in the moment of contracting his muscles . . . can possibly determine the content' of the description of the action *A*. Hence no causal condition of the man could determine the content of that description. And hence no causal condition of the man could be the intention to do *A*.

If it is fair to interpret Miss Anscombe in this way, and I can find no other interpretation which makes her conclusion an interesting one, then she is using what I call the argument from distinct existences. She is using more than this. She points out that an action may be intentional under one description and unintentional under another. This point would not carry the conclusion of the argument under the second interpretation. The argument from distinct existences is still needed. For let us suppose that *doing A* is one complex relational property of agents while doing *B* is another.[4] And let us suppose that the intention to do *A* (or *B*) is a certain kind of causal condition of agents which tends to result in their doing *A*. (This is not begging the question. I wish only to show that Miss Anscombe's observation is compatible with this supposition.) Now frequently a man may do *B* in doing *A*, and sometimes he will do both *A* and *B* when he has the intention to do *A*, but not the intention to do *B*. So that his action will be intentional under the description 'the action *A*', but not under the description 'the action *B*'. To rule out as not even possible this account of how an action may be intentional under one description and unintentional under another, we need to be able to rule out the assumption that intentions are causal conditions. To rule this out, Miss Anscombe uses the argument from distinct existences (if she does).

The argument from distinct existences is not confined to the philosophy of mind. In *Principia Ethica* (Cambridge, 1903) G. E. Moore argues in the following way: the word 'good' whenever it is predicated of something stands for some property which all good things have in common. There are 'natural' properties, such as *pleasant*. The word 'good' does not mean the same as any expression which stands for a natural property. (This follows from the fact that it always makes sense to ask of such a property whether it is good.) Hence, the property that the word 'good' stands for is not identical with any natural property.

This argument differs from those so far considered in that it depends not on principle II but on its converse. But the considerations which I shall use against the arguments of Professor Melden and Miss Anscombe could be used against Moore's argument. I do not mean by this to imply that I think that 'good' does stand for a natural property.

It should be clear how the argument would dispose of central-state materialism. We have seen it applied to acts of volition, for which I have no affection. It has been applied as well to kinaesthetic sensations and to intentions (if that was Miss Anscombe's intention). It can be generalized for any mental event, condition, or what-not. This means that it would be fatal to dualism as well as to materialism.

Central-state materialism and interactionist dualism share a common framework. According to both doctrines, states of mind are causal conditions having behavioural manifestations. When I talk of dualism hereafter I shall, unless I say otherwise, mean a special kind of dualism. I believe that a state of mind is a condition of the person which tends to produce behaviour falling within a roughly determinate range. And I believe that to characterize a state as a mental state is to characterize it as a condition which tends to produce behaviour of certain kinds. This can be put by saying that mental states are defined in terms of their behavioural manifestations. (I am not concerned to argue for this thesis in the present paper, only to defend it from a specific rebuttal. Nor am I concerned here to state the thesis in any but a rough-and-ready manner.) The kind of dualist I have in mind is one who agrees with me on this point. He maintains, in disagreement, that mental states are not physical states. There may be other kinds of dualist who maintain that in characterizing a mental state *as* a mental state we make no reference to behaviour. Such dualists will have other troubles, but the argument from distinct existences will not worry them.

Let us denote an arbitrary mental state by '*M*' and call its characteristic behavioural manifestations *P*-type effects. How does the argument from distinct existences work against interactionist dualism? It will be said that, according to the dualist, the inner cause *M* which tends to produce *P*-type effects is:

a) distinct from *P*-type effects and from any tendency of the person to manifest *P*-type effects; and

b) not describable independently of *P*-type manifestations.

As we shall see later, the dualist need not allow *b*) at all. But for the moment we shall say that *b*) is forced upon him if the mental state *M* is to do the logical job of producing *P*-type effects, if it is to have what Melden would call 'the required logical consequences'.

For *M* just *is* what produces *P*-type effects. Now, the argument continues, if *a*) is true, *b*) is false, and if *b*) is true, *a*) is false. If the supposed inner cause cannot be described except in terms of its effects, then it is not distinct from them and hence not a cause of which they are effects. If it is distinct from them as a cause, then it cannot be that of which (as manifestations of a state of mind) they are manifestations.

Central-state materialism involves at least the claim that the inner cause M is:

a') distinct from P-type effects and from any tendency of the person to manifest P-type effects; and

b') describable quite independently of P-type manifestations.

But against this it may be claimed that if either a') or b') is true, then the mental states M cannot do the job they are supposed to do. It cannot be an accident that, for example, an intention to do A 'makes' me do A. There is some *logical* connection between intention and intentional action. In general, there is some logical connection between a mental state and its manifestations. But this cannot be so if the mental state is distinct from its manifestations.

The argument from distinct existences has used us roughly. Before we retaliate, let us look at a passage in which Professor D. M. Armstrong, then in his unregenerate pre-central-state-materialistic days, flirts with the argument. The passage (*Perception and the Physical World* (London, 1962), pp 90–1) has the virtue that it comes near to showing what is wrong with the argument:

> There is another line of attack on this attempt to distinguish sense-impressions from beliefs or inclinations to believe we are (immediately) perceiving something, which may in the end come to the same thing. If there is only a contingent connection between the having of a sense-impression and the belief or inclination to believe we are (immediately) perceiving something, then it ought to be possible to characterize the sense-impression in other ways than by appealing to the belief (inclination to believe). Thus, there is a contingent connection between father and son, for the father is the cause, or at any rate a part cause, of the existence of the latter. But the characterization 'father' is not logically independent of the causal relation a father has to a son. However it is possible to characterize the being that begets a son in a way that is independent of this causal relationship, e.g. as a man. Now it may well be that, on any showing, the most *convenient* way of characterizing our sense-impressions or perceptual experiences would be to say 'It is the sort of experience that makes me believe, or inclines me to believe, that I am perceiving an object of a certain sort'. But if there is only a contingent connection between sense-impressions and beliefs or inclinations to believe, it must be possible to give the former an independent characterization, however inconvenient it may be for us, or however little interested we may be in doing so.
>
> But is such independent characterization in fact possible?

What are Armstrong's reasons for doubting that the required independent characterization is possible? He gives none. That nobody has been able to provide such an independent characterization might make one think that the job couldn't be done. But without begging the question this could not be used against a theory which purported to give an independent characterization. There is one objection which Armstrong cannot bring against the view that sense-impressions are distinct from 'beliefs or inclinations to believe we are (immediately) perceiving something'. He cannot say that since sense-impressions are defined in terms of the beliefs they are alleged to produce, they cannot be characterized independently of those beliefs, and that this means that sense-impressions cannot be distinct from those beliefs and hence cannot produce them. For just this sort of thing could be said about father and son. And there the same argument would be clearly invalid. It is true that 'the characterization "father" is not logically independent of the causal relation a father has to a son'. Yet, as Armstrong remarks, it by no means follows from this that a man's father cannot be characterized except as the thing which begot him. If it did, then it might be argued that the father could not be distinct from the son. What I have called the argument from distinct existences cannot, then, produce the conclusion that Armstrong desires. That argument, at any rate, is unsound. If it were not, then we would have also the undesirable conclusion about fathers.

The argument from distinct existences is so obviously unsound that we are entitled to feel that Professor Melden and Miss Anscombe are not relying on it in the way I have suggested. If we do not feel this, then we ought to feel at least that there are certain features absent from the case of father and son which are present in the cases they consider and that these features give some plausibility to their reasoning. What are these features? On the hypothesis that 'sense-impressions are distinct from beliefs or inclinations to believe we are (immediately) perceiving something', we may be tempted to say that sense-impressions just *are* those things which are related to the beliefs in question in a certain way. We may feel that we cannot say in the same way that a father just *is* that thing which is related to his child in a certain way. A father is an independent entity; we can recognize him as a man without knowing that he is a father. Indeed, if we were not able to recognize men as men we would not have the idea of the relation *fatherhood,* for this relation holds between men. On Armstrong's view, the case is quite different with sense-impressions and the belief or inclination to believe we that are perceiving. We do not observe these separately and then notice that a certain relation holds between them. What we know is that people form certain beliefs (or inclinations to believe), and we then suppose that these beliefs are 'based' upon sense-impressions. But if this is so, it may be said, sense-impressions are characterizable solely in terms of their relations to certain beliefs and hence cannot be distinct from them.

If this argument is acceptable, then it will dispose of central-state materialism and interactionist dualism. For according to these theories, as I have sketched them, to characterize a mental state *as* a mental state is just to characterize it as a state which is causally responsible for its behavioural manifestations (if any). From this it would seem to follow that mental states can be known to us only through their manifestations and hence that they cannot be distinct from their manifestations.

The trouble with this argument is that it would also dispose very neatly of the pretensions of molecular biologists and geneticists. We could say with Professor Melden, 'No account of alleged genes is intelligible which does not involve a reference to the relevant transmission of hereditary characteristics'. We could say with Miss Anscombe, 'Clearly our symbol "gene" must be interpreted as a description of or as having an internal relation to a description, of the transmission of some hereditary characteristic'. We could conclude thence that a gene cannot be a DNA-molecule. A DNA-molecule cannot do the logical job of a gene for the reasons that *a*) 'DNA-molecule' is a characterization completely independent of any reference to the transmission of hereditary characteristics and *b*) the gene is *defined* as that which is responsible for the transmission of hereditary characteristics.

The argument required to force the conclusions that Professor Melden and Miss Anscombe draw from their cases turns out to be the argument from distinct existences, as I have stated it. We have seen already that this argument is generally unsound, since it would produce the conclusion that a father is not distinct from his child. We all know the following passage from Hume's *Treatise* (book I, part III, section III):

> They are still more frivolous who say, that every effect must have a cause, because it is implied in the very idea of effect. Every effect necessarily presupposes a cause; effect being a relative term, of which cause is the correlative. But this does not prove that every being must be preceded by a cause; no more than it follows, because every husband must have a wife, that therefore every man must be married. The true state of the question is, whether every object which begins to exist, must owe its existence to a cause; and this I assert neither to be intuitively nor demonstratively certain, and hope to have proved it sufficiently by the foregoing arguments.

Under instructions from the twentieth century, we can see now that Hume radically mistook the nature and power of the argument in his hands. Instead of using it to question the necessity of the principle that every event has a cause, he should have used it to establish that *no* event has a cause. And about husband and wife he should have said something like this: 'Take a married man Jones and consider Mrs. Jones. Now Mrs. Jones can only be characterized with reference to Jones. If she could be characterized independently, she would be unable to do the logical job of Mrs. Jones. This job is to be Jones's wife, the woman who is married to Jones. This means that Mrs. Jones cannot be distinct from Jones. If she were, she could be independently characterized.'

It is no good objecting to this reasoning that the cases considered by Professor Melden and Miss Anscombe are different from the cases of father and son, of husband and wife. The point is that by considering these latter cases, we can show that the argument from distinct existences is unsound. This means that Melden and Anscombe cannot properly use this argument to produce their conclusions when they consider cases of a different kind. And I have shown that the argument is needed to produce their conclusions. Admittedly, it would be proper for them to use the argument if they could show that their cases differed from the straightforward ones in some way that allowed the argument to go through. But they cannot do this. For there is another case which resembles theirs closely, the case of gene and DNA-molecule. If the argument were allowed to go through for their cases, then we would have to conclude as well that a gene cannot be characterized as a DNA-molecule and hence that the recent identification of genes as DNA-molecules (in certain arrangements and in certain wider physical contexts) involves a gross philosophical blunder.

At this point it may be felt that there is a great difference between the case of gene and DNA-molecule and the cases considered by Melden and Anscombe. The difference is that it is after all possible to characterize a gene as a DNA-molecule, while it is not possible to characterize the intention to do *A*, say, independently of the action *A*. But this begs the very question at issue. The thesis I am opposing is just the thesis that mental states cannot be characterized independently of their behavioural manifestations. I am not in this paper concerned to show that they can be. I am concerned only to refute the argument from distinct existences which would establish that they can't be. We cannot defend that argument simply by invoking its conclusion. For that matter, if we had an independent argument to show that mental states could not be characterized without reference to their manifestations, we would not need the argument from distinct existences.

The argument from distinct existences depends on an interpretation of principle II which manifests a large misunderstanding of the logical connections involved in the cases to which it is applied. It may pay us to trace these connections. We need to understand how postulation functions in the construction of a theory. The gene gets into genetics first of all as a theoretical entity. No reasonable man can believe that hereditary characteristics just *are* inherited—there must be some mechanism whereby they are transmitted. We call whatever it is that is responsible for their transmission a gene. Because of the nature of the hereditary phenomena, it was possible for Mendel, publishing in 1866, to say that genes must satisfy certain general conditions. And because of this both Sutton and Bovari were able in 1902 to locate the genes in the chromosomes. Then in the 1950s Watson and Crick were able to say that genes were DNA-molecules. (This is rather simplified history.)

Certainly, in a sense, there is a logical connection between the gene and the transmission of hereditary characteristics. For, by definition, only what is responsible for the transmission of hereditary characteristics can be a gene. But just as certainly, in another sense, there is no logical connection between genes and hereditary characteristics. For as we know, genes are DNA-molecules and the connection between DNA-molecules and hereditary characteristics is a contingent one. The fact that DNA-molecules are responsible for the transmission of hereditary characteristics is the fact that genes are DNA-molecules. And this, of course, is a contingent matter. What is not a contingent matter is the fact that *if* genes are DNA-molecules, *then* DNA-molecules are responsible for the transmission of hereditary characteristics.

According to the two theories I am defending, states of mind function in psychological theory in much the same way as genes function in genetic theory—that is, as theoretical states (not entities). I repeat that it is not my purpose, in this paper, to establish this claim. I have given some argument for it elsewhere.[5] I am concerned only to defend the claim from the argument from distinct existences. To be sure, there are differences between states of mind and genes. States of mind are 'given'; they are 'introspectible'. I have also discussed this matter elsewhere.[5] Another difference is that the theory in which states of mind figure is mere common sense: there is no conscious or self-conscious postulation. It is not easy to see how this could affect the logical structure of the theory.

Now let us look at the notion of intention from the point of view of the central-state materialist. Certainly, in one sense, there is a logical connection between intentions and intentional action. For, by definition if you like, only a state of the person tending to produce intentional action can be an intention. But just as certainly, in another sense, there is no logical connection between intention and intentional action. For intentions are states of the central nervous system and the connection between such states of the central nervous system and behaviour is a contingent one. The fact that such states are causally responsible for our intentional behaviour is the fact that intentions are states of the central nervous system. And this, of course, is a contingent matter. What is not a contingent matter is the fact that *if* such states are intentions, then such states are causally responsible for intentional behaviour.

Notice that even though intentions are—according to the theory—'defined' in terms of intentional behaviour, we may say that an action *A* was intentional if and only if it sprang from the intention to do *A*, that an action is intentional in virtue of the fact that it proceeds from an intention. Since the intention to do *A* is simply that state of mind, whatever it may be, defined (appropriately) in terms of *A*, our remark is a conceptual one. But that does not mean that the intention cannot be a state of the person which causes him to behave in certain ways. In particular, it does not mean that the intention cannot be a central nervous condition. Nor does it mean that our remark has no empirical content at all. For at least it implies that intentional behaviour does not just happen without being influenced in any way by any state of the agent.

Nothing much hangs on the word 'empirical'. It depends on the kind of theory within which the postulation occurs, just what is the nature of the identification. Complex numbers were postulated to give a closed field for root extraction. They were subsequently identified as pairs of real numbers. But the identification was not the result of an empirical inquiry.

I have talked about postulation. But earlier examples should make it clear that what I have said applies for all expressions which may be relationally defined. Let us call x an R of y where xRy. Suppose we have an object b in the range of some arbitrary relation R. If the argument from distinct existences were sound, it would be impossible to identify any object distinct from b as an R of b. Thus it would be impossible to discover either the causes or the effects of any event. Neither our wives, husbands, fathers, mothers, or children would be known to us. We would not know our own names, nor where we lived, nor anything else at all. Indeed, we can use the argument to establish materialism provided that we are allowed two very plausible assumptions.

1) There is at least one material thing m.
2) Every thing that exists bears some relation to anything else that exists.

It follows from 1) and 2) by the argument from distinct existences that there exists exactly one thing, the material object m. (This is a long way from anything I believe; but it will hardly please a non-materialist.) By the same argument if follows that m cannot have distinct parts. We arrive then at the implausible conclusion that there exists only one material point in the universe.

We should pay close attention to the charge that a mental state cannot be further characterized than as that state which produces its manifestations. We have seen that this charge cannot be supported by the argument from distinct existences. (We have *not* seen that it cannot be supported at all.) According to the views I am defending, what is true is that an intention, e.g., cannot be characterized *as a mental state* otherwise than as that state which tends to produce certain behavioural manifestations. It does not follow from this that a particular intention could not be characterized without any reference, explicit or implicit, to behavioural manifestations. The gene is completely characterized as a theoretical entity once we have said that it is that which is responsible for the transmission of hereditary characteristics. A particular gene is completely characterized as a theoretical entity once we have described the hereditary phenomena for which is is responsible. Any further account of it (e.g. as a molecule with certain chemical properties and having a certain locus) constitutes an identification of the particular gene, complete or partial. Similarly, any further account of an intention as a brain process constitutes an identification of that intention, though it says nothing about it in a phenomenological way.[6]

Dissatisfaction over our inability to describe or identify mental states except in terms of the behaviour they are postulated to account for has found expression in the claim that, regarded as causes, they are *occult* causes. It is said that on our kind of theory, states of mind—or at any rate those of other people—are inevitably unknowable. Ryle argues from here that since states of mind are clearly not unknowable, a state of mind cannot be a cause (*Concept of Mind* (London, 1949), p 21 and *passim*). It must instead be some sort of disposition to behave in certain ways. (This is an over-simplified account of Ryle's position, but I believe it to be essentially correct.) This argument is presented as a general refutation of causal theories of mind. But against a theory like central-state materialism it merely begs the question. Clearly, there is nothing occult about a state of the brain. According to that theory, particular mental causes are merely unknown at this stage of the history of science. This does not imply either, as Ryle might suppose, that we cannot, at this stage of the history of science, know what state of mind a man is in. I can, for instance, know that a man is in whatever state of mind it is that produces in him a tendency to behave angrily. I can know that he is angry, though I do not know what anger *is* (that it is, as the theory asserts, a certain state of the central nervous system). Similarly, I know that my cat had what I called a crooked gene because she herself had a crooked tail and produced large numbers of kittens with crooked tails. I knew this long before the gene was identified as a DNA-molecule. Even now I do not know how a crooked gene differs from a straight one.

This counters Ryle's principal general argument against causal theories of mind. It may be that Ryle's argument does demolish that brand of dualism which he describes as the Official Theory. But even if it does, there is much more to be said for dualism than Ryle imagines.

Among those dualists who regard states of mind as causes of behaviour we may distinguish two kinds, the *philosophical* and the *scientific*. Both say:

a) mental states (or entities) are distinct from the behavioural phenomena they explain; and
b) mental states are not identifiable with physical states.

The philosophical dualist asserts *b*) after only *a priori* arguments. The scientific dualist asserts *b*) on probablistic evidence. He backs a different empirical horse from me and is prepared to see the question finally settled by the scientists. These are ideal positions, certainly, but Ayer in *The Concept of a Person and Other Essays* (London, 1963) advocates philosophical dualism. Dr. John Beloff, as he appears in *The Existence of Mind* (London, 1962), approaches to scientific dualism.

Ryle's argument may work against some philosophical dualists. But against scientific dualism, it doesn't even get started. Beloff could say to Ryle, 'Perhaps it is a matter of fact that we can never know the real causes of human behaviour. At any rate, we don't know them now. Yet, as you would say, we can tell one state of mind from another. The supposition that we cannot amounts to radical scepticism concerning causes. We do not have to succumb to such scepticism, merely because there are some causes we cannot identify.' Central-state materialism gives us the strongest possible assurance for the existence of other minds, an assurance of equal strength with our 'guarantee' that nature is uniform—there is for central-state materialism no *special* problem of other minds. But central-state materialism is not alone in this; scientific dualism gives us the same assurance. So does philosophical dualism, provided only that the philosophical dualist states his position in such a way that he is not committed to saying *on special grounds* that it is impossible to determine another man's state of mind. Given that he can do this, and Ayer, for example, can, then he can make to Ryle much the same reply as Beloff can.

I have not refuted behaviourism. I doubt the possibility of demonstrative refutation on any important philosophical question. But behaviourism is not the sort of thing we are going to accept without powerful reason. Many of the arguments supporting behaviourism are variations on Ryle's theme. Behaviourism is often the result of panic flight from scepticism concerning the mind. I would say this even of what I take to be Ryle's behaviourism, in spite of his apparent contempt for scepticism. But as we have seen, if a behaviourist can escape from scepticism concerning the mind, so can a dualist. It need be no more difficult to determine that there is present in Jones something tending to produce angry behaviour than it is to determine that (for some or no reason) Jones is disposed to behave angrily. The difficulty of determining the former is not increased by the assumption that what is present in Jones is not (or is not necessarily) a physical something. The troubles for dualism lie not here but elsewhere.

In conclusion, I wish to repeat what I hope I have said often enough already. I have not attempted in this paper to establish central-state materialism, nor any other theory of mind. I have attempted to defend a group of causal theories from a particular argument which I have called the argument from distinct existences. I have set out to refute this argument and I take myself to have done so. The question whether the theories I have defended can resist other attacks is irrelevant to the question whether I have done here what I set out to do.

NOTES

[1] This paper was read at a class on Materialism conducted by Professor D. M. Armstrong and myself in New College, Oxford, in 1962. It was accepted for publication in this anthology in that year and revised in 1966. No attempt was made, in the revision, to provide more recent examples of the argument from distinct existences.

The argument from distinct existences is discussed briefly by Professor

Kurt Baier in Section IV of 'Pains', *Australasian Journal of Philosophy* (May 1962), pp 18–23, and more briefly in Miss A. A. Stoop's review of Professor Melden's 'Free Action', *Australasian Journal of Philosophy* (August 1962), pp 247–9. This paper was written independently of the work of Baier and Stoop; yet what I say here is certainly foreshadowed by their papers.

[2] This term is suggested by Feigl's article 'The "Mental" and the "Physical"', eds. Feigl and Scriven, *Minnesota Studies in the Philosophy of Science,* vol. II, (Minneapolis, 1958). See also U. T. Place, 'Is Consciousness a Brain Process?', *British Journal of Psychology* (February 1956); J. J. C. Smart, 'Sensations and Brain Processes', *Philosophical Review* (April 1959).

[3] This thesis needs much refinement. See my 'Ryle and the Mechanical Hypothesis', in C. F. Presley (ed.) *The Identity Theory of Mind* (Brisbane, 1967). The unrefined theory is presented in more detail in my critical notice of Ayer's *The Concept of a Person and Other Essays* in the *Australasian Journal of Philosophy* (November 1964).

[4] For a discussion of this view see my 'Ryle and the Mechanical Hypothesis', *loc. cit.*

[5] In 'Ryle and the Mechanical Hypothesis', *loc. cit.*

[6] For a discussion of the phenomenological aspects of mental states see my 'Ryle and the Mechanical Hypothesis', *loc. cit.*

MORALITY AND NEEDS

KAI NIELSEN

I

TO SAY THAT something is the case is one thing, to say that it ought to be is another. To say that something is desired is not to say, or even to imply, that it is desirable. To say that something is sought or admired is not to say that it is good or admirable. An adequate classification of basic human needs would further our understanding of that complex animal we call 'the human animal', but it would tell us *nothing* about what is ideally worthy of achievement.

It has been said that 'the basic human needs fall broadly into three groups'.[1] There are the needs of the body (food, drink, sex, exercise, rest, sleep); there are the needs of the mind (the need to understand, construct, appreciate, and the like); and finally there are the social needs (the need for other human beings, the need to respond to others and to have them respond to us). To point out that there are such needs is to make an observation about what is the case and not to say anything with direct normative significance.[2] All norms involve, directly or indirectly, a reference to what ought to be and are not reducible to psychological or sociological facts. Moral discourse is a form of practical discourse concerned with directing behavior and guiding attitudes. It is only incidentally concerned to describe how men act. Morality is an autonomous activity with its own distinctive rationale; and the language that is distinctive of this activity cannot, even in principle, be identified with or assimilated to factual statements about the behavior of man in society. There is a clear divide between the *de facto* and the *de jure*; normative and factual uses of language are disparate. No moral questions can possibly be answered by discoveries, no matter how fundamental and how well confirmed, about what men need and what they seek.

In spite of its paradoxical air, this by now traditional picture of morality is in some ways a compelling picture and reveals some major insights into the nature of morality. These insights have, in our time, been exploited to the full. Until we realize that talk about right and wrong or good and evil is not simply talk about human psychology, about what people seek and avoid, we have not even begun to understand morality. Yet this traditional picture is in certain respects a distorted one. The divide between the *de facto* and the *de jure* is not so great and not so clearly marked as this picture prompts us to believe. I shall try to show how this is so by examining the logic of 'needs'. Where the picture I have just described has a firm hold, such an elucidation of 'needs' (even if it were fuller and more accurate than any I am able to give) will not be sufficient to break its spell, but it may do something to weaken it or to bring it into question.

In carrying out my analysis I shall be concerned to establish the following: 1) Sentences in which 'need' or 'needs' occur have several uses, including a normative use. 2) For a large and important range of cases, the connection between '*x* needs *y*' and '*x* should have *y*', though not an entailment, is still non-contingent. 3) In moral contexts, as well as in other contexts in which value judgments are made, to establish that someone needs something or that something is needed is also to establish that there is a *prima facie* good reason for his having it or for claiming that it should be done. In sum, for a significant class of cases, we are entitled to infer that, everything else being equal, if something is needed it should be done.

II

Consider these sentences:

a) He needs a permit to park here.

b) He needs more exercise to get in shape.

c) He, like everyone else, needs rest and relaxation.

a) asserts that something is required by a certain regulation. Sentences such as *a*) are characteristically used to make factual assertions that are true when there is some rule, regulation, or prescriptive law to the effect that what is asserted must be done.

b), on the other hand, asserts that something (getting more exercise) is a means to something else (getting in shape). It is important to recognize that what is needed is a means to an end or goal that people adopt or espouse. If, in fact, it is an effective means to the end or goal in view, then the assertion is true, if not, not.

c) might be thought to be very like *b*) for, after all, don't we assume a reference to ends in *c*) too? When we utter *c*), do we not intend something like this: 'He, like everyone else, needs rest and relaxation, if he wants to be healthy and happy'? Here health and happiness are our ends. Well, in some sense they may be our ends, but if they are, they are certainly far more pervasive ends than the particular and specific ends involved in *b*). If health and happiness are ends human beings seek, then they at least are ends we all assume in normal circumstances without question. If someone says 'I need to run a couple of miles each day' we can quite naturally ask him 'Why?' and take as an answer something like 'I want to run the mile this year'. Here there is an end—one among many that he might have had—that needs to be specified if we are to understand his action. But it is decidedly odd to ask someone 'Why do you need rest and relaxation? What end does that serve?' To say 'My end in mind is health and happiness' is to say something very peculiar indeed, but is the peculiarity due to any logical or conceptual oddity or is it due to the fact that health and happiness are such obvious and pervasive human ends that they are usually simply assumed? Though I am inclined to think that the oddity is conceptual, I do not want to argue that issue here; here I only wish to note that even if we do contend that *c*), like *b*), asserts that a certain state of affairs is a means to a certain implied end, it remains the case that the 'end' in *c*) (unlike the end in *b*) is of a very general order.

Even if we stress the above-mentioned similarities between *b*) and *c*), it is also important to notice that *c*) refers directly to a pervasive tendency on the part of people to try to achieve a certain result (i.e. rest and relaxation) at reasonably definite intervals even when various things stand in their way, that is *c*) refers to a conative disposition on the part of human beings to seek rest and relaxation. The three groups of 'basic human needs' (bodily needs, needs of the mind, and social needs) also refer to conative dispositions, but in sentences like *a*) and *b*) there is no reference to dispositions to act in a certain way.[3]

It is important to note that while *a*), *b*), and *c*) are sentences that would in normal circumstances be used to make factual statements —statements that are perfectly open to confirmation and disconfirmation—*b*) and *c*) are also sentences which function at the same time both factually and normatively. They both tell us that something is the case and direct us to make something the case. That statements made by the use of *b*) and *c*) would in the normal case be normative can be seen by observing that in each case if 'ought to have' or 'should have' replaces 'needs', the sense of the sentence is not appreciably altered. The traditional picture has been disturbed; we have normative statements that are also factual.[4]

III

Let us now see how useful our distinctions are in classifying a sampling of sentences in which 'need' or 'needs' occurs.

I shall introduce sample sentences under six groupings (groups A, B, C, D, E, F).

A.
1. She needs a ticket to get in.
2. The dog needs a licence.
3. You need a licence to get married.
4. He needs a jack of spades to have a straight flush.
5. You need not register until Monday.

The sentences in group A seem to me to be naturally classifiable as being of the same type as *a*), i.e. 'He needs a permit to park here'. They hold in virtue of a regulation, rule, or law. For all but 5 it would be natural to substitute 'must have' for 'needs' or 'need'. Moreover, 5 will not upset the apple-cart, for 'You need not register until Monday' implies that if you are going to register at all you need to (must) register at least by Monday.

B.
6. She needs a tutor.
7. The team needs a new coach.
8. A traffic light is needed here.
9. I need to be reminded.
10. I need a vacation.
11. He needs a new suit.
12. He needs to work harder.
13. He needs a psychiatrist.
14. The Bolivian Army needs to be mechanized.

The sentences in group B seem to be naturally classifiable as the same type as *b*), i.e. 'He needs more exercise to get in shape'. They all say or imply that the something which is needed is a means to attaining a certain end or goal. To use 12, 9, or 7 is to assert or imply something like the following (just *what* is asserted or implied will, of course, be context-dependent): 'He must work harder to do his work effectively' (12), 'If you want me to do it you had better remind me' (9), 'To get a well-coached winning team you must get a new coach' (7); 6 and 8 are not so clear-cut, for it is true that 6 and 8 could, without strain, be used so as to fall under A instead of B. If there were a regulation that in certain circumstances a traffic light must be erected and if 8 asserts that these conditions are satisfied, then 8 is being used so that it belongs in group A. But it could also be taken to mean that though there are no regulations which make it imperative that a traffic light be placed there, it would be a good thing—the pattern of traffic being what it is—if a traffic light *were* placed there. Similar things could be said of 6. But while 6 and 8 could be so used that they function as the sentences in group A normally function, they could also naturally be taken to function as the other sentences in group B normally function. We can gain no sure clue to the use of a sentence from simply gazing at it. We must look for its use (function, rôle) in live contexts ('where the engine isn't idling'), and as contexts differ, the use will also tend to differ. But for all of that, it remains true that the normal contexts in which these sentences are used are sufficiently standardized to allow for A and B to be natural, non-arbitrary groupings.

C. 15. Adults as well as children need to be loved.
16. People need to be entertained.
17. Men need women.
18. One needs a goal in life.
19. Hitler had an overwhelming need to find a scapegoat.
20. Her needs are not extensive.
21. The needs of the Plains Indians were few.
22. Children of divorced parents often need very special care.

D. 23. Human beings have destructive needs.
24. People have many needs.

25. Human beings have needs of which they are not aware.
26. The needs of the human animal are more complex than the needs of any other animal.

Groups C and D, though in certain respects interestingly different, both bring together sentences of the same general type as our sample sentence *c*), i.e. 'He, like everyone else, needs rest and relaxation'. In both C and D we are referring directly to certain conative dispositions of human beings. The sentences in Group C, unlike those in D, are reasonably (though in varying degrees) specific. Those in D are very general. They are either platitudes (truisms), such as 24 and 26, or psychological generalizations, such as 23 and 25.

E.
27. The house needs to be painted.
28. My car needs gas.
29. Plants need water.
30. The meat needs salting.
31. Sailboats need wind.

Group E seems not to fit into my classification. It does not, of course, make sense except in some very extended sense to attribute conative dispositions, ends, or goals to houses, cars, meat, sailboats, or even to plants. The sentences in Group E get their use by courtesy of sentences of the types we find in A, B, C, and D. Only if there were prior and well-understood uses of the types described in A, B, C, and D could sentences such as those in E be understood. 'Needs' is at home with people or other animals and only derivatively with things. But in an anthropomorphic way we can apply it to things, too, and this common way of speaking is perfectly well understood. When we say that cars need gas and sailboats need wind, we mean that they can't perform their function without gas or wind.

27 and 30, on the other hand, are very like the sentences in B. 'If you want the house to look good and weather well, you had better paint it', and 'The meat will not taste good unless it is salted' give the cash-value of 27 and 30, respectively.

F.
32. She needs to be in by midnight.
33. He's not aware of how much she needs him.
34. There is no need to go there.
35. He needs it like a hole in the head.

F is not meant to designate a common group, except in the sense that all the sentences in it call for special comment, one way or another. 32 (like 6 and 8) could be placed, depending on just how it is used, in either A or B. 33 could go under group B or C, though I should think it would more naturally go under C. 34 is so context-dependent that one cannot tell, apart from a definite context, whether it belongs under A or B. 35 is, of course, ironical. It is in effect saying 'He does not need that at all. It's exactly the sort of thing he doesn't need.' Here these sentences replacing 35 are functioning like sentences in group B.

IV

What about the normativeness and non-normativeness of the sentences in these groups? The sentences in B could all be replaced with little (if any) alteration of meaning, by sentences which are quite obviously normative. 'She should have a tutor' could do duty for 6; 'There ought to be a traffic light here' for 8; 'I should have a vacation' for 10. Similar substitutions could be made for the rest of the sentences in B, for these sentences are normally used both to express a judgment about what should be and to state facts. Thus, if someone asserts one of the sentences in B and if what he asserts is true, we are entitled to conclude that, apart from some defeating circumstances, what is needed should be done.[5]

The sentences in D, on the other hand, seem to have a purely *de facto* use. 'People find many things good' or 'People should do many things' is not even a near equivalent to 'People have many needs'. In D we seem to be just talking about the conative dispositions of human beings.

Group C is a mixed lot in this respect. It is very natural in some contexts to substitute 'should' for 'needs' in 15, 18, and 22, e.g. 'Children of divorced parents often should have very special care'. While it is indeed difficult to decide if sentences with the appropriate substitutions do exactly the same job as the original sentences, the use is so close that it would be logically odd, a deviation from a linguistic regularity, to say (for example) 'Human beings need some security but they ought not to have it'. Such a sentence is logically odd in the same sense that 'That is wrong, but I don't disapprove of it' or 'I know you thought he was the best candidate but why did you vote for him' are logically odd. In each case we are puzzled over the very *meaning* of what is being asserted or asked. Such utterances do not have a clear use. We cannot begin to answer such questions or assess such assertions until we have an explanation of what is at issue. It is indeed true that 'Children need to be loved but they ought not to have this need fulfilled' is *not* self-contradictory, but it is logically odd. We balk at such a sentence. We do not understand without some special context what it *means* to say 'Though they need love, they *ought* not to have it'. It is too much like saying 'It's wrong, but I don't think it's wrong'. No doubt a use could be supplied, as a use could be supplied for 'He has an unconscious toothache', but as it stands it doesn't have one.[6] In other words, we do not understand what it *means* to assert that such an utterance is a *moral* utterance. We can't, in such a context, assert that someone needs something and still assert that he *ought* not to have it, unless we can show that contrary to our usual expectations his having it would harm him or others or stunt his development or clash with some more fundamental moral claim.

If someone said 'Though children need love they ought not to have it, for to get on in this world, to become mature, self-reliant individuals, children must have this need frustrated', we would indeed understand that the speaker had made a moral claim, even though we might believe that what he said was absurdly false or in some way ridiculous. But if we did not have some such explanation, we would not understand what it could mean to call 'Children need to be loved but they ought not to have this need satisfied' or 'One needs a goal in life, but one ought not to have one' *moral* utterances. The 'ought', understood as a *moral* ought, is out of place here, though we do understand what is being advocated. If in a normal context I assert 'The sun is shining', you are entitled to assume that I believe the sun is shining. Similarly, if I assert 'One needs a goal in life', you are entitled to assume that I believe one ought to have a goal in life. That, of course, is a factual report of my moral convictions, but we can go further. Given the way native speakers of English speak, we are entitled to conclude that if human beings need a goal in life they ought, generally speaking, to have one. If we assert 15, 18, and 22, and if what we assert is needed is really needed, then we can conclude that what is needed ought to be done, everything else being equal. Though there are many conditions that could defeat the claim that what is needed ought to be done, there is a less-than-contingent connection between saying something is needed and saying this need should be satisfied. This being so, to establish that something is needed is, in effect, to give a good reason why what is needed should be done. It may not, however, be a sufficiently good reason in a given situation for actually doing what generally speaking needs to be done.

Keeping in mind Nowell-Smith's difficulties with 'logical oddness' in his *Ethics*, it could be argued, against what I have said above, that 'logical oddness' and 'conceptual connection' do not get us very far. It is indeed true that I do not analyse these notions here, but one can hardly analyse all one's concepts in any single essay or one would never finish or be able to articulate anything. However, I do give clear paradigms of what I mean and there are two very careful accounts of concepts of this type in the literature.[7] Moreover, by now it should be abundantly clear that there are stronger than contingent connections between statements which still are weaker connections than entailments. To the remark that a certain utterance is odd, the appropriate response should be 'So what?' But if the utterance is so deviant that we do not understand what, if anything, is being asserted or uttered, then a comment on its oddness is appropriate. It is also worth keeping in mind that intelligibility admits of degrees and that a puzzling utterance which also sounds odd may turn out on inspection to be a disguised piece of nonsense. Oddness remains an important symptom of conceptual *malaise*, but it must not be taken for more than that.

19 is the lone exception in C to what we have just been saying. This seems to be just a psychological statement about Hitler. But even here we would be entitled to say this: '*Given* Hitler's psychic economy, *if* Hitler's aims are to be furthered and *if* Hitler's homeostasis is to be preserved, then Hitler ought to have a scapegoat.'

Generally, we can conclude from the host of 'need-statements' of type C that if it is true that people need what it is said they need, then we are entitled to assert that (everything else being equal) they ought to have it. For such a range of cases, that x is needed is a good reason for saying x ought to be.

For sentences of the type classifiable under A, 'must' can be substituted for 'needs' without an appreciable shift in meaning, e.g. 'The dog must have a licence' for 2. Since this is so, there is a sense in which there is no 'should/should not' about them since there is no alternative that does not involve infringing a rule, regulation, or law. But statements made by the use of these sentences are (in their appropriate contexts) good reasons for the claim that what is needed should be done. In contexts in which it is wise, or in some other way desirable, to act in accordance with the law (rule, regulation) in question, then the only reasonable thing to do is to do that which the law (rule, regulation) requires. 'Reasonable' here has a directive, that is, a normative, force. A friend of mine wishes to take his family on an outing at Mulberry Park. I tell him that he should have a ticket. He looks at me in surprise and queries 'A ticket—to get in a park?' I reply 'Yes, there is a guard-house at the entrance and you need a ticket to get in. There is no other way you can get in.' If what I say is true, this settles the matter. 'You need one to get in' is a good reason for claiming you should have a ticket. 'I fully intend to go and I know I need a ticket to get in, but should I have one?' is logically odd. Statements made by the use of sentences of the kind grouped under A state relevant reasons for saying that what is needed should be done.

I think it is also evident that sentences grouped under E or F could be adequately handled in the ways already suggested. If this is so, then all the 'need statements' classifiable under A, B, and C, and the analogous ones in E and F, are either themselves normative or state good reasons for asserting that what is needed ought to be. Thus, for a large and familiar class of cases, the connection between '*x* needs *y*' and '*x* ought to have *y*' is non-contingent and *x*'s needing *y* is *eo ipso* a good reason for claiming that *y* ought to be.

Group D remains recalcitrant. As I said earlier, the sentences in D do not seem to have a normative use. It appears as if they are employed simply to make factual statements about pervasive conative dispositions. That we have many needs or needs of which we are unaware is not to say that these needs ought to flourish. That people have certain dispositions is one thing, and that these dispositions ought to flourish or be inhibited is another.

Here we are back to 'the great divide'. And isn't it apparent here that there is a rational point in saying that talk about the basic needs (conative dispositions) of man is one thing and talk about how man ought to act or what kind of conduct is reasonable human conduct is another? Psychological discoveries about basic human needs can have no *direct* normative implications. The needs of man may be such and such, but it remains an open question whether these needs are good or ought to be satisfied.

I think that even here such a division is unrealistic. The logic of 'needs' in its more typical uses (A, B, C) carries over to D. After all, in C there is also a direct reference to conative dispositions and we have seen that such statements have normative significance. Consider a platitude like 24. To honestly assert 'People have many needs but *none* of them should be satisfied' is to assert something that is logically odd. If, by and large, people's needs aren't to be satisfied, what, pray tell, is to be satisfied? 'Man's basic needs are S, P, and T' is normally taken to be a good reason for saying that men ought to have S, P, and T. After all, who would seriously assert that man ought not to have food, drink, exercise, rest, and sleep, that he ought not to gain some understanding and appreciation of his fellows and his world, that he ought not, sometimes at least, and if certain conditions could be realized, have human companionship and love?

A certain kind of Christian or Moslem ascetic, or a Hindu or Buddhist seer, might say that we ought to have no more of these things than is absolutely necessary to 'keep body and soul together'. We should seek a *samadhi* or a *satori* in which we completely escape the world of the senses and the push and pull of mundane human needs.

I am not at all sure that we have intelligible descriptions of these so-called states, but let us assume such 'descriptions' are in some sense intelligible. (After all, intelligibility admits of degrees.) It is rather common for religious men to say that for certain men, at least, there are further, deeper *needs* which must be satisfied—a mystical goal, a need to be with God, etc. These needs are deeper and more fundamental than those needs that I have called 'man's basic needs'. The theists among them might say—as did Pascal—that man is miserable without God and that his deepest needs are only realizable when he turns aside from the things of 'the world' and seeks God with his whole heart and his whole mind. If such beliefs are held, there would quite naturally be a question about whether man's basic (mundane) needs ought to be satisfied; but it is crucial to realize that the reason for *not* satisfying them is that by denying them, or inhibiting them, one could satisfy what is believed to be a still deeper need. But this is logically on a par with saying 'Though Nielsen needs a vacation in the Barbados he ought not to have it, for he needs still more to make his mortgage payments.' To so reason is not incompatible with what I am trying to maintain about the normative implications of statements of type D, but is more grist for my mill.

I am trying to suggest that even with general statements, such as 24, it remains the case that if a human being needs something or has a certain kind of need, unless it is characterized as bad (as in 'destructive needs'), the presumption is that what is needed should be realized. 'A woman needs sexual fulfilment' is typically normative, while 'A woman's need for sexual fulfilment is manifest' is not. But it still remains logically odd to say 'A woman's need for sexual fulfilment is manifest but that need ought never to be satisfied', *unless* some justification is provided that would explain why such a need ought never to be satisfied under any circumstances, e.g. 'God wills that only the male should enjoy sex'.

Generally, to say '*x* is needed' or '*x* is a need' or '*s* needs *x*' is also to make a claim that there is a good reason for doing or having what is needed. Where the 'need-statement' in question is itself a normative claim, we have a normative statement that is also a factual statement. These two claims, if correct, count heavily against the traditional and in some ways very gripping picture of morality mentioned at the beginning of my essay. If what I have said here is at all right, the traditional picture is a distorted one and, as the discussions centering around the emotive theory and Hare's analysis have brought out, it engenders a paradoxical conception of morality. Yet it has its insights, too, e.g. morality is morality and not something else. Without throwing the baby out with the bath-water, we need to correct this distorted picture and come to see how some moral notions, at any rate, are linked to and in some ways are inseparable from certain factual notions about human beings and what human beings need.

V

Let us now look at some objections to the line of argument I have taken. I have argued that given the use of 'moral' and 'needs' which is built into our moral discourse, we would not understand 'All human needs should be frustrated', if this statement were taken to be a moral claim, any more than we understand 'All memory beliefs are illusory' (only if some memory beliefs were not illusory could we understand what it would be like for some to be illusory). I readily acknowledge that it is perfectly sensible to claim that *some* needs ought to be overridden or that *some* needs ought not to be satisfied. For a given need we can always ask, 'He needs it but should he have it?', but if we are reasoning morally we cannot ask, 'Should any human needs be satisfied?'

Not so, it is natural to object. You grant that sadistic needs should be inhibited and, if possible, eradicated. But we can surely *conceive* of a world in which all human needs are sadistic or in some similar way destructive—that is, we can conceive of a world in which all human needs would be of the type now regarded as undesirable. You grant, the objection would continue, that if a person has a need of this destructive sort that it is perfectly correct to claim it ought to be inhibited. Why can't we *generalize* this for a world in which all needs are destructive needs. In such a world it would be perfectly sensible to assert, as a moral belief, that all human needs ought to be frustrated. This certainly appears to be a perfectly intelligible thing to say, given the fact that we would say of a given destructive need that it ought, where possible, to be inhibited. We are only generalizing this. If this is so, you are then mistaken in claiming that we would not understand how 'All human needs ought to be frustrated' could be a moral utterance, given the use of 'moral utterance'.

Let us assume that the above hypothesized situation is sufficiently intelligible to be capable of exemplification. Assuming this, it would be correct to say that such destructive needs should be satisfied. Here the needs in question would be something that everyone would have. In fact, they could have no other needs. Since such needs are their only needs, they would be the only dominant conative dispositions to seek something out that people so situated and so constituted could have. There could be no needs which would be incompatible with their destructive needs, for if someone were strongly disposed to avoid the pain brought out by the destructive need, if he had a conative disposition to avoid the pain brought out by destructive needs, he would, by that very token, have a need that wasn't destructive and the situation would no longer be the hypothesized one. To keep the hypothesized situation intact, everyone must have a dominant conative disposition to behave in what we now call a destructive way and in this way only, and no one could be strongly disposed to avoid such behaviour.

If this were so, what grounds would we have for claiming that in this Alice-in-Wonderland situation such needs ought not to be satisfied? Our reason for calling them destructive or harmful needs, and by so labelling them to give them a bad mark, is that they normally are needs that frustrate other needs, other desires, and other wants. But in our situation they no longer can function in this way or they can only frustrate us to a lesser degree than if those needs were not satisfied. If this is so we have now lost our rationale for calling them destructive or harmful needs where these grading labels continue to have their usual normative force.

We are tempted to believe the above objection to my thesis is well taken because we, on first hearing the objection, think of a world in which, since all human needs are destructive, people are miserable, hedged in, made to suffer things they are not disposed to suffer. 'Destructive needs' continues to have its usual normative force even though we are now in a context in which it could not do its usual normative job. *But in the context in question such words could no longer grade*. Everyone would have these and only these needs; no one would have a dominant disposition to strive against them if *all* needs really were destructive. People could still conceive of people having other needs, so 'destructive needs' would not be a redundancy, but it would no longer have a disapprobative force. 'Destructive needs' could not exhibit its normal negative normative force, by showing that such needs were the object of an anti-attitude, for then we would have a dominant disposition to react against these destructive needs, and if this were so, then there would be at least one need that was not destructive. But *ex hypothesi* when we so generalize this cannot be so. If *all* our needs were destructive, 'destructive' would lose its negative normative force; that is to say, its very meaning would change.

Taken literally, 'All human needs ought to be frustrated' can be seen to be nonsense when we consider carefully 'needs', 'ought', 'frustrated'. To frustrate a person is to make him or try to make him do something that he is not *disposed* to do or to prevent him or obstruct him from doing something he is disposed to do. Now to speak of human needs is to speak of our pervasive, conative dispositions (tendencies to strive for or against). Juxtapose against this the fact that moral utterances by definition typically function to guide conduct. They are not just orders or blunt 'tellings to'. But guidance makes sense only where people have certain dispositions or wants. Moral guidance takes place against a background of conflicting wants, both personal and interpersonal. But '*All* human *needs* ought to be frustrated', presumably tells us to frustrate *all* dispositions. But then there could be no guidance, no telling one to seek one thing rather than another, for that very *seeking* would be the exercise of a disposition, but supposedly *all dispositions* are to be frustrated. It purportedly guides conduct, yet it withdraws one of the presuppositions of guidance. So 'All human needs ought to be frustrated' is a disguised piece of nonsense.

It is natural to continue the argument against the position I am maintaining by arguing that whether in an ordinary way a need is graded as destructive or not ultimately depends on the *pro-attitudes* we just *happen* to have, the things we want and desire. Here the problem of the great divide breaks out all over again: that we want something is not sufficient reason for asserting that we ought to have it.

That we want something is indeed not a sufficient reason for saying we ought to have it, though to grant this is not to deny that there is a conceptual connection, that is, something more than a purely contingent connection, between 'wanting something' and 'affirming that having it would be desirable'. But to acknowledge this does nothing to gainsay the claim that *x* needs *y* is, for a large range of cases, both a *de facto* and a *de jure* statement or that human beings have a certain need is, in many contexts at least, a *prima facie* good reason for claiming this need should be satisfied. To find out that we need something is to find out something which has a direct relevance to coming to a decision about what it is that we ought to have.

I am not by any means out of the dark woods yet. In reasoning as I have, I have perhaps done little more than serve as an unwitting and very unscientific ethnographer of our tribal mores. The linguistic regularities I have uncovered, it might well be argued, show little more than that we live in a society which just happens to have adopted a moral code which dictates that most needs ought to be satisfied. Our tribe has, as one of its leading and fundamental moral principles, the principle that most needs ought to be satisfied. But we could perfectly well understand an alternative *morality* which rejected this principle and did not assume that the satisfaction of human needs was, generally speaking, a good thing. *We* might well believe that such a morality would be unrealistic, absurdly false, and totally inhumane. But—and this is the significant thing—we would still recognize it to be (in a descriptive sense) a morality, and if a people were actually to adopt such a code of conduct we would without any difficulty recognize it as a moral code. The argument I have made, it might be continued, confuses a particular moral code with what, given the use of 'a moral code', could count as a moral code. Indeed, in our Western Greco-Roman, Hebraic-Christian culture, we are entitled to assert that if x is a need, then generally speaking x ought to be satisfied, but it remains the case that we could perfectly well understand a moral inconoclast's denying such an implication. It is ethnocentric to claim that a system of human conduct that sought to inhibit and repress *all* human needs because it held that man was evil was not really a morality.

Even if it is the case that what I have said holds only for all extant moralities, or even if it only holds for Western morality, it is still important to see that it does hold for that—that given extant moral codes, or given our moral code, if something is a human need, then it has a *prima facie* right to be realized.

Someone in the grip of 'the great divide picture' might counter: 'But why adopt our *conventional* moral point of view or the moral point of view embedded in any extant morality? There are many very different moral codes connected with many very different ways of life. Logically speaking, which one you adopt or whether, by your own decision of principle, you create, in Nietzsche's phrase, "new tablets", is in the last analysis up to you. It all depends on what choices you are willing to make and stick by. The point of the "traditional picture", as you call it, is to bring out the necessity for choice here. What you say about the conceptual connection between "needs" and "ought" in conventional morality does nothing to break the hold of this "picture". Your analysis only confuses matters.'

There would be a considerable force to this objection if there were any adequate reason for believing that opting for what is misleadingly called the 'conventional moral point of view' is without a sound rational point. But rational beings will want to have their basic needs satisfied and their interests respected. Given the fact that human beings tend, broadly speaking, to be roughly equal in strength and intelligence, it is plain enough that to insure as well as they can that their needs and interests will be safeguarded, they need some social device which will fairly and equitably adjudicate their conflicting interests. Such an adjudication is a central function of morality and that any culture will have some stabilized ways of doing this is a perfectly natural and reasonable thing to expect. Without it rational living would be impossible. That human beings generally have a stake in such a point of view is perfectly understandable. No arbitrary decision of principle is involved here.[8]

Yet it seems to me that in answering my critic in the way I have above, I have, in effect, conceded too much to him. It is not the case that I have simply been talking about Western morality or about 'old tablets' that just happen to exist. It seems to me that the conceptual connections I have been describing hold for anything that would be recognized as a morality, given the uses of 'morality'. I do not deny that the concept of morality could be *stretched* so that these connections might no longer hold; but such an extension would have to be *made*. We do not now know what it would be like for a morality to exist which taught that the satisfaction of *all* human needs was evil, or regarded it as a matter toward which a moral code could remain completely indifferent.

Suppose someone were to try to argue that *all* human needs ought always to be inhibited and wherever possible destroyed, for human beings are evil and the purposes of this depraved, lustful, sinful creature, man, are all evil. Such a conception of man is not just frantically pitiful and absurd, it is in an important sense morally unintelligible. It is a definitive feature of moral judgments and value judgments generally that if someone makes a value judgment we can always ask him to justify it. If I say 'You ought to do so and so' you can always, with perfect logical propriety, ask me' Why should I?' and I must (and the force of the 'must' here is logical) in principle at least be able honestly to assert something that would count as a 'good reason' for the moral judgment in question. (I would myself have to take it as a good reason for so acting.) In a context in which I tell you something ought to be done or should be done or that it would be a good or admirable thing if it were done, I am not simply telling you, ordering you, or just trying to get you to do it. Instead, I am making a claim which must be supportable by reasons. (These remarks are what Wittgenstein would call grammatical remarks.)

Now consider the following snatch of a dialogue where K is advocating a 'morality' such as I have described above.

K: Human needs! Root out all those stinking needs. Man is a cesspool of depravity. The satisfaction of our deepest and most pervasive needs is just what should be avoided at all costs.

L: Why? Why shouldn't we satisfy them when satisfying them does not hurt others or lead to an even greater deprivation of the things we all need?

K: Why? Why—because man is evil, everything about him is vile.

L: But why is man so thoroughly evil? I understand how some men—Franco and Molotov, for example—are evil, but how are 'All men evil'? I don't understand that at all!

K: They are evil because they don't do what the Ruler commands.

L: But on your own grounds if the Ruler is a man (and you said a while ago that he is), then he, too, is evil. Why then should we do what he commands?

K: The Ruler is evil, but what he commands is supremely good. What he commands is always the right thing to do.

L: Why?

K: Because what he commands is always right.

L: How do you know? It certainly isn't contradictory or in any way logically odd to deny it.

K: I know his commands are always right simply because they just are right, that's all.

L: But why are they right?

K: They just are!

L: How do you know?

K: One just apprehends their rightness.

L: But what makes following his commands the right thing to do? Why are these right acts right? What reason do you have for claiming this is the right thing to do?

K: No reason, and nothing makes them right. They just are right, that's all. One must just see or apprehend their rightness.

K is not just being arbitrary; he is saying something that does not make sense. Rightness is not a name for some property or relation that can just be apprehended.[9] When we say of x that x is right or good, there must be some natural features that are referred to, in virtue of which it is right or good. It can't be 'just right, that's all'. In spelling out why something is right—and that question is, as I said, always logically appropriate—we would at least if pressed end up talking about the natural features of the situation in question. When pressed to justify why certain properties are right-making properties rather than others, we would eventually end up referring to certain pervasive human needs and interests. Without such a reference our moral talk would be groundless and finally, like K's talk, unintelligible.

Suppose someone took a less frenetic line than K, our Kafka-like candidate for the underground. Suppose our milder man said: 'Conventional morality is indeed so constituted that if something is a need, it is something that has a *prima facie* claim to be. But human needs are actually morally neutral. Whether they should flourish or be inhibited is finally a matter of what the moral agent in question decides he ought to do.'

Such a claim appears to be much more reasonable. Isn't it a perfectly intelligible moral view? But again, couldn't we properly ask of anyone, who claimed to be asserting that we ought to deny as many human needs as possible, what reasons he had for his odd claim? He could not justifiably reply: 'Because we ought to, that's all'. What could he say that would not, when he was pressed, finally involve an appeal back to human needs and interests (human conative dispositions) and to the assumption—he is supposedly challenging—that these needs should be satisfied?

It does not seem to me that he could avoid such an appeal. The case here for human needs seems to me in some important senses like some of the things we would say about memories. We can challenge the correctness of any given memory belief, but in doing this we must assume that most memories are reliable. It makes no sense to ask if memory beliefs are *generally* reliable.[10] Similarly, though any given need (unless it is described as 'a destructive need', 'a sadistic need', 'and the like) has a *prima facie* claim to be satisfied, it may turn out that it ought not to be satisfied due to some other overriding considerations (the harm its satisfaction would do to others, etc., etc.). But to say that generally human needs ought *not* to be satisfied makes no sense at all, if we try to take it as a *moral* claim. Given the way the word 'morality' functions, such an utterance couldn't be a *moral* utterance. (In certain Gellnerish moods, we want to say 'But to understand the use—no matter how well—of the English word "morality" and all its important connections may not really be to understand morality. Morality, in essence, might be something entirely different.' But this is nonsense, for it is unintelligible to say that morality is something entirely different than what the use of 'morality' can sanction as morality. If morality isn't this, it is nothing.) If such an utterance could not be a moral utterance, then no grounds have been given for asserting that I have been ethnocentric, taken what is simply Western morality as the whole of what could even in principle count as 'morality' or simply talked about extant moralities. It seems to me that I have not done these things, but I have made a conceptual remark about the nature of morality which (if correct) seriously undermines our traditional picture of the nature of morality.[11]

NOTES

[1] Morris Ginsberg, *On the Diversity of Morals* (New York, 1957), p 134.

[2] *Ibid*, pp 134–8.

[3] I am, in part, indebted to Paul Taylor for the way I have made these distinctions, though he does not make them exactly in the way I do. See Paul W. Taylor, '"Need" Statements', *Analysis*, vol. 19 (April 1959).

[4] I do not mean to suggest that what is by now the traditional picture does not allow what Hare or Nowell-Smith would call descriptive elements in normative utterances. But this picture would still stress that a normative utterance has a very different logical status than a factual one.

[5] To object that if the need statement is construed as normative there is of course no problem is to miss the point on at least two counts. 1) There is no question of 'construing them normatively', for their standard use *is* normative, as my argument shows. 2) Even though 'I need a vacation' is normative, it doesn't follow that I should have one, any more than 'He is rude' entails 'He ought not to be rude', even though 'He is rude' is normative. What does follow is that, everything else being equal, I should have one. But everything else may not be equal, so there might be a problem.

[6] It is a mistake to argue that in both cases we can guess what the speaker *intends* and so the sentence has a use. We might guess what a speaker means by 'I have an unconscious toothache' or 'I have my soul in my wallet', but this would not establish that the sentence in question has a use, has a function in a form of life, but only that the speaker, if we had guessed correctly, had *given* it a use. But there is a sense in which we cannot give a use—though we might give a *new* use—to something which already has a use. What is crucial to see here is that to give a word-string a use does not show how we could understand it as being a part of, having an integral rôle in, the *Sprachspiel* we call 'moral discourse'.

[7] Isabel C. Hungerland, 'Contextual Implication', *Inquiry*, vol. 3, no. 4 (winter, 1960), pp 211–59, and P. H. Nowell-Smith, 'Contextual Implications and Ethical Theory', *Proceedings of the Aristotelian Society,* supplementary volume (1962).

[8] I have tried to show this in my 'The Functions of Moral Discourse', *The Philosophical Quarterly,* vol. VII (July 1957). 'Appraising Doing the Thing Done', *The Journal of Philosophy,* vol. LVII, no. 24, (November 24, 1960): 'Appealing to Reason', *Inquiry,* vol. V, no. 1 (spring, 1962); 'Wanton Reason', *Philosophical Studies,* vol. XII (1963); 'The Good Reasons Approach Revisited', *Archiv für Rechts- und Sozialphilosophie,* vol. L/4 (1964), pp 455–83; and my 'On Moral Truth', *Studies in Moral Philosophy,* Nicholas Rescher (ed.), (Oxford: 1968), pp 9–25.

[9] See P. H. Nowell-Smith, *Ethics*, chapters 3–6, and E. W. Hall, *What is Value?*, chapters 1–3.

[10] See Sydney S. Shoemaker, 'Personal Identity and Memory', *The Journal of Philosophy,* vol. LVI (October 22, 1959).

[11] I am indebted to Professor Paul Taylor and Messrs. Robert Hoffman and Wade Savage for their helpful criticisms of earlier statements of this essay. Imperfections that remain are of course mine.

DISPUTES AND VALUES

BEDE RUNDLE

ANALYSES OF THE terms 'value word' and 'value judgment' or 'evaluation' generally involve both a positive characterization and a contrast with words and judgments of an allegedly different type. Positively, they are said to express or evoke feelings, emotions, or attitudes, or to be associated with certain speech acts, such as commending and prescribing. Negatively, it is claimed that they are not empirical or descriptive, that they do not state facts, cannot be said to be true or false. The difficulties associated with these and related characterizations are familiar enough: they may be obscure—does 'attitudes' include beliefs?—or, to the extent that they are not, it may be questioned whether they do in fact apply to the judgments and/or words which they are thought to characterize—is 'good' always, or even typically, used to commend? Again, there may be some doubt whether a positive and a negative characterization are jointly applicable: we might agree that a certain value judgment expressed a feeling and yet hold, perhaps for this reason, that it stated a fact; indeed, if usage means anything at all, there is no case for saying that 'is a fact' and 'is true' cannot be attached to, say, a statement that something is good. They often can be applied, both meaningfully and truly. Moreover, even when the characterizations do fit, there is still the question of the significance of this fact. Perhaps there are value judgments which do not combine happily with 'is true' or 'is false', but if the point of this observation is to show that there is no hope of settling disputes over values, it may also be necessary to show that other terms from the same family, e.g. 'correct', 'justified', 'is so', are likewise out of place.

The negative aspect of the usual analyses is perhaps their most important feature, whether they present a sharp dichotomy—'not descriptive, but prescriptive'—or a weaker distinction—'not purely descriptive, but also prescriptive'—since it is at this point that the dispute concerning naturalism arises. It is also at this point that the analyses are most questionable; indeed, the alleged contrasts are so dubious that there is considerable difficulty in even *stating* the naturalistic fallacy. Thus the naturalist claims that, for some word w, if x is w it follows that x is good, say, even though w is not a value word, while his opponent replies that, as a matter of logic, the entailment holds only if w is a value word. Sometimes it then begins to look as if the anti-naturalist's criterion for whether w is a value word is whether or not it entails a judgment of goodness, or, if this circularity is avoided, he falls back on the unsatisfactory characterizations mentioned above. At any rate, it is so unclear what can and what cannot be the premise for an inference here that we may be inclined to abandon altogether the terminology of 'value word', 'value judgment', and 'evaluation'. However, while particular philosophical uses of these expressions may recommend this counsel of despair, it is a reasonable presumption that these expressions have *some* meaning, independent of philosophical theories. After all, if I am asked to write a review of a book, but not to venture any value judgments upon it, I have at least a rough idea of the sort of expression that would be out of place. For instance, I should be debarred from describing the work, or aspects of it, as 'boring', 'trivial', 'incoherent', 'wrong-headed', 'unoriginal', or 'worthless', on the one hand, or, on the other hand, as 'stimulating', 'important', 'clear', 'cogent', 'original', or 'valuable'. Admittedly, there are borderline cases. Can I say that the author does or does not succeed in establishing a certain contention? Can I describe his approach as 'scientific'? As 'unscientific'? There is no lack of difficult cases, but by and large it is easy enough to extend the list of words which would be inappropriate, so we might inquire what principle or principles determine membership in this list, and, of course, in lists of value words arising in other contexts. However, although I shall occasionally rely on an intuitive understanding of 'value word', my aim here is not to give an accurate characterization of such words, but I am interested in certain features of words and their uses which are commonly taken as central in discussions of value. The main philosophical issue around which the argument will develop is the question of the decidability of value judgments.

I begin with a feature of certain judgments which is closely related to decidability, namely disputability. It might be suggested that the words which we are inclined to call 'value words' are words whose applicability may be a matter of dispute or controversy, so that the instruction to make no value judgments on a book would be tantamount to the instruction to refrain from saying anything controversial, anything that anyone might take issue over. This may or may not be essential to such words; it is clear that it does not define a sufficient condition for being a value word, if such words are to form a proper sub-class of words in general; the dating or authorship of a work may be a matter of controversy, but to assert that it was published at such and such a time or written by so and so is surely not to make a value judgment. Again, disputes may arise over the applicability of a word in borderline cases, but once more this phenomenon is too general to serve as a distinguishing mark of value words. I do not suppose that anyone has ever explicitly claimed disputability as a distinguishing mark, but there is a tendency to argue as if it were: if the question is whether 'kind' or 'generous', say, are value words, it is sometimes thought sufficient for an affirmative answer that we should be able to describe cases where there could be reasonable doubt as to whether they were instances of kindness or generosity. I should have thought there was no doubt that these were value words, but this test is applied to show that they are value words in a sense such that being a value word is not being, or is not merely being, a word of some other sort. Clearly, though, disputability by itself is of little significance, but it must be disputability of a more specific kind, disputability backed by the right reasons. To meet this objection, the argument might be developed in the following way. There are words which we use regardless of how we are disposed towards the persons, things, or behaviour which they describe; regardless, that is, of whether we view them favourably or unfavourably. In contrast to such 'neutral' words there are words which embody some sort of pro- or con-attitude; such are 'value' words. Vagueness or lack of knowledge may lead to controversy concerning judgments containing words of either of these types, but in the case of value words a further source of controversy is present; a judgment featuring such a word may be disputed by two people as a consequence of the fact that the relevant attitude is not shared by both. In such cases the only rational course is for the two parties to agree to differ, each being at liberty to maintain his own judgment in keeping with the attitude or disposition which he has. Or so it might seem. Whether or not this is the position in a given case is going to depend in part on what is meant by a word's embodying an attitude. It may be true that to describe a person as 'kind' we must satisfy ourselves as to the goodness of his actions over a certain range, and to that extent it may be true that the word embodies a favourable attitude; but it may also turn out that such implicit judgments can be established as right or shown to be mistaken. Just as it is premature to take disputability as a sure sign that 'kind' is a value word in a sense in which such words are to be distinguished from words of some other sort, so the fact that a word has an attitude built into it may not guarantee the possibility of irreconcilable disagreement. Again if the claim is that the logic of value words is quite personal, in the sense that we are not required to take into account the beliefs or attitudes of others in order to defend our use of such words, then it may turn out that to speak of irreconcilable *disputes* is to misrepresent the matter, the apparent disputes being on this hypothesis no more than verbal.

What, then, seems to be wanted is not simply a word which embodies a favourable or an unfavourable attitude or disposition but a word which *a*) embodies such an attitude and *b*) is such that its applicability can *on that account* be indefinitely disputed. But now it is far from clear that value words are invariably of this sort. Apart from the possible exception just noted, there is the further possibility that a word should fail to satisfy *a*) and yet count as a value word simply because it named a quality which we are likely to regard as of positive or negative value, as a good or a bad point. For instance, to describe a book as 'unoriginal', 'unintelligible', or 'boring' is to advert to features which we are likely to regard, or perhaps inevitably regard, as failings or bad points in a book. It seems reasonable to call these 'value words', but it is doubtful that they satisfy *a*), and even more doubtful that they satisfy *b*). Perhaps 'boring' is in some way expressive of an attitude, but neither it nor the other words satisfy *a*) in the sense that their use presupposes an unfavourable disposition on the part of the speaker towards the features which he thereby describes. It is not because I dislike or have a low opinion of certain features of a book that I describe it as 'unoriginal', 'unintelligible', or 'boring', but I have this opinion because I consider these descriptions applicable. Now it may be granted that these words can be regarded as value words, simply because descriptions in such terms are commonly a prelude to an explicitly unfavourable judgment, but the anti-naturalist would presumably maintain that if these descriptions are in fact neutral, then they cannot entail an explicit evaluation: if a judgment of a book as poor or bad, at least in certain respects, is not implicit in a description of it, then as a matter of logic no such evaluation can be derived. This may seem trivially true, but it is in fact inconclusive (taken in the relevant sense). For the statement that *x* is bad to follow from the statement that it is *w*, it is not necessary that in order to describe *x* as *w* the speaker must first satisfy himself of *x*'s badness in the relevant respect. As far as logic is concerned, it may be that, for things of *x*'s sort, being bad just is a matter of being *w*, and a person, though capable of applying *w* correctly, could be unaware of this. The entailment might require further information about the nature of the sort of thing in question, but there is no *a priori* reason why this information cannot be given in equally neutral terms.

Definitions of 'value word' which involve something like conditions *a*) and *b*) suffer from the obscurity of the notion of 'embodying an (un) favourable attitude', a defect which we might try to overcome by adopting the apparently more precise terminology of different kinds of speech act. Earlier attempts to explain what is characteristic of value words in terms of the expression of feelings have largely given way to analyses in which the explanatory weight is borne by such notions as *commending*, *praising*, *criticizing*, and *condemning*, and this approach seems to be an advance, if only because emotivism is so implausible. My own impression is that an appeal to such speech acts is almost always misguided: some words are intimately associated with the performance of certain speech acts, but attempts to use this association in defining value words require us to regard as essential a feature of the use of a word which arises only in certain contexts. This has, of course, been said before, but the question still merits some discussion, since it is not clear that the powerful form of argument currently invoked against the speech act analysis is in fact conclusive. The argument which I have in mind is the following: against R. M. Hare's claim that the primary function of 'good' is to commend, P. T. Geach and J. R. Searle have maintained that the possibility of commending arises only when 'good' is used assertively, only when we actually call something 'good'.[1] However, since 'good' can be used non-assertively, as in questions, conditionals, and indirect speech, and since it has the same meaning in these contexts as when used assertively, the observation that 'good' is used to commend cannot tell us anything of substance about its meaning. Searle considers rephrasals of the troublesome contexts in terms of 'commend', e.g. 'I wonder if I commend this electric blanket' for 'I wonder if it is a good electric blanket', but concludes that such reformulations differ in meaning from the original versions. Nor is this surprising. After all, the claim is not that the meaning of 'good' can be explained *solely* by reference to its commendatory function, and it is obvious that even when used assertively, 'good' cannot be replaced by any part of the verb 'commend'. What is wanted is a proof that *no* reformulation can show how this function of 'good' is to be invoked when explaining its meaning. But what about 'I wonder if this is what one would call a "good" electric blanket', or 'I wonder if this is what would be called a "good" electric blanket'? These versions appear at least to escape the charge that we have expressed only that force of 'good' which is conveyed by the verb 'commend'. Similarly, 'I don't know whether it is a good electric blanket' could be rephrased as 'I don't know whether it is what one would call a "good" electric blanket', not 'I don't know whether I commend this electric blanket'. Or, perhaps in some contexts it would be appropriate to replace 'good' by 'what I would call "good" '—if, say, there is no generally agreed standard of goodness for things of the sort in question. At any rate, to say that to call something 'good' is to commend it may not contribute much to our understanding of the word, but in view of the possibility of such translations there is some case for saying that whatever contribution it does make it makes with respect to non-assertive uses of the word no less than to its assertive use. However, even granted that it is possible to counter the Geach–Searle argument along these lines, the counter may be no more than temporary, and it still seems that Hare's analysis is a reversal of the true position: it is because 'good' means what it means that it may be used to commend; its meaning is not to be explained by an appeal to the fact that it is so used, but this is an additional function imposed upon its use only in certain contexts. What holds for 'good' holds for other value words; commending and its opposite do not serve to characterize the use of such words in general, but they apply only to words descriptive of qualities or behaviour of a restricted sort. Moreover, even when a word is eminently suited to a commendatory rôle, both its being a value word and its aptness for such a rôle may be explained simply by reference to the general predilection for the features which it describes. Consider first the case where what is commended is a person, or something ascribable to a person. Commendation is in place here only in so far as it is a question of something for which the agent is responsible, typically actions or qualities performed or manifested in the face of difficulties or contrary inclinations. Thus industriousness, courage, and fortitude come immediately to mind as qualities which we frequently commend. To a lesser extent, we may commend a person on his kindness, generosity, impartiality, patience, or tolerance, though only, and then not necessarily, if these qualities are displayed in adverse conditions, or are in some way notable or exceptional. At the other end of the scale, we have a person's talents, his wit, charm, intelligence, and good looks; these we may value highly, but we are not likely to commend a person on them. If the idea of an accomplishment in adverse conditions is implicit in the meaning of a word, as perhaps it is with 'courageous', it is very likely that its assertive use will constitute a commendation; at any rate, we could scarcely fail to appreciate that the disregard for personal safety implied by 'courageous' is an exceptional quality. However, apart from the explicit performative, I cannot find any expression whose assertive use can invariably be described as a commendation. A casual remark or musing is not likely to qualify, but commending involves *calling attention* to the relevant behaviour with, accordingly, a certain aim, e.g. to make known one's recognition, or to invite from others recognition of the person's behaviour. Again, the question of authority may arise. When the teacher says that Tommy is a good boy he may be commending Tommy, but Tommy is hardly in a position to commend the teacher by calling him '(a) good (teacher)'; indeed, even when the speaker is an adult, it may be presumptuous of him to say that he was commending someone in saying, for instance, 'It was good (kind, generous) of you to do that', and we would wonder just who he thought he was if he took himself to be commending a saint in calling him a good man. Commending would be about as appropriate as the patronizing attitude suggested by 'Ah yes, Saint Francis, a good man (chap)'. In listing a person's virtues we may be doing any number of things—we may be expressing appreciation, praise, admiration, reverence, and even gratitude—but the only descriptions which stand any chance of being generally applicable are the dispassionate 'describing' and 'stating', along with others which apply irrespective of any reference to the worth of the attributes named.

Although 'good' *may* be used in commending people, the sense in which commending pertains more generally to the use of the word is not the same as the sense just discussed. Pots and pans cannot *do* anything to earn commendation. We may of course commend things which people do, as when the teacher tells Tommy that his writing is good or that he sang well. Similarly, perhaps, a poem could be commendable through being a commendable achievement. But can we commend a scene, a sunset, or a strawberry? Certainly, we cannot speak of a 'commendable sunset'; however, it is thought that, by calling them 'good', we can commend such things, where commending is an activity which has as its point the guiding of choices. Now it is true that 'commend' often means something like 'pronounce or judge favourably upon', with, as before, the aim of inviting some sort of response from others. However, the use of 'good' in this connection is limited, and the response aimed at may be no more than recognition of the merits or good points of the object concerned; in so far as the aim is to guide choices, 'recommend' rather than 'commend' gives the appropriate speech act description. So, for instance, we may commend a type of car, soap, or television set by pronouncing them 'good'—things designed for a purpose and which may or may not come up to standard. On the other hand, there is no question of commendation when speaking of good luck, good fun, good health, a good recovery, or a good chance.

Apropos of commending, Hare makes the further claim that, no matter what descriptions of a person we accept, commending that person is a further step which we are never logically compelled to take.[2] With regard to many descriptions this is no doubt true, since we can often drive a wedge between describing and commending by making the latter depend on the speaker's intention. Someone may wish to commend a person in describing him as 'strict', while the same description may be a condemnation in the mouth of another. The word is not reserved for any particular rôle, but to know the appropriate description of a person's speech act you must know more than the language, you must know something of the speaker's intentions. What holds for 'strict' certainly holds for at least most other descriptions; however, what is being maintained is the strong claim that *no* description can carry a commendatory force, where this is advanced not as an empirical truth about actual descriptions but as a logical truth guaranteed by the meaning of 'description', which brings us back to the familiar difficulties of establishing the required dichotomy in the intended sense. It may be possible to elaborate and generalize the intention–description distinction so as to yield the desired conclusion, but, leaving aside this approach, there is a sense in which it is true that commending someone is a step which we are never logically compelled to take. Commending and condemning are things which we do, and things which we do in a sense of 'do' in which we are never compelled to do anything. Suppose, for instance, that to call a person 'courageous' is to commend that person. Now it may be that, given what I know and claim with regard to a person's behaviour, I cannot consistently deny that he acted courageously. It is true that actually commending him is a further step which I am not logically compelled to take, but the step in question is actually *saying* 'He is courageous'. I think that other conditions would also have to be fulfilled, but suppose it possible that on a given occasion all that remains for a commendation is the utterance of these words. Here *utterance* must be stressed; it would not be enough if I just had the *thought* 'He is courageous'. Even to think that a person's behaviour is *commendable* is not thereby to commend him. Similarly, given the fulfilment of certain necessary conditions, it may be that the utterance of 'You played well' automatically counts as a commendation, but once more logic is powerless to extract this acknowledgment. Again, to call a person a 'liar' may be to condemn that person, but although the facts may force me to the conclusion that a certain person is a liar, condemnation does not reside in the mere drawing of this conclusion; in stopping short of actually calling the person a liar I stop short of condemning him. This is especially obvious when condemning is understood as a perlocutionary act—the person being condemned by my remark, irrespective of how I intended it—but it also holds for condemning as an illocutionary act. It is true that a condemnation cannot be derived from a statement of fact: as a performance it cannot be derived from anything. Similar remarks apply to complimenting, congratulating, praising, boasting, reproaching, and rebuking; in all these cases the liberty we have is the liberty to speak or remain silent.

While 'good' may be used in order to guide choices, the same purpose is often served by informing the person making the choice that such and such an object has the features which he wants. For instance, instead of calling a medicine 'good', we might simply state that it did cure what it was claimed to cure. Conversely, we could discourage choice of a medicine by saying that it brought death within minutes, or that its curative powers were no greater than those of water. This is obvious enough, but it may be urged that the possibility of using these descriptions to guide choices rests on the fact that, by accepted standards, a medicine which can be so described just is good (bad, poor), the suggestion being, perhaps, that we might have adopted different standards—not very plausible in this instance. However, although the step to 'good' or 'bad' may be immediate from the description given, it is not necessary that the guidance of choices should depend on this step being taken by the chooser, but he need only recognize that what is described is what he wants. It is of course likely that a good x and the sort of x wanted coincide, but they may not, and in general, descriptions bearing on the latter will serve better to guide an individual's choices than descriptions relating implicitly or explicitly to the goodness of something. On the other hand, the connection between being good and being what is wanted is often not merely contingent, and in many cases the divergence can be put down to the fact that what is wanted is wanted for a special purpose, whereas 'good' connects with what is typically wanted of things of the sort in question. It would be difficult to say that something was not a good x if it had everything that anyone wanted of an x. If a knife has all the properties which we want of or look for in a knife (of a certain sort), and none which is not wanted, then it is not merely a good but a perfect knife; here Moore's 'open question' is surely an illusion. Again, 'want' seems to provide the generality which a definition of 'good' requires. Hare has argued that the different descriptions associated with 'good' vary so much from one class of objects to another that the word cannot be thought of as primarily descriptive; hence the attraction of regarding its commendatory function as primary, as the source of its identity in diverse contexts.[3] However, although at one level of generality what makes a car good is quite different from what makes a pen good, it may be that the particular specifications both fall under some more general description, such as 'having what one wants of an x'.

An analysis along the above lines is given by Paul Ziff (*Semantic Analysis*, chapter VI), who claims that 'good' means 'answering to certain interests'. 'Interests' is perhaps in general more appropriate than 'wants', and the evidence which Ziff offers in support of his analysis is pretty substantial, though it more convincingly supports a version of the analysis which differs slightly from the above. Thus, for the most part, Ziff is content to say that 'good' has associated with it the condition of answering to certain interests; only in conclusion does he make the less cautious claim that this associated condition gives the meaning of 'good'. In the great majority of cases, the argument for an association is overwhelming; on the other hand, the result of replacing 'good' by 'answering to certain interests' often sounds very odd, even when 'certain' is supplanted by a more specific reference. This may not be much of an objection to the alleged synonymy; still, it could be that while Ziff's formula gives the most general approximation to 'good', it is not entirely adequate to particular occurrences of the word. That is, it could be that 'good' is 'polymorphous', that it has a number of central meanings, e.g. 'enjoyable', 'useful', 'kind', 'effective', and so on, and that Ziff's formula gives the highest common factor of each use without quite doing justice to any particular use. At any rate, supposing that whether or not something is a good x is in some way the same question as whether or not it answers to certain interests, I want now to consider the question of *whose* interests. This question Ziff regards as essentially irrelevant, since the appropriate answer is: 'Whichever one has the interests in question' (p 236). As a general observation this response may be correct, but in particular cases the question does become important, especially if our concern is with disputes about the goodness of something. Take as an example the phrase 'good news'. In the context of the statement 'A social scandal is good news', 'is good news' has roughly the sense of 'is newsworthy'. In this sense, what is good news is what makes good news, and it is clear that what counts as news is relevant to what counts as good news. It is a question of the value of some incident *qua* news, not for any other feature it might have, and that is a matter of what is required of news as such: that it should arouse interest, report something out of the ordinary. And, of course, the most horrifying or regrettable happenings may qualify for that. Consider now the case when, on learning something to my advantage, I say 'That is good news'. What I am then commenting on is not necessarily something which makes good news, but it is a matter of welcome news; it is not so much that, as having the characteristics of news, something is good, but good news here is simply news of something good. In the first case, my own preferences have no bearing on the question of what counts as good news; it is a question of a general concern with features of news established independently of the wishes of any given individual. In the second case, however, it may be that my preferences are the only ones relevant, or at any rate that I can speak of good news just in so far as the incident reported meets an interest of mine, is good as far as I am concerned.

Unless some qualification is introduced or is understood from the context, what holds for 'good news' in the first sense holds for most instances of '(a) good f'. Whether or not x is a good f depends on whether or not x has or does what is typically wanted of f's, and this is true not only when f specifies a certain role, as 'driver', 'accountant', 'watchdog', or names an object designed for a certain purpose, as 'radio', 'watch', 'lock', but also when f belongs in neither of these classes, as 'bargain', 'weather', 'recovery'. Again the goodness of an f may be a matter of its answering to the interests of people in a certain position: the goodness of a poison is to be judged from the standpoint of those wishing to poison, not of those wishing not to be poisoned, while whether the victim is making a good recovery is determined from his point of view, not that of those hoping to gain by his death. On the other hand, as with the second interpretation of 'good news', or with 'I had a good holiday (time, meal, swim, bath)', it may be that only the speaker's interests are in question, and when, in this case, 'good' means 'pleasant' or enjoyable', the speaker's word is often the last word.

Suppose that the results of a lottery are announced and that I find myself the winner. If I say 'That's good news' and a less fortunate ticket-holder says that it is not, have we contradicted one another? In this instance I am inclined to say 'No', if it turns out that neither of us meant anything more than that it was or was not good as far as he was concerned. However, the question is often not even as clear as that, but it may be far from obvious just what interests of what people are at issue. Consider the case where a difference of standards arises. Someone who is a good tennis player by my standards may not rate as such by the standards of a Wimbledon champion; a car good by yesterday's standards may not be good by today's; what is deemed good weather by an Englishman may not be considered such by an Australian. The difference in standards which we speak of here can be understood in two ways. On the one hand, it may be that each party looks for the same characteristics, though within this common framework one requires more than the other for his standards to be met. In such a case there is at least the possibility of an absolute comparative judgment: 'A is a better tennis player than B', say. On the other hand, the two parties may differ not about the degree to which certain features should be present but about the sort of feature required. In such cases the area of disagreement is likely to be restricted by the description of the object which is being judged good: no matter how much I wish my car could fly, the fact that it cannot does not give me grounds for saying that it is not a good car. But even within these limitations there is often ample room for disagreement: I rate safety factors in a car more highly than you who value speed, in which case even an agreed comparative judgment is unlikely. In both cases, disagreement at a verbal level may be considerable, but in so far as it is possible that each disputant should recognize a claim relativized to certain interests as being what he intended in saying that something was or was not good, to that extent it seems inappropriate to speak of any real difference of opinion, though the matter is, of course, likely to be further complicated by a lack of requisite information or by disagreement about the truth or probability of some relevant claim.

So far I have been assuming that Ziff's analysis is substantially correct. As Ziff himself recognizes, there are uses of 'good', as in 'a good two miles' and 'a good hour', which the analysis does not appear to accommodate. Other more or less similar examples are given by 'good' in conjunction with 'sackful', 'handful', 'ton', 'dose', 'distance', 'height', 'hiding', 'thrashing', 'number', 'proportion', 'chance', 'scolding', 'talking to', 'look', 'fright', 'scare', 'slap', 'hit', 'push', 'bite'. The sense of 'good' when it prefaces these nouns may vary, but it usually means something like 'full', 'complete', 'sizeable', 'considerable', or 'substantial'. So understood, the connection with interests is not obvious, but a case can be made out for some sort of connection. First, a more general point. While a thing's being good may be ultimately a matter of its answering to certain interests, when trying to ascertain whether *x* is a good *f* we generally need not bear in mind the relation to interests, but our immediate concern is likely to be with more specific characteristics of *x*. Consider how we determine whether something is a good copy, a good fit, a good example, or a good question. In many cases, *x* is a good *f* to the extent that it has what it takes to be an *f*, is complete or in no way lacking as an *f*, or possesses to some degree features associated with being an *f*, such things being as we want them only in so far as these conditions are fulfilled. Again, certain actions, e.g. a push, a rub, a bite, must not be tentative or half-hearted if they are to have the effects desired by the agent. In general, the notion of being complete, full, thorough, and so forth gives a fairly minimal condition for being a good *f*, but it is very commonly applicable, and it is understandable that it should carry over to cases such as 'a good hour', which is at least analogous to those cases where the interest is obvious. Even here a case could be made out for a connection with a very general interest; at any rate, 'good' is seldom if ever *just* an intensive, but interests come into the picture in some way. A 'good' chance seems to mean no more than a 'considerable' chance, but we do take some account of interests when using this phrase—I would not say that there is a good chance that I shall be killed. Similarly, I may say that I gave someone a good hiding, but I am less likely to say that someone gave me a good hiding. The expression 'a good fright' is interesting here, since it may be that a good fright is a bad fright. Something is a good fright because it is a success as a fright, but for the same reason it is a bad fright, though once more the standpoint adopted is likely to lead to the use of one description rather than the other. While a difference in standpoint can lead to a difference in the use of 'good' and 'bad' here, when 'bad' is an intensive, with the sense of 'serious' or 'severe', it is often not possible to use 'good' in its place. Consider 'cold', 'pain', 'mistake', 'scar', 'accident', 'sprain', 'difficulties', 'wound', 'indigestion', 'lack', 'lapse', 'failing', 'delay', 'nightmare', 'injury'. It is sometimes said that anything can be called 'good', but it is generally far from clear what '(a) good *x*' would mean when *x* is replaced by a word from this list.

Although what is considered good need often be considered good only from the point of view of the speaker, in the majority of cases a more general or typical interest must be met for the use of the word to be justified. What holds for 'good' also holds for most uses of words associated with the expression of feelings, as 'boring', 'engrossing', 'exciting', 'irritating', 'pleasing', 'shocking', 'interesting'. These words, which may figure as particular values of 'good' and 'bad', can be said to express or embody an attitude, but it is doubtful that they satisfy condition *b*), and they do not presuppose a favourable or unfavourable attitude, in the sense that we have to satisfy ourselves that something is good (bad) before describing it in such terms. Consider 'boring'. Typically, to describe a film, say, as 'boring' is to generalize one's own reaction to the film: I found it boring, it bored me. In so far as it is reasonable for me to suppose that my own reactions are not idiosyncratic, to that extent it is reasonable for me to use the impersonal formulation, though there is, of course, frequently the risk that this wider claim will prove wrong—what bores me may engross others. There is, too, considerable vagueness about the scope of the impersonal judgment: just what section of the populace need be bored by the film for my claim that it is boring to be vindicated? Similarly with 'exciting'. A film cannot be said to be exciting if it excites no one, but it is not necessarily not exciting if there is someone whom it does not excite. If deaf people or idiots fail to find it exciting, this does not of itself oblige me to retract my claim that it is. I can reasonably say there is something wrong with such people; for one reason or another they are incapable of being excited by certain aspects of films in general, so their reactions may not count for much in a particular case. But there are limits to which that form of defence may be carried, and these limits are overstepped if I can be rightly accused of elevating to the norm my own peculiar capacity for being excited. The indeterminacy implicit in such judgments gives rise to problems of verification, but they are not alone in this; a similar difficulty besets many statements involving general terms which are not explicitly quantified, e.g. 'Frenchmen prefer wine to beer'. This does not mean 'each and every', nor just 'some' Frenchmen; it is as imprecise as 'By and large, Frenchmen prefer wine to beer'. Even though the indeterminacy in 'x is boring' or 'x is exciting' may complicate their verification, it is important to note that such statements stand or fall accordingly as people do or do not react in a certain way. This trivial fact is often overlooked, especially with regard to the words 'disgusting', 'appalling', 'shocking', and 'revolting', which some people persist in using even when it is obvious to them that they are in a minority. If a person describes something in these terms, then he is simply wrong if others do not concur in finding it so. If he wants to go on using these words despite the preponderance of dissenters, he must face the fact that they are in his mouth no more than expressions of personal distaste; in dismissing the reactions of others as irrelevant to his judgment, he is in effect only voicing the claim that he finds something disgusting, appalling, shocking, or revolting. Such a person is likely to round on dissenters with the claim that they *ought* to be disgusted, appalled, shocked, or revolted, but whatever we think of that, it is a different issue, and does nothing to vindicate the use of the impersonal formulation. It is also clear that such judgments are unlikely to enjoy any lasting validity: matters which shocked our forefathers no longer shock us, though they may conceivably shock future generations, and jokes which our parents found amusing may draw no response from us.

The words just considered are all of the same grammatical form, but there are others to which the same remarks apply, e.g. 'dull', 'tedious', 'attractive', 'likeable', 'pleasant', 'enjoyable', 'agreeable', 'repulsive', 'outrageous', 'disagreeable', 'impressive', 'strange', 'funny', 'easy', 'difficult', 'nice', and 'nasty'. A statement that something is dull, etc., may be personal to the extent that it is based on the speaker's own reactions (responses, feelings, sensibilities, abilities), but not personal in its logic, in the sense that the reactions of others are irrelevant to its truth. Once more this is important, in view of the tendency to overemphasize the autobiographical element in such assertions to the point that it becomes conflated with their truth-conditions. Of course, to a greater or lesser degree, most statements which are not explicitly personal are at the mercy of the findings of others; it is just that this vulnerability is more real in the case of statements based on reactions and feelings. Personal differences are unlikely to be the source of disagreement over the claim that something is spherical, brown, wet, glistens, and is made of rubber.

The logic of the words just discussed has much in common with that of 'good', with differences in reaction corresponding to differences in interest as a source of dispute. Another source of dispute which was in evidence with 'good' and which is more generally applicable is the possibility of differing standards. I suggested earlier that some words might be held to embody a pro- or con-attitude, when in fact they do no more than name features which are, or are likely to be, the objects of such attitudes. Possible examples of such words are 'modest', 'honest', 'polite', 'tidy', 'considerate', and 'punctual'. In a given case, the value or desirability of, say, honesty or punctuality may be undeniable, since these may be in the interests of all concerned. On another occasion, a conflict of interests may make an unqualified assertion about their value or desirability impossible, but in either case it would seem that we need take no account of our dispositions or the value which we place upon the relevant behaviour in deciding whether the terms 'honest' or 'punctual' apply. However, it might be argued that this is to overlook an important point, namely that the applicability of any of the above words may be disputed by people who hold different standards as to what counts as an instance of the relevant behaviour. One man may set his standards of tidiness or politeness much higher than another, but when they accordingly give opposed judgments, there is no question of the one being right and the other wrong. This is, I think, sometimes true, though we are at liberty to adopt differing standards only within certain limits, and a person who adopts idiosyncratic standards does so at the risk of misusing the relevant words, whether it is a question of quantity—how much regard need you show others in order to be classed as 'considerate'?—or of quality—what sort of behaviour counts as 'considerate'? In fact, it is doubtful whether the possibility of conflicting standards is a point of much significance with respect to any of the above words, since words in general may be similarly affected: whether a man is bald, poor, fat, or strong are questions to which in some cases there can be no right or wrong answer. It is true that, within a certain range, no statement of the number of hairs on a persons' head entails that he is or is not bald, and in general, that a description of something over a range in which the criteria for being *f* are not precisely fixed may not entail that the thing is *f*, or is not *f*. The fact that *f* may name a feature of value is of no further account.

I mentioned at the outset that a common source of disagreement could be the vagueness or ill-defined character of the terms in which a description is couched. The type of dispute just mentioned is to some extent a particular instance of this, and another relevant case is that of words used in an analogical or transferred sense. Names of certain animals, 'ass', 'pig', 'nit', 'skunk', 'louse', 'cow', and 'bitch', have an uncomplimentary sense when applied to people, and indeed it is this sense or force which tends to be uppermost, the resemblance to animal behaviour *qua* undesirable overriding the question of a more specific likeness. Though rather indeterminate in meaning when so used, such words are not applied altogether indiscriminately: the type of behaviour which might prompt me to call someone a 'louse' is quite different from the behaviour which might lead me to call him a 'pig', though as it is never a question of anything more than a purported likeness between human and animal attributes, no one could claim that he had literal truth on his side in describing someone in such terms; at best the description might be eminently suitable. Other examples: in saying the Smiths descended upon us I may be likening them to vultures or other unwelcome predatory creatures; in saying that certain people were exterminated I suggest a regard for them as pests or vermin. Of course, it is not just the animal kingdom that is fruitful in the comparisons which it offers, but words may be drawn from any sphere and reapplied in extended or analogical senses. Consider the various uses of 'thick', 'polished', 'smashing', 'smooth', 'wet', 'dregs'. The use of these words is never entirely arbitrary, but it tends to become a matter of choice when they are released from more or less definite truth-conditions.

So far we have not met with any clear-cut examples of value words which satisfy both *a*) and *b*), but the sources of possible disagreement noted may infect words which have little or no bearing on values. Indeed, we may even begin to wonder whether there are any words which have the features thought to characterize value words, since in many cases a pro- or con-attitude is no more than suggested by the use of a word, and in other cases, even though a word may in some sense embody an attitude, this may be no bar to the testability of a statement in which it figures. What seems to be wanted is a word which does not commit the user to anything as explicit as, say, a judgment of goodness or badness, but which merely carries overtones indicative of a favourable or unfavourable attitude. This description fits some of the words mentioned in the last paragraph, but the fact of their non-literal use rather complicates the issue. What about 'upstart', 'old maid', or 'newfangled'? These carry derogatory or disparaging overtones, but perhaps nothing which amounts to anything as definite as a testable claim. Similar examples are 'nigger' and 'dago'. These have a pejorative sense, but while we would not use them unless we regarded the relevant races as inferior, their use does not involve anything as precise as a statement to that effect. Note that the claim that 'nigger' is used pejoratively easily survives the test of non-assertive contexts: I betray an attitude if I say 'I wonder if he is a nigger' just as much as if I say 'He is a nigger'. Moreover, even though the attitude which the use of the word betrays is not embodied in any precise claim-making form, still it might be argued that the use of the word is not defensible, since it does in a roundabout way give expression to beliefs which are unjustified.

This last example brings us to wider questions concerning language and the choice of words. In the sorts of dispute so far contemplated, I have been supposing that the disputants would each be prepared to use the problematic description on some occasion or other, even though they may disagree in a given case. However, as the example of 'nigger' shows, there are words which one person may use but which another may not, not even to deny what the former person has said. Further examples are given by various 'non-standard' locutions; for instance, colloquialisms, obscenities, archaisms, neologisms, children's talk, officialese, slang, jargon, and cant. Even if I am prepared to praise something in the highest terms, I would not say that it was 'fab'. Nor would I say that someone did or did not behave in a 'dastardly' fashion, or that someone was 'made the recipient' of something. In a given case I may feel compelled to agree to such descriptions, but they are not descriptions which I would volunteer. Again, I may be diffident about using an obscene expression, but not on the grounds that it misrepresented the situation. If it were a case of disagreement, I might still be reluctant to voice my disagreement in the opposition's terms. Of course, in some contexts we may not hesitate to use words from the above classes; we talk unashamedly about 'moo-cows' and 'doggies' to children, and use certain colloquialisms in speech but not in writing. The reasons why we are reluctant to use or refrain from using non-standard expressions vary from case to case; perhaps we do not wish to risk association with the sort of people who use such expressions freely, perhaps we regard a word as ill-suited to a certain context because of the solemnity or frivolity of the contexts in which it typically occurs. As far as I know, no one has suggested that there is a fallacy involved in inferring non-standard from standard statements, and I do not think that any general argument against the possibility of such inferences would hold, though with slang and highly colloquial language the difficulties generated by loose and figurative language are likely to arise. Perhaps in general the situation is similar to that which I claimed for the case of commending. I may not be able to deny that x is g if it is f, where g is a non-standard term for f, but nothing actually compels me to use g. If Smith is a policeman, then of course he is a cop, though I do not have to put it this way.

Non-standard expressions are interesting for the parallels which they offer to traditional philosophical controversies, but there are other more relevant cases where a person might refrain from using a word. For instance, in her article 'Modern Moral Philosophy' (*Philosophy*, 1958, pp 1–19), Miss G. E. M. Anscombe has argued that in certain uses the terms 'right' and 'wrong' are empty, notably when they are detached from a law-based conception of morality which gives them content. Similarly we might argue that disputes as to whether people do or do not have rights to private property or freedom of speech are meaningless when there is no question of a body which might confer or withhold such rights. Again, I suspect that both affirmations and denials featuring 'deserve', 'merit', and related words often rest on an untenable retributive theory of punishment. These and many more words and issues remain to be discussed; they are likely to be complicated, but I doubt that the fact-value dichotomy will shed any light on the problems involved.

NOTES

1 P. T. Geach, 'Ascriptivism', *Philosophical Review,* vol. LXIX (1960), pp 221–5; 'Assertion', *Philosophical Review,* vol. LXXIV (1965), pp 449–65; J. R. Searle, 'Meaning and Speech Acts', *Philosophical Review,* vol. LXXI (1962), pp 423–32.

2 R. M. Hare, 'Descriptivism', *Proceedings of the British Academy,* vol. XLIX (1963), p 121.

3 *The Language of Morals,* p 118. We can say that 'good' in 'good news' means 'welcome', while 'good' in 'a good approximation' means 'close', even though the word in general means neither of these. Nor is 'It is a close approximation, so it is a good approximation' thereby made altogether trivial, but finding the value of 'good' in a given case is analogous to solving an equation.

PRIVATE LANGUAGES AND LINGUISTIC STIPULATION

M. J. SCOTT-TAGGART

IN THIS PAPER I propose neither to attack nor to defend the private language argument. I shall give a short account of two methods of deploying the argument, and show how the two prohibitions against a private language which these erect are in large part definitional. I must insist in advance that I do not believe this makes it a trivial matter: philosophy must end in definitions, but definitions which are made with a purpose. I shall indicate briefly the different purposes to which these definitions relate, and which I shall call the demand for communicability and the demand for a linguistic super-ego. In this way, having clarified the argument, I shall hope to show that its essential features express demands concerning our statements about the world which are shared by demands of traditional theory, and thus how the private language argument can with benefit be brought into relation with that theory.

I. THE DEMAND FOR COMMUNICABILITY

The private language argument has been deployed, with effect, in connection with the *prima facie* private language that nests within our own: the language of sensations, where there is such a marked difference between first- and third-person statements. I shall, however, only be concerned with the closely related problem of a totally private language. We are to examine the supposition that there might be a being who uses his words to 'refer to what can only be known to the person speaking, to his immediate private sensations'.[1]

Such a use of words has sometimes been called impossible, sometimes pointless. Its pointlessness has even been used covertly as a reason for its impossibility. Thus Flew argues cogently that Locke was inconsistent in holding 1) that language is for communication—it is to be the 'common tie of society'—and 2) that 'the use of words is to be sensible marks of ideas; and the ideas they stand for are their proper and immediate signification'. Flew charges that Locke's view takes for granted 'that it is possible for people to communicate, while at the same time denying a presupposition of any common language', and claims that it is only through 'a systematic failure to launch and press home a really determined attempt to state the position consistently that its fundamental impossibility is concealed'.[2] Of course Locke was right in what he wanted to say, namely that we should try to have first-hand experience of what we are talking about, but he certainly chose an unfortunate way of expressing it. And it seems to me true that if all the entities talked about in a language were to be private, then we should have a language in which it was not possible to communicate. It also seems to me plausible to say on this basis that we have shown the impossibility of a private language, if 'private language' is defined as a language in which all the entities spoken about are private. But it does not seem to me compelling. For strictly all that we have shown is the impossibility of a communicable private language. If we define a language as communicable, then we have shown the impossibility of a private language—by definition. The purpose of such a definition would be to draw our attention to the conditions which have to be satisfied for different people to attach the same meaning to an expression. We express crudely a necessary condition for communicability if we say: the proposition expressed by '*x* means the same by this word as *y*' is one that can only be asserted if it is logically possible for the two speakers to agree that the word has been correctly used. To appreciate the value of a firm grasp upon this condition is to appreciate some of the most important contributions to contemporary philosophy. The recent work of Quine can be viewed as throwing light on this conditional by following out its implications for the theory of translation, and thus, incidentally, teaching us a great deal about our relation to our own language.[3] Again, Strawson's stimulating discussion of the concept of a person also illuminates the conditional by making use of it in another context.[4] Instances could be multiplied of the fruits borne of an appreciation of this point of view from which we see the rôle of objective particulars in conditioning and regulating language.

The definition, then, is important, but if we are not interested in communication (either because there is nobody to communicate with or just because we are not interested in communication) the argument based on the definition would not be binding upon us. To refute the private language proponent in this way would be to suppose that his purpose was to throw light on the question of communicability, but could not his purposes have been different? Perhaps Locke was interested in communication, but he need not have been. A proponent of a private language might uphold his position by arguing that his purposes were entirely different, as, for example, to construct a model for certain specific purposes, and it is inappropriate to dismiss the product of the model-maker's activities in all cases by saying something akin to 'It will never carry passengers'. So if this is all that there is to the private language argument we can learn its lesson and go our way, although a little more carefully. But there is more to it, for the impossibility of communicating has been thought to entail more vicious consequences than loneliness. Let us look at these.

2. THE DEMAND FOR A LINGUISTIC SUPER-EGO

The lack of communicability is at the core of the present objection to a private language, although it starts from two apparently independent premises. The first is that to possess a word is to be capable of indulging in some form of controlled behaviour. For a word to have a use it must also be open to misuse. If there is no restriction on its use, then it cannot be said to be a word. This I take to be plainly true. The second premise is that if a word is to be open to use and misuse, then there must be some independent standard which determines, of its uses on at least some occasions, whether they are correct or incorrect. This seems to be implied by the use of the word 'correct', which, being an evaluative word, implies something about conformity to or violation of a standard. How these two premises relate to the dispute can be seen from Malcolm's article on the subject. He says about a case of a presumptive private ostensive definition that 'I did not establish a connection if subsequently I applied that word to sensations other than pain or to things other than sensations, e.g. emotions. My private definition was a success only if it led me to use the word correctly in the future. In the present case "correctly" would mean "consistently with my own definition", for the question of whether my use agrees with that of others has been given up as a bad job.'[5]

The question is: could we have a use for 'I am using *W* as I used it before' without also having a use for 'I am using *W* as everybody else uses it'? I could not have a use for the former statement unless there was a way of discovering whether I was using *W* as I used it before: there has to be the possibility of error and there must also be a decision procedure. This decision procedure must consist, Malcolm claims, in an appeal to something which is independent of my impression that I am using the word correctly, although the notion of independence is one which he leaves unclarified, beyond implying that 'in the nature of the case there cannot be such an appeal'. Granted that an independent check is required, why is it 'in the nature of the case' that there cannot be one? This raises the questions:

1) What is the independent check that Malcolm demands?
2) Is this the only sort of independent check?

While if there are other sorts of independent check, we must also ask:

3) Do the other sorts also rule out the possibility of a private language?
4) Why does Malcolm demand the one that he does?

As to the first question. Malcolm expresses the demand for an independent check, the demand for 'some other way' of expressing my recognition, on another occasion, and again he says that 'the notion of the private language doesn't admit of there being "some other way". It doesn't allow that my behaviour and circumstances can be so related to my utterance of the word, that another person, by noting my behaviour and circumstances, can discover that my use of the word is correct or incorrect.'[6] This implies that an independent check must consist in correction by other people. Malcolm appears to suggest that this need not be actual correction by other people, but that a referring in imagination to other people will do, although I think that this referring in imagination is taken to presuppose that there has been actual correction. The only way, we are told, that I might discover for myself whether I was using the word correctly would be to 'presuppose that I have a conception of correct use which comes from outside my private language and against which I measure the latter'.[7]

It seems that, for Malcolm, an appeal to an independent check is an appeal to a consensus. This explains his thinking that 'in the nature of the case there cannot be such an appeal'. That this is indeed his view is further confirmed when he says, echoing Wittgenstein's 'whatever is going to seem right to me is right', that 'a sound I can use *as I please* is not a *word*'.[8] This locution, in the normal use which is here being employed, we find in sentences like 'You can do as you please', which carry the implication that other people are in some way not relevant to whatever is going to be done. Taken together, these points make clear that Malcolm construes the 'independent' in 'independent check' to mean 'independent of my own decision'. If we define 'independent' in this way, then a private language is indeed impossible.

What is the purpose of adopting such a definition? It does have a value, just as the definition in the first form of the private language argument had its value. It draws our attention to the way in which our language does normally work: that 'I am using this word correctly' implies 'I am using this word as I used it before' only in so far as, in general, it also implies 'I am using this word like everybody else'. More generally, it draws our attention to the fact that language is a homoeostatic system, albeit an open one, in which departure from correct use is quickly corrected or more slowly followed. This definition emphasizes the homoeostasis, as the first emphasized the regulative function of physical objects. This new emphasis has been used by philosophers to throw light on certain corporate, democratic activities as well as upon traditional problems.[9]

Although this reference to a consensus is valuable, we must not take it for more of a necessity than it is. Morality is, like language itself, a social activity; and just as concentration on the morals-learning situation led to the concept of the super-ego, the introjection of parental symbols to form the conscience or moral disciplinarian, so one might guess that it is a concern with the language-learning situation which has led to this notion of the linguistic super-ego. The analogy, while it cannot be pressed too far, brings one point to our attention: just as questions of moral philosophy cannot be reduced to questions about how we learn moral rules, so philosophical questions about meaning cannot be reduced to questions about how we learn to use certain words.

If we adopt the sort of independent check that Malcolm requires, then we are quickly led to overemphasize the importance of learning situations for philosophical problems. Thus Rhees argues that there could not be a language unless meanings were independent of the speaker, which he defines, in part, to mean that they *have to be learnt.*[10] On the basis of this definition he argues, correctly of course, that a child Robinson Crusoe, never brought into relation with a language, could not *have* a language, a conclusion which is also entailed by Malcolm's position. The demand for a linguistic super-ego, like the demand for communicability, yields the result: a person who cannot communicate cannot have a language. The two demands are not, however, equivalent. The demand for communicability forbids a language to those people who cannot communicate with others because their words have a purely private reference; the demand for a linguistic super-ego forbids a language *not only* to these people *but also* to those who cannot communicate with others simply because there is nobody to communicate with. The demand for a linguistic super-ego turns the demand for communicability into the demand for actual communication.

A linguistic super-ego is demanded because, Malcolm and Rhees believe, 'linguistic behaviour' entails 'learned behaviour'. The entailment is sustained by the implicit definition of the form that an 'independent check' would have to take. Need we accept this definition? The child-lost Crusoe, we may agree, would not have a language. It is not, however, true that 'would not' and 'could not' are generally coincident, and to say that the Crusoe 'could not' have a language is merely to draw our attention to the various reasons which might be given for the 'would not'. A matter of fact can always be turned into a matter of logic, but it is not at all clear that we are obliged to follow Malcolm and Rhees in the present case. We would only be logically constrained to agree with their position if 1) we allowed the necessity of an independent check, and 2) could not produce any other sort of independent check than that stipulated by Malcolm. In the following section, however, I shall willingly concede 1) while arguing that there is another answer to the question implicit in 2).

There are many things which I am not constrained to do which it would nevertheless be wise to do, and it might be argued that if we do not become disciples of Malcolm, then we are foolishly indulging our freedom. I shall not argue this at all fully here, for I am mainly concerned to keep the roads open, and not to recommend one particular route. I will point out only that Malcolm's position has all the ingredients of a classical metaphysical system. If not in itself, then in the hands of its followers it acquires its own mystique, idiom, parables, and its own particular exaggerations. I have shown that the main concern of Malcolm in the present instance is to insist on the connection of 'linguistic behaviour' and 'learned behaviour'. He does this for various reasons. We are, none of us, really interested in the fate of Crusoe, for the question does not really concern the relation of a possible Crusoe to a possible language, but our own relation to our own actual language.

The main question is not so much 'Can a man alone have a language?' as it is 'Can a man have a private language in the sense of a language such that all the entities talked about in this language are private?' It is with the second question that I am mainly concerned. But if we answer the first question negatively, then this carries consequences for the second question as well as for other questions involved in the dispute over private languages. Thus if a man alone cannot have a language, then we have exhibited that there is a need for the conditions to be satisfied in virtue of which other people can learn a given person's language, and so we answer the second question negatively as well as preparing the ground for later argument about the concepts by means of which we talk about our epistemologically private life, since there must be observable conditions associated with the occurrence of a private entity, and these conditions will in some way form an ingredient in the meaning of the concepts by which we talk about private entities.

With this later line of argument I am not, as I have said, here concerned. I am concerned with the connection between 'linguistic behaviour' and 'learned behaviour' that sets up this later argument, and with the appeal to learning situations that such a connection causes to be philosophically respectable.

The appeal to learning situations has certainly proved its value.

There is, for all that, a temptation to use the question 'How would you learn?' in the same way that philosophers were recently tempted to use the question 'How would you verify?' The analogies between the two questions, as things are, have been largely unremarked because of an historical accident. The question 'How would you verify?' fell into disrepute because of its close association with the various forms of reductionism, and in its fall it took with it the tradition upon which it was based. But this link with reductionism was only a contingent feature of the question, and when the link is broken it becomes clear that the question 'How would you learn?' is only an idiomatic variant of the earlier question 'How would you verify?' and this question, of course, has ancestors in its turn. The latest form of the question differs from its predecessors mainly in its being accompanied by the repudiation of reductionism and by an affirmation of the democratic nature of language.

The question 'How would you learn?' has thus become the *modus operandi* for people working with a certain view of man's relation to language and to the world. This attitude is, in a certain way, rationalistic: Rhees and Malcolm insist on man's dependence on others for his language, an insistence which reminds one of Kant's conception of the enlightenment as release from tutelage, where 'tutelage' is defined as 'man's inability to make use of his understanding without direction from another'.[11] Perhaps it is time for an English *Aufklärung*.

We have now looked at two versions of the private language argument. The first ruled a private language out of existence because it was claimed that a language must admit the possibility of the statement '*x* means the same by this word as *y*'; and this possibility was ruled out if there was no publicity. The second argument ruled a private language out of existence because it was claimed that a language must actually involve the statement '*x* means the same by this word as *y*'; only through actual communication can someone have the required check over the use of his words. I have indicated the way in which this argument is used as clearing the ground for some of the more interesting conclusions to come out of the private language argument, but I want now to see if this is the only sort of independent check that we can discover.

3. THE DEMAND FOR AN INDEPENDENT CHECK

To put the problem once more in terms of the child-lost Crusoe, the question, as we can take it from Malcolm, is whether he could give a sense to 'I am using this word according to my definition'. In order that he might do so, we have agreed, he must have some way of checking whether he is using the word in the same way on the present occasion as he did on some previous occasion. We posit as contrast to Malcolm's argument that this check cannot be constituted out of appeals to other people, and ask: can a check be provided in any way out of the nature of that about which we talk in a language?

In order to decide whether it might be, I propose to consider two different sorts of language: one in which all the entities talked about are *sensations*, and another in which all the entities talked about are *physical objects*. The first will be a private language, and the second a public language. As I want to keep the two sorts of language clear and separate from one another, I am going to make a further and unreal supposition, which is that there is no correlation between any group of sensations and any objective states of affairs, where these include natural behavioural expressions which may be known to the possessor of the sensation kinaesthetically. This supposition is clearly necessary if we are to have a private language (i.e. a language in which all the entities talked about are private) that is also a language that nobody else could understand, for if there were such correlations, then other people could come to use the words that I use in the situations in which I use them. The term 'private language' has, under Wittgensteinian auspices, often been used of a language which is to be defined as one that nobody else could understand, but it is clear that a private language in a sense other than that I have defined is not necessarily a private language in this further sense. Because this supposition does not actually obtain, other people *can* learn to use a sensation or feeling word in the same situation as I, although the basis of their judgment is different from the basis of my judgment that this situation is to be characterized in a certain way. It is because this supposition is false that we have our ordinary talk about sensations and other private phenomena, and one effect of the private language argument has been to stop us thinking of these two bases either as providing different 'senses' of a sensation concept or as one having a certain priority over the other (although the argument has been taken to excess and often been used to invert the priorities). This effect has been the product of the argument that other people *must* be able to speak my language, so that these two 'senses' *must* be reconciled within one concept. It is the force of this argument that I wish to consider, and in order to do so it is necessary to make the supposition, however unreal it may be.

Could a person have a language if all that was talked about in this language was sensations, and would his position be any different from that of the child-lost Crusoe who is going to talk about physical objects rather than sensations? Have we a check on the use of concepts that we apply to sensations as well as a check on the use of those concepts that we apply to physical objects? And have we, indeed, cut off from the linguistic practice of others, a check on those concepts that we apply to physical objects?

Let us suppose that a person is presented with a sensation that has a certain quality which he picks out by the word *E*, and that at a later time he is presented with another sensation which he believes is also an *E*. How can he check his belief that he is using *E* as he used it before? We might first of all suppose that he could do so by referring to concomitant sensations, but under the terms of the supposition that we have made this is not possible. By cutting off an objective reference we have also cut off all coherence between one experience and another: if there were coherence, then there would be objective reference. This follows from what I take to be the truth in Kant's *Transcendental Deduction*. We therefore have a person who claims that an experience is of the same kind as a previous experience, and needs to be able to confirm this by reference to something else, and who cannot do so by saying that both experiences, besides being of this kind, are also of some other kind.

It might be thought that memory images would do. The possibility is worth looking at in view of the important rôle that images play in traditional theory, and it is worth contrasting physical objects in this respect with images. One of the most important features of the contrast springs from the different methods we employ in individuating physical objects as opposed to images. Thus a physical object exists in a spatial dimension, and it can therefore be numerically identical with an object whose perception belongs to an earlier time. Images, on the other hand, are individuated by reference only to a temporal dimension, although we also require specification of the owner, and so a mediate reference to a spatial dimension. An image, therefore, cannot be numerically identical with an image from an earlier time.

What follows from this? Most importantly, a physical object can, quite literally, be reproduced. It is only in a metaphorical sense, the sense in which a picture can be said to be the reproduction of reality, that we can speak of an image as a reproduction of a past situation. I cannot produce numerically the same image on different occasions, but only an image which is a reproduction of, or qualitatively like, an earlier image.

Let us relate these facts to the person for whom we are trying to provide a private language. It is surely clear that because the only sense in which he can say of an image that it reproduces the past situation is that it is qualitatively like the past situation, it follows that any problems that he might have about saying that the new experience is like the old will reappear in saying that the image-experience is like the old. To say that the image-experience is like the new experience does nothing to relate either of them to the past experience. Images are thus not an independent check on whether we are using a word in the same way as on a previous occasion.

The case is *prima facie* different for physical objects. If someone produces a print of a picture, I can always ask if it is an accurate reproduction of the original, but if the original is itself produced there is no sense in which I can ask if it is an accurate reproduction. It is its own model. Thus a Crusoe, who is to have a language in which he talks about physical objects, might be able to produce numerically the same object to which he applied the word on a previous occasion, and in doing so he would, in an almost literal sense, be holding the past alongside the present. Physical objects, because of their insistence through time, are much more plausible candidates for the rôle of an independent check.

It will be objected that if I produce a picture, rather than a print of it, then we can still ask 1) 'Is it the original picture?' and 2) 'Is it just as it was, or has someone been touching it up in the interval?' It will be claimed that if we are to use physical objects as a check, then we presuppose answers to these questions, and these answers will presuppose that we are able to use the concept of qualitative similarity, whereas it is precisely our ability to handle qualitative similarities that is in question. The appeal to physical objects is thus, it is said, eventually as circular as an appeal to images.

Kant or Hume would meet this objection by saying that there are ways of determining whether an object is the same as one previously perceived which are not available in the case of images, namely reference to 'causal rules'. In order not to distract attention through begging exegetical issues, I shall deal with the wider concept which embraces any rule of the kind, 'Generally, if *F*, then *G*', so that these may include such rules as 'Generally, if people utter "The snow is white", then the surrounding scene is decked in snow'. It is the traditional view that a sub-class of these statements is essentially constitutive of our concept of the numerical identity of physical objects, and it is certainly true that some imprecisely defined sub-class of them must be involved every time I make a particular identity statement.

I shall designate by *L* the sub-class of law-like propositions which are involved in the making of some particular identity claim, as, for example, 'It is the same cherry'. Just as there are different ways in which this statement might be challenged, so there are different justifications that might be produced. Thus someone might, in response to one particular challenge, say 'It has the same scar on the side, and besides, it was on the top of the bowl when I left it'. If this is to justify him in saying 'It is the same cherry', he must be prepared to make the universal statement which will be a specific instance of the more general rule, 'Generally, whenever an object has the same distinguishing marks as one previously observed, and is in the same place as that object, then it is the same object'. This, therefore, is one element of *L*.

Traditional philosophy has been much concerned over the essential structure of *L*, but here I shall only require its existence. And that it exists is clear from the fact that if there is an objective reference to an experience, then this is constituted out of the relationship of various experiences to one another, and this in a law-like way. If we now relate this to our Crusoe and his attempt to confirm the particular statement 'This is *E*', we find that he can now appeal to two things: 1) the standard cherry, or whatever it might be, which is the same object to which he previously applied the word *E*, and which he can now hold alongside the new object to be qualified in this way, and 2) the body of reasons that justify him in saying that this is the same object to which he applied the word previously. 1) provides the basis for the perceptual similarity that we found in the case of images also, while 2) provides the relating of experiences to one another that, under our supposition, we did not find in the case of images. These two are independently necessary and conjunctively sufficient for the provision of an independent check upon the use of *E*.

The factual insistence of physical objects is required in order that we might meet an objection which is sometimes drawn from the question 'What is the feature of the world which *E* signifies?'[12] It is claimed that if the feature cannot be specified without reference to the word, then any object can be a proper instance of it: this is essentially the argument that we applied against images construed as an independent check. The argument moves forward, however, to meet the present case, for, it is held, if we have two objects, and the relevant similarity between them can only be specified by reference to the word, then, since there must be some feature that they have in common, it will once more follow that they provide no check on the use of the word. Fortunately, however, the argument cannot be extrapolated in this way. It is true that I cannot define a similarity by reference to a single particular, but I can define one, within certain pragmatic limits, through a partial exhibition of the similarity. The idea that a complete exhibition is required, or else an illicit backward glance at the word will be involved, is a mistake that is made because people allow themselves to be logically pushed beyond the limits of practical endurance. The similarities which we pick out in language are objective similarities, and because of this a finite sample of instances can sufficiently define the similarity.[13]

The argument from similarity is therefore not legislative against our Crusoe, for by the same means that he adopts to equip himself with one standard object he could equip himself with any practicable number, and so exhibit the similarity to his own satisfaction. By increasing the number in the standard set he would be able to assess his performance as reliably as we can assess that of the child. The difference between the child's situation and that of our Crusoe is that the child possesses his set of standard examples in the convenient form of the linguistic practice of others. In order to check whether he is using '*E*' as he used it before, the child need only ask someone, whereas Crusoe must check back to his store of *E*-instances. This difference seems to be one to which we can be logically indifferent, but let us confirm this by looking at the situation of the child a little more closely.

Let us suppose a child reaching linguistic maturity who asks himself 'Am I using "*E*" as I used it before?' A first step for him would be to discover if other people would also be prepared to use '*E*' in the situation in which he is using it, and we are also inclined, with our respect for authority, to accept this as a sufficient check. We must notice, however, that 'He and I are both using "*E*" on this occasion' does not confirm the statement 'I am using "*E*" as I used it before'. That my usage is, on this occasion, consistent with the usage of others does nothing to show conclusively that my present is consistent with my own earlier usage. The linguistic practice of others is only a check on 'I am using "*E*" as I used it before' if I can both assert 1) 'He and I are using "*E*" in this situation', and *also* 2) 'He and I did use (or would have used) "*E*" in the past situation'. But 2) is clearly not entailed by 1), for it is related to it as inductive premise to conclusion. We can only get to 2) from 1) by means of generalization, where 1) provides us with only a single confirming instance of the generalization through which we can be certain of 2).

When we examine the child's situation, therefore, we discover that 'I am using "*E*" as I used it before' is confirmed through an appeal to the law-like statement 'He and I always use "*E*" in the same situations'. The confirmation is thus floated upon the conjecture of an objective solidarity, and the authority of the linguistic patriarchs to which Malcolm implicitly appeals is nothing but the hypostatization of this conjecture. We must stand passive before our linguistic betters in the same way that we stand passive before physical objects (which is not to say that in either case we are altogether passive).

I have examined the case of the child to secure my earlier use of the body of law-like statements which I have said are involved in every identity claim. I take it that I have shown this by showing that law-like statements are also a presupposition of the utility of the other sort of independent check required by Malcolm. To show this is not only to give warning against careless *ad hominem* arguments but is also to prove by complete induction the necessity, and therefore the legitimacy, of an appeal to law-like statements. That the validity of these law-like statements is, as I have said, conjectural does not invalidate their use. Although conjectural, these law-like statements can be empirically reputable, if and because they are disconfirmable. We know, of course, that a lot of linguistic jostling goes on at this point, but it is still true that recalcitrance must be met somewhere, and it is this potential disconfirmability which makes a law-like statement independent of ourselves, and thus able to perform in the rôle of an independent check. Since the law-like statements which the Crusoe might forge have this character, there is nothing in the demand for an independent check which would preclude his possession of a language.

4. CONCLUSION

We have looked at two modern forms of the private language argument, and shown how they articulate with disputes about the nature of the concepts in which we talk about mental events. The two forms might well be called the mild and severe forms, although I have called them the demands for communicability and for a linguistic super-ego. The first of these made communicability a necessary condition for the application of the title 'language', and with this I have been but little concerned, for it is relatively trivial apart from the demand for a linguistic super-ego.

I have dealt mainly, therefore, with the private language argument in its severe form. I have shown that this argument, when stripped of definitional strength, does not legislate against, although it is *prima facie* inconsistent with, a more traditional argument that can be built upon the same premises. For both the traditional argument which I have outlined and also the position that Malcolm adopts make use of a premise that has been used although not examined in this paper, which requires there to be a check or control over any use of words. The two arguments differ in the form of control that they provide.

This conclusion is important in that it shows Malcolm's position to stand within a tradition, and not opposed to one, as it has so often seemed. This appears partly in the fact that the question 'How would you learn?' is intimately involved in Malcolm's position and is also a logical outgrowth of the tradition of empiricism. It appears more importantly in the fact, which I have remarked, that the traditional theorists were extremely concerned to clarify the essential structure of the body of law-like statements involved in every identity claim: for the traditional theorists the most important class of law-like statements were those they called 'causal rules', and for Malcolm the most important class are what we might call 'linguistic congruence rules'. It would be premature to argue over the relative importance of these two types of rule, and it is only if we dogmatize about their importance that the two insights bear the appearance of inconsistency. Concern with the rules of linguistic congruence is a fairly new phenomenon in philosophy, and it is important. But, I would insist, these rules must be complementary to the more traditional 'causal rules' and not a replacement for them. Traditional theory has as much to give to contemporary philosophy as this philosophy has to add to the older views.

NOTES

1 Wittgenstein, *Philosophical Investigations,* §243.

2 *Hume's Philosophy of Belief* (Routledge & Kegan Paul, 1961), p 47.

3 *Word and Object* (New York, 1960), esp. chapters 1–3.

4 *Individuals* (Methuen, 1959), chapter 3.

5 'Wittgenstein's *Philosophical Investigations*', *Philosophical Review,* vol. LXIII (1954), p 532.

6 *Op. cit.,* p 537.

7 *Loc. cit.*

8 *Op. cit.,* p 536.

9 Cf. Bennett, *Rationality* (Routledge & Kegan Paul, 1964), esp. §§8–10, and Malcolm, *Dreaming* (Routledge & Kegan Paul, 1959).

10 *Proceedings of the Aristotelian Society,* supplementary Volume, vol. 28 (1954), p 93.

11 *Akademie* edition, vol. VII, p 35.

12 Cf. Rhees, *op. cit.,* p 81.

13 Cf. A. Quinton, 'Properties and Classes', *Proceedings of the Aristotelian Society,* vol. LVIII (1957–8).

UNDERSTANDING A WANT

C. C. W. TAYLOR

IN RECENT YEARS a particular form of dispute has become depressingly familiar in moral philosophy. This dispute concerns itself with the word 'want' or with the word 'good', and may be schematized in the following dialogue:

A. 'If anyone were to say that *that* was good (or alternatively that he wanted *that*), no one would understand him.'

B. '*I* should understand him perfectly well.'

A. 'Oh, no, you wouldn't! You only *think* that you would understand because you are in the grip of a particular theory of what it is to think something good (or alternatively of what it is to want something).'

B. 'I know when I understand something and when I don't. You *say* that I don't understand only because *you* are in the grip of a particular theory, etc. In fact, not only do I understand, but so do you, if only you would admit it.'

And so the debate continues; not in the sense of going on to a further stage, but by grinding endlessly round the same well-worn track. No resolution of the dispute appears in prospect, since it seems to have gone beyond the reach of argument and to have petrified itself in the blank confrontation of conflicting claims about understanding. In this dispute it appears to be assumed that the central point at issue, viz. what is being claimed when one claims to understand a want, is entirely unproblematical. It will be the task of this paper to show that this is not the case, and to attempt to tease out some of the tangles in the notion of understanding a want, in the hope that this analysis may contribute to the solution of the original deadlock. It will, however, first be useful to see how this dispute comes to arise and why it should have a certain importance for ethics.

UNDERSTANDING A WANT

I

Though, as we have seen, the dispute may be over the word 'good' as well as over the word 'want', the argument about wanting is more fundamental, in that the dispute about 'good' can always be taken back a stage, and so turned into a dispute about 'want'. The course of the argument is as follows: in the controversy between the 'naturalist' philosopher who claims that in any given case the meaning of 'good' is wholly determined by the factual characteristics in virtue of which the object in question is called good and the 'prescriptivist' who maintains that 'good' always has an evaluative meaning independent of the descriptive meaning which is alone determined by the 'good-making' characteristics, a stage is reached at which it is agreed that anyone who recognizes the particular interest which establishes the 'good-making' characteristics has logically no choice but to call the object in question good if it does in fact have the appropriate qualities. This recognition of the interest is quite independent of whether or not the man in question *shares* the interest; thus a man with no interest whatever in horsemanship, having once understood the interest which the practitioners of that skill take in it, is logically committed to the judgment that a horseman of the appropriate sort, viz. one who rides gracefully, keeps the saddle, treats his horse well, etc., is a good horseman. Thus far play has gone in favour of the naturalist, but the prescriptivist has a ready counter in the claim that, since the goodness or badness of an object is determined by the interest which most people take in it, it is always open to anyone to propose a deviant interest in any object, which will enable him without logical error to assign it a different value from the normal on the goodness–badness index. This process, he will with justice maintain, is the very one by which changes in moral and other values have always been brought about. Now the notion of interest seems to be analysable in terms of wants; e.g. the interest which people have in horsemanship is the reason or reasons which they have for going in for horsemanship, which reasons are without distortion specifiable as what they want from the activity. So when the prescriptivist claims that it is always open to anyone to have and to recommend to others a deviant interest in an object, he is claiming that it is always possible to want from an object something different from what other people want from it.

The naturalist need not be seriously alarmed by this claim, since he can with perfect consistency concede that for many objects or perhaps even for every object there is a range of possible interests in accordance with which the object may be differently evaluated; he may even concede that this range may be capable of extension without limit. What he cannot concede, however, without the sacrifice of his whole position, is that there is no limit to the range of characteristics in virtue of which it would be correct to call an object of a certain kind a good one of that kind, for that would be just to concede that a value could be assigned to an object independently of its factual characteristics. His position depends on a distinction between something's being a good *x* from someone's point of view and its being a good *x simpliciter*. The former characterization may be equivalent to 'the sort of *x* which I have a fancy for', and there appears to be no limit to the range of fancies, whims, or likings which anyone may have. The latter is, however, subject to restriction, in that it presupposes a particular interest in *x*'s capable of being shared by the majority of people who are concerned with *x*'s, and the range of that sort of interest is logically restricted. But how, demands his opponent, can he restrict the range of possible interests? For since an interest is reducible to a want, to attempt to circumscribe the range of interests is to attempt to restrict *a priori* the range of possible wants. But since that someone wants something is a matter of fact, any such attempt is an attempt to establish truths about the world by armchair reasoning instead of by observation, a procedure which has been out of favour since that regrettable business of Hegel and the number of the planets.

To this the naturalist must reply that his thesis asserts not that any description of a recognizable state of affairs can be shown necessarily to lack application but that certain forms of words which purport to describe states of affairs fail in fact to do so. In this particular case the contention is that certain forms of words of the form '*X* wants *Y*' do not constitute a description of any situation which can be recognized as that in which a human being wants what he is said by the form of words to want. In order to show that a form of words is not a genuine description it is necessary to show that the purported description cannot be understood.

Hence the insistence of the naturalist that certain descriptions of, or claims to have, wants are incomprehensible as they stand and hence, too, the insistence of the prescriptivist that all such descriptions and claims are comprehensible; this seems to be the point where their dispute must be decided.

It should be emphasized that the naturalist is not committed to denying that any grammatically and syntactically well-formed utterance of the form 'I want an *x*' or 'I want to *ϕ*' is comprehensible as the expression of a whim, fancy, or craving, but only that certain utterances of that form are incomprehensible if they purport to express a want common to and consistently held by a group of people, such that the satisfaction of that want would be grounds for regarding a particular object or a sort of object as a good one of its kind or as a sort of good ones of their kind. In order to examine this contention it will be helpful first to consider the general conditions under which expressions of wants can be understood.

II

The most puzzling task for anyone considering whether some utterances which purport to express wants are incomprehensible is to determine exactly what sort of incomprehensibility is being alleged and denied. It is, however, at least clear that the cases in question are not those in which *a*) someone purports to express a want by emitting a string of non-significant sounds or a concatenation of words which do not constitute a significant sentence, or *b*) someone utters the words 'I want *x*' where *x* is not the name of any object, state of affairs, activity, etc., real or imaginary. Typical utterances of the sort in question, e.g. 'I want a saucer of mud', are grammatically well-formed sentences in which the purported object of the want is a recognizable object. Clearly, then, the naturalist is not claiming that such sentences are incomprehensible in the sense in which 'Cat thoroughly the if' and 'I want a tonk' are. Yet it may be suspected that his opponent is sometimes prepared to regard the fact that the dubious sentences are not incomprehensible in that way as a criterion for their comprehensibility *tout court*. This is an obvious error, since it is commonplace that not every grammatically well-formed sentence is significant, as can be seen from such an example as 'I defy a saucer of mud'. So the sort of incomprehensibility which is attributed to the dubious 'wanting' sentences is the sort which characterizes sentences of the kind represented by our last example. What sort of incomprehensibility is that?

At this point it might be objected that there is an obvious difference between the cases typified by this last example and the disputed cases of wanting, in that nothing could be recognized as a case of defying a saucer of mud, whereas nothing is easier than to describe someone's wanting that or any other object. But why should we not describe someone whom we came across shaking his fist at a saucer of mud and shouting 'You can't scare me!' as defying it? Well, it isn't really defying unless you believe that the thing which you are defying has the capacity and the intention to harm you, and it is just senseless to attribute those propensities to a saucer of mud. That is to say, no one who understood what kind of thing a saucer of mud is could be said or could claim to be defying it, though someone with queer beliefs about things being the abode of powerful and malignant spirits might defy the spook which he regards as animating this saucer. But, now, what differentiates the case of wanting the saucer of mud from the case of defying it? For wanting a saucer of mud is mysterious, not when a man wants it to mix a certain sort of pigment with, or as a mud-bath for his canary, or in general for any recognizable purpose, but in the case where he claims seriously to want it for itself, and is insistent that only a saucer of mud, and not just any old thing, will satisfy his want. The oddness of this situation seems quite parallel with the oddness of defying the saucer; in either case we have the appropriate utterances ('I defy . . .', 'I want. . . ') and some of the appropriate actions, fist-shaking, hunting about, and so on, and yet in each case part of the context necessary to constitute this as a genuine case of the purported activity appears to be lacking. To be more precise, what is lacking is in each case a belief on the part of the agent about the relation of the object in question to his purposes and interests, in the first case, that this is an object which is capable of and minded to harm him, and in the second, that it is one for which he has some sort of use. Our example about defying the saucer indicated that it may indeed be possible to supply the appropriate context about any object by building in a sufficiently far-fetched set of beliefs about it. The cost of this, however, is to change the concept of the object; thus the man who really believes that saucers of mud are the abode or rather the embodiment of malign spirits and hence appropriate objects of defiance has a different concept of a saucer of mud from the everyday one. The fact that he can recognize saucers of mud and teach the use of the phrase 'saucer of mud' in the same way as everyone else is not sufficient to show that he has the same concept, but merely that his concept is to a certain extent parallel with the normal one; for a disagreement as to whether or not an object falling under the concept is alive is surely a sufficient criterion of a conceptual difference. On the other hand, anyone who claimed to have precisely the same concept of a saucer of mud as everyone else and yet maintained that such a saucer was an appropriate object of defiance would be unable to be understood. The contention of the naturalist is that anyone who seriously claimed to want a saucer of mud just for itself would be in the same state.

III

Here the prescriptivist may well claim that his opponent has illegitimately shifted his ground. Instead of the original assertion that it is impossible to understand someone who says that he wants a saucer of mud just for itself, the naturalist is now content with the far weaker thesis that in certain circumstances it may be impossible to make out what someone wants a saucer of mud *for*. Characterizing the situation in that way, however, entails the admission that the man in question does indeed want the saucer of mud, though not for anything. But to admit that is surely to admit that his want can be understood, for it is a sufficient condition of understanding a want that one should be able to say what it is that is wanted. And to admit so much is to abandon the original naturalist position. The naturalist has chosen instead to retreat to a supposedly safer position, maintaining now that in order to understand a want it is necessary to be able to say what the thing wanted is wanted for. The safety of this position is, however, illusory, for it is a perfectly familiar situation to want something but not to want it for anything. Indeed, unless this were so, all explanation of wanting would involve an infinite regress, since one could never know what it was to want anything without knowing what it was to want the thing *for* which the first thing was wanted, and so on *ad infinitum*. Tactical retreat has thus degenerated into total rout.

The naturalist's reply to this attack involves three parts. His first move is to reject the dichotomy, which he is accused of ignoring, between understanding someone who says that he wants *X* and understanding what he wants *X* for. Secondly, he denies that it is a sufficient condition of understanding a want that one should be able to say what it is that is wanted. Finally, he examines the notion of wanting something for nothing at all and that of wanting something for nothing other than itself, and endeavours to show significant differences between standard examples of those sorts of wants and the kind of cases under dispute. We may take these three points in order.

III *a*

The substance of the first point is the denial of the thesis that there is any criterion of understanding what someone says when he says that he wants *X* other than understanding what he wants *X* for. Here the naturalist has another opportunity to take the offensive. Either the prescriptivist merely asserts that there is such a criterion, in which case he is begging the question, or he must be able to say what it is and to show that it is a genuine criterion. Now the criterion cannot be just the comprehensibility of the sentence expressive of the want according to the rules of grammar and vocabulary of the language of the sentence (the basic sense of comprehensibility discussed earlier). The only other criterion, however, which has so far even been hinted at is that covered by the second point of the reply, viz. that one should be able to say what it is that is wanted. The answer to the first question is thus seen to depend on the answer to the second.

III *b*

The question of whether it is a sufficient condition of understanding a want that one should be able to say what it is that is wanted is rendered obscure by the fact that saying what it is that is wanted is itself not an unambiguous concept. One interpretation of this notion requires merely the ability to repeat the form of words expressive of the original want. But this is too hospitable, since it allows 'I want a tonk' to count as intelligible; one can say what is wanted here, viz. a tonk, whatever that is. In addition to being able to name the purported object of the want, then, one must understand what the name means. Now our earlier discussion of the man who defied the saucer of mud indicated that understanding what a name means is not simply a matter of being able to identify examples of things to which the name applies; to put the matter in the broadest terms, one must be able in addition to give some account of how the object affects and is affected by the other objects, including human and other agents, in its environment. Thus one must know whether or not the object is itself or is a part of a living organism, and in the case of a functional object, whether an artefact or an organic element, one must have at least some concept of its function. Further, having a concept of the function of an object implies knowing at least to some extent what wants are satisfied by the object. To all of this the prescriptivist might well assent, while maintaining that this still gives a criterion of understanding a want independent of understanding what the object of the want is wanted for, since it is one thing to understand what an object is wanted for by most people and another thing to understand what this particular object is wanted for on this particular occasion by this particular person.

Acceptance of this criterion, however, produces awkward results. Consider the case of a man who says 'I want a wife'. Now we understand what a wife is, viz. a woman married to some man, and we understand what marriage is and at least in a rudimentary fashion what the function of a wife is within the institution of marriage. So we introduce to him a paradigm example of a wife, viz. a woman who is married to some man and who fulfils the normal functions of a wife. Imagine our surprise, then, not to say indignation, on finding that instead of being grateful to us for so exactly satisfying his want he accuses us of having totally misunderstood what he wanted. Yet we did understand what the name of the object of the want means; our criterion has therefore proved insufficient.

One might attempt to save the criterion by suggesting that we have simply misidentified the object of the want. 'I want a wife' does not mean 'I want some woman who is already a wife', as 'I want a beefsteak' means 'I want something which is a beefsteak', but rather 'I want some woman *as my wife*' or 'I want some woman to be my wife'. In picking on some woman who was already a wife as the object of the want we simply hit on the wrong sort of woman. But 'a woman as my wife' or 'a woman to be my wife' are not alternative sorts of woman to a woman who is a wife, as a woman who is a spinster is an alternative sort of woman. The phrases 'a woman as my wife' and 'a woman to be my wife' do not pick out sorts of women at all; rather their function is to specify *the kind of want* which I have for a woman. That is to say, in the kind of case typified by wanting a wife there is no distinction between understanding what it is that is wanted and understanding what that thing is wanted for. In this sort of case it is the kind of want which determines the description which is given of the object. Obviously there are other descriptions which properly characterize the object of the want; thus in the present case what is wanted is a woman, and also a human being, an animal, an inhabitant of the planet Earth, and so on. Yet equally obviously none of these descriptions conveys the essence of what is wanted in wanting a wife. One might be tempted to think that wanting a wife could be analysed into two components, wanting a woman and wanting her in order to be one's wife. But this supposes that there is some state which can be recognized as that of wanting a woman, but not as a wife or as a mistress or as a shorthand-typist or as anything else, and that to this neutral state there can be added the specification that in this case she is wanted as a wife. When, however, one tries to describe the case of someone who wants a woman in this neutral way one sees that this supposition is vacuous, since any description turns into a description of wanting a woman as something or other, even if it is only as someone to talk to or something to look at. It will certainly not do to suppose that one can isolate this neutral wanting by means of the locution 'wanting a woman as a woman', since in these uninhibited days the particular implications of that phrase are especially obvious. Since, then, there is no such state as that of just wanting a woman *simpliciter*, it follows that one cannot claim to have understood what it is to want a wife simply in virtue of having observed that the object which satisfies this want is in fact a woman; one must also be able to see *how* the object satisfies the want, which in this case is to see how the woman fulfils the rôle or function of a wife.

A further attempt might now be made to save the suggested criterion via a distinction proposed earlier between two analyses of the sentence 'I want an *X*', viz. 'I want something as an *X*' (or 'something to be an *X*') and 'I want something which is an *X*'. The foregoing discussion might be agreed to have established that in cases where the former analysis is the correct one the distinction between understanding what is wanted and understanding what it is wanted for embodies a false dichotomy, since in these cases the want is understood if and only if one understands what the object of the want does in satisfying the want. In cases of the second sort, however, the original criterion, that one should understand the meaning of the name of the object of the want, is sufficient. Further, this class is the more important, since in most cases the object of the want already fulfils the appropriate description before it begins to satisfy the want.

Yet even over this reduced range of wants the suggested criterion proves inadequate. To consider our previous example, suppose the man who said 'I want a beefsteak' (i.e. 'I want something which is a beefsteak') is supplied with one, encased in a container which allows him no access to it but lets him look at it to his heart's content. Surely the misunderstanding of this want is as gross as that which thought to satisfy the man who wanted a wife by producing someone else's. Again, someone who wanted something which is a pen would hardly be satisfied were the thing which is a pen so tampered with as to prevent him from writing with it. These examples indicate that the distinction between wanting something as an *X* and wanting something which is an *X* is a mistaken one. It is indeed the case that in some cases where an *X* is wanted the object which satisfies the want is an *X* before it begins to satisfy the want and in other cases it is not, but in either case it satisfies the want only in so far as it functions or behaves *as* an *X*. Thus all cases of wanting something, and not merely one sort of case, as had been suggested, are cases of wanting something as an *X*. This is what makes the saucer-of-mud case so puzzling, that one has no idea what counts as functioning or behaving just as a saucer of mud, and hence has no conception of what will satisfy this want. Thus it is not clear whether it will be sufficient to let the man see the saucer whenever he wants to, or whether he must handle it or daub himself with the mud or what. In ordinary cases of wanting something out of the way, as, for example, someone's asking for a stick of a specific but unusual size and shape, one has some partial understanding of the want against a background of similar but more usual wants; it is, for instance, a fair guess that the stick is wanted as a tool for some particularly intricate job, such as clearing a difficult drain. But in the saucer case any such background is stripped away, and one is left merely with the assertion that the saucer is wanted for itself, which in this context is quite uninformative.

The analysis of all wanting something as 'wanting something as an *X*' enables this sort of wanting to fit naturally into a more general account of wanting, which includes not only wants whose natural form of expression is 'I want an *X*' but also those expressed in the form 'I want to . . .' and 'I want you to . . .'. This general account may be briefly stated as follows, that in the expression of a want, 'I want' functions as an operator governing a proposition signifying the state of affairs which constitutes the satisfaction of the want.[1] Thus 'I want a beefsteak' is fully analysed as 'I want (I eat a beefsteak)', 'I want to be Prime Minister' as 'I want (I am Prime Minister)', 'I want you (him) to shut the door' as 'I want (You (he) shut(s) the door)'. In terms of this scheme we can restate our reason for the exclusion of certain wants as incomprehensible, viz. that there is no proposition signifying a state of affairs constitutive of their satisfaction. In the saucer-of-mud case, for instance, the place of the verb in the propositional schema 'I . . . a saucer of mud', which once filled in would specify the particular sort of want which the saucer would satisfy, must be left blank; hence this propositional function has no values, and hence the operator 'I want', since it governs no proposition, fails in this case to specify a particular want. It will not do to suggest that the blank in 'I want (I . . . a saucer of mud)' might be filled by 'have' or 'possess'; for these verbs do not themselves signify particular states of affairs, but in the context of propositions expressive of wants have the rôle of variables to which the particular activities in which the satisfaction of wants consists are assigned as values. Thus wanting to have a wife is wanting to be married, and wanting to have a good dinner is wanting to eat a good dinner. But in a case where no particular value can be assigned, as in wanting to . . . a saucer of mud, it is obviously wrong to try to press the variable itself into service in that rôle. This is not to suggest that it is never possible to make a distinction between having or possessing a thing and using or enjoying it, and that certain wants are not properly to be described as directed towards the former but not the latter. Thus someone may want to own a picture but have no interest in looking at it, since he values it merely as an investment or as a status symbol. But this case, so far from being one in which the variable 'having' has no value other than itself, is simply one in which its value is different from the normal; instead of wanting to be able to look at the picture whenever he likes, the man in question wants to save money or to impress other people through his ownership of the picture. It does, however, suggest that there is no wanting to have a thing which is not wanting to have some use of it or other, since even wanting to own something for the sake of owning it seems to involve wanting to think of one's importance being enhanced by the number of one's possessions and to be able to congratulate oneself on having this particular thing. We see, then, that in general the dichotomy between understanding what it is that is wanted and understanding what that thing is wanted for is a false one. The only criterion of understanding a want is understanding what state of affairs would satisfy it, which is equivalent to understanding what use the person whose want is in question expects from the object of his want.

The notion of understanding what state of affairs would satisfy a want may itself be interpreted in either a weak or a strong sense, a distinction which is crucial for the original dispute. The weak sense is simply that one should understand the proposition which, in the most exact specification of the want, occupies the bracket following the verb 'I want' in the schema adopted above. The difficulties so far encountered in the saucer-of-mud case arise from failure to meet this condition; the failure to specify in what way the saucer was wanted left the bracket empty, while the attempt to fill this gap with the notion of 'having' a saucer succeeded in putting into the bracket not a proposition but a propositional form, which itself required completion. This deficiency is, however, easily supplied by more detailed specification; provided that the bracket is filled by any proposition which can be understood as specifying a recognizable state of affairs, the weak condition is satisfied. Thus wanting to eat a saucer of mud and wanting to hold one in one's hand are both in this sense comprehensible, while wanting to sing a saucer of mud is not. This condition is certainly acceptable to prescriptivists, since it rules out as incomprehensible only those purported expressions of wants whose satisfaction does not consist in any describable state of affairs. The naturalist, on the other hand, requires a stronger condition, viz. that some expressions of wants, whose satisfaction consists in a recognizable state of affairs, should none the less be judged incomprehensible. How this sort of want is to be marked off from other wants seems obscure; the idea seems to be that some states of affairs, while certainly describable in themselves, could not be the object of comprehensible wants, in that such states of affairs could not be recognized as serving any purpose of the agent who claimed to want them, and hence could not sensibly be wanted for anything. To take up a distinction mentioned earlier (p. 247), it would be maintained that, while any describable state of affairs may be the object of a whim or craving, only states of affairs recognizable as serving some purpose can be the object of the shared interest necessary to constitute some object a good one of its kind, since the recognition of a shared interest requires that one be able to recognize a purpose common to those who share that interest.

This account of the distinction seems, however, not to lack difficulties. Firstly, the common purpose which one has to recognize in order to recognize a shared interest may be just the satisfaction of that interest. Thus if a number of people happen to share some want, the fact that that want may seem a very odd one to someone who does not share it does not prevent that person from recognizing the satisfaction of that want as a common purpose of that group. Secondly, we are perfectly familiar with the ideas of wanting something for no reason at all and of wanting something for nothing other than itself. What is there to prevent any want, however odd, from coming under one or other of those classifications?

If the naturalist is to block this move, he must show differences between these familiar types of wants and the odd wants under review, differences significant enough to preclude the classification of the latter under any of the former headings. It is therefore necessary to examine in turn the notions of wanting something for no reason at all and wanting something for nothing other than itself.

III *c*

The characteristic feature of situations in which something is wanted for no reason is their triviality; the thing that is wanted, whether an object or an activity, is of small importance, and the want one of the sort which arise suddenly and depart as suddenly whether satisfied or not. In fact the answer 'For no particular reason' given to the question 'Why do you want that?' often indicates not that the person questioned has considered the matter and come to the conclusion that there is no reason for which he wants whatever it is that he does want but that the matter is so trivial that he can't be bothered to think what the reason might be. But it might well be the case that even if made to think over the incident, he could find no reason for having wanted the thing. (Wanting to pluck a leaf or to cut the head off a plant with a stick as one walks along are ordinary examples of this sort of thing.) Here it might well be accepted both that he did indeed want the thing and that he wanted it for no reason, though familiarity with psychoanalytic theory has made us much more alive to the possibility of unconscious reasons for even the most casual actions. If, however, the want were one whose satisfaction required even a moderately complicated chain of activity, if it were persisted in and if it were seriously expressed, then one would be very reluctant to admit that there was no reason for which the thing was wanted. The natural response to such a situation would be to say 'If it means as much as that to him there must be some reason for which he wants it', and to assume that if no reason could at present be found, nevertheless advances in psychology would reveal one. The situation has an analogue in causal explanation, where it is presupposed that every event has a cause and assumed in the face of any apparently uncaused event that further investigation will reveal some cause. But while that analogy emphasizes the central place which the notion of wanting things for some reason holds in psychological explanation, it does not seem to justify the insistence *a priori* that nothing can be seriously wanted for no reason; for if detailed investigation revealed a body of wants for which no reason could be assigned, psychological theory ought rather to try to accommodate that fact than to go on for ever looking for explanations in terms of reasons. Nor does it seem that such an accommodation would necessarily overthrow all psychological explanation; its effect might rather be to demarcate the area of conduct which admits of explanation in terms of reasons, and to contrast with that an area in which some other sort of explanation is operative. Yet this question, however interesting to the speculative psychologist, is not at this stage of the argument central to the dispute between the naturalist and the prescriptivist, since the latter, even if prepared to concede (as there seems no compelling reason that he should be) that nothing can be seriously wanted for no reason, may still maintain that any state of affairs whatever may comprehensibly be wanted for no reason other than itself. Only if that assertion could be refuted would it be necessary for him to establish conclusively that some things (viz. at least those things which cannot be wanted for nothing other than themselves) can be seriously wanted for no reason.

Turning, therefore, to things wanted for the sake of nothing other than themselves, we find them commonly falling under two main headings. Firstly, there are ultimate ends or ideals of conduct, e.g. the pursuit of knowledge, the improvement of the human condition, the establishment of the Kingdom of Heaven on earth. These things are not wanted for the sake of anything further; rather they serve to explain the particular organization of detailed wants and pursuits which an individual imposes on his life. This is sufficient to differentiate these cases from those originally under discussion, which presented the picture of someone's wanting a particular object for itself in isolation from the general pattern of his wants and interests. But why should not the disputed want itself have the status of an ultimate principle? Why should not someone claim, for instance, that the possession of saucers of mud was his ultimate end in life, and organize all his activity to that end? Yet a special sort of incomprehensibility seems to attach to the assertion that something *prima facie* pointless is wanted not merely for itself but as the ultimate good in life. It is a necessary condition of seriously holding that something is such an end that one should be able to say something about why it is worth pursuing, not in the sense of recommending it as a means to anything further but by showing that this end subsumes those features which are recognized as making them worth choosing; an example of this process would be to show that some end allowed for the practice of activities which are fun, exhilarating, interesting, or productive of content. This is not to rule out the possibility of far-reaching modification of and divergence from commonly accepted ideals of life; but if any attitude is to count as a serious attempt at such a modification it must connect at some point with the accepted standards. Otherwise there seems to be no reason for regarding it as an attempt to introduce a new ideal of life, as distinct from a resolution to behave in some arbitrarily selected way.

This leads naturally on to consideration of the second sort of things commonly wanted for themselves, i.e. objects and activities falling under the several desirability characteristics mentioned in the previous paragraph, e.g. fun, interesting, pleasant, exciting, enthralling. To these the same restrictions apply as we saw to apply to ultimate ends, viz. that one should be able to give some account of the desirability of the thing which relates it to conventional standards of that sort of desirability. For example, anyone who claimed to want a saucer of mud for the fun of it and for nothing else would be logically committed to some attempt to say, if required, in what the fun of it consists, and to show that this bears some recognizable relation to the sort of thing that is generally reckoned as fun; thus nothing could count as fun which does not offer scope for some more or less energetic activity providing diversion from the cares of everyday life. It does indeed seem very implausible that merely having (perhaps holding in one's hand) a saucer of mud could fulfil those conditions, but not perhaps so odd that it should be satisfying, or restful, or somehow comforting.

The last sentence gives us a hint that it is going to be extremely difficult for the naturalist to maintain that any object could not fall under some desirability-characteristic or other, and so properly be wanted for itself. This is due in part to the vagueness of the notion of a desirability-characteristic itself. The idea of such a characteristic seems to be that it is a feature of an object which can be recognized as providing a good reason for wanting that object. But from this it would seem to follow that any feature of an object whatever could be such a characteristic, provided that the person wanting the object has a taste or a liking for things which have that feature. In that case, any object whatever can be wanted for itself, and the naturalist case falls. Or is it suggested that there is some limit to the tastes and likings that people can have, so that anyone who claimed to like anything outside that range could be convicted of logical error? How is this limit to be drawn? It is a matter of common observation that people like all sorts of quite different things, without being able to give reasons for liking one thing rather than another. One man's tastes are often 'incomprehensible' to another, in that one man finds it impossible to understand how the other likes the things which he does like, yet that fact provides no justification for the assertion that either has committed any logical error in the statement of his tastes. Again, since it was admitted that anything could be the object of a whim or craving, it would seem very difficult to maintain that it is not the case that anything could be the object of a taste or liking, since the latter share with whims and cravings the important feature that they do not have to be supported by reasons. And since it is logically possible that any liking should be shared by some group, it seems that the members of that group would be justified in evaluating any x as a good x on the ground that it satisfied their liking.

It might be objected that, if any group evaluated x's on the basis of their liking for a certain sort of x, while the standard ground of evaluation took no account of that liking, then the members of that group must have a different concept of x from the standard one; thus the fact of their evaluation would not tend to show that it is possible to evaluate x's as commonly understood on the basis of a mere liking. This objection appears sound to this extent, that where the concept of an x includes specification of the function of x's as commonly recognized, then any evaluation of x's made without reference to that function is not an evaluation of x's but of something else. Thus if any group evaluated the objects which we call knives without any reference to their cutting qualities, then we should say that they had no interest in knives, but regarded those objects as something else, say, as ornaments. If, on the other hand, while using knives for cutting, and regarding their efficiency in cutting as relevant to their goodness or badness, they nevertheless thought blue knives the best sort of knives, on the ground that that was the sort of knife that appealed to them, it would not be plausible to suggest that they had a different concept of knife from our own, but simply that they looked at knives from a different viewpoint. Where the concept is not explicitly functional, it seems that any difference in evaluation could be accounted a difference in viewpoint, since it would always be possible for supporters of conflicting evaluations to agree *a*) that they were evaluating *x*'s and *b*) that *x*'s could be defined and recognized without reference to the conflicting standards of evaluation.

IV

Our conclusion is, then, that the naturalist has made out his case only as far as concerns functional concepts which themselves specify the interests which can be taken in the objects falling under them. The importance of this conclusion for ethics is that it seems unlikely that the concepts which are the principal subjects of ethical evaluation, e.g. man, action, human life, are such concepts, which implies that the prescriptivist account of ethical evaluation is the right one. In order to substantiate his own view of ethical evaluation, the naturalist would have to show, e.g. that if any agent took as his predominant interest in life some satisfaction falling outside a specified range of interests, then that life could not be recognized as a human life. But if the agent could be identified as a language-using member of the species *Homo sapiens*, the refusal to recognize his life as human appears quite arbitrary. Yet though the naturalist has, strictly speaking, failed to establish his case, his challenge has made the prescriptivist aware of the true nature of his own position, and thereby performed a considerable service to ethical thought. Largely thanks to the naturalist's insistence, it has been made clear that in normal conditions of human life the criteria of moral evaluation may be established with certainty, and moral judgments characterized as true or false in the ordinary, underivative sense of those words. That being so, is it not time to recognize that the interest of the original controversy has been exhausted, and to turn instead to the many detailed questions concerning ordinary criteria of evaluation which still await clarification?

NOTE

[1] This analysis was originally suggested to me by Mr. T. C. Potts, who has developed it elsewhere in much greater detail.

INDEX